Responses to Miscellaneous Questions

Miscellany of Eighty-Three Questions
Miscellany of Questions in Response to Simplician
and Eight Questions of Dulcitius

Augustinian Heritage Institute

www.augustinianheritage.org

THE WORKS OF SAINT AUGUSTINE

A Translation for the 21st Century

Part I – Books

Volume 12:

Responses to Miscellaneous Questions

THE WORKS OF SAINT AUGUSTINE
A Translation for the 21st Century

Responses to Miscellaneous Questions

Miscellany of Eighty-Three Questions
(De diversis quastionibus octoginta tribus)
Miscellany of Questions in Response to Simplician
(Ad Simplicianum de diversis quaestionibus)
and Eight Questions of Dulcitius
(De octo Dulcitii quaestionibus)

1/12

introduction, translation and notes by
Boniface Ramsey
(series editor)

editor
Raymond Canning

New City Press
Hyde Park, New York

Published in the United States by New City Press
202 Cardinal Rd., Hyde Park, New York 12538
© 2008 Augustinian Heritage Institute

Library of Congress Cataloging-in-Publication Data:

Augustine, Saint, Bishop of Hippo.
     The works of Saint Augustine.

     "Augustinian Heritage Institute"
     Includes bibliographical references and indexes.
     Contents: — pt. 3, v .15. Expositions of the Psalms, 1-32
—pt. 3, v. 1. Sermons on the Old Testament, 1-19.
—pt. 3, v. 2. Sermons on the Old Testament, 20-50 — [et al.] — pt. 3,
v. 10 Sermons on various subjects, 341-400.
     1.   Theology — Early church, ca. 30-600.   I. Hill,
Edmund.   II. Rotelle, John E.   III. Augustinian
Heritage Institute.   IV. Title.
BR65.A5E53   1990   270.2   89-28878
ISBN 978-1-56548-055-1 (series)
ISBN 978-1-56548-277-7 (pt. 1, v. 12)

Printed in the United States of America

In gratitude to
Lee and Maidie Podles

Contents

Miscellany of Eighty-Three Questions

I. Whether the soul exists of itself — 29; II. On free choice — 29; III. Whether it is by God's causality that humankind is evil —29; IV. Why humankind is evil — 30; V. Whether an irrational animal can be blessed — 30; VI. On evil — 31; VII. What the soul should properly be called in an ensouled being — 31; VIII. Whether the soul is moved by itself — 31; IX. Whether truth can be grasped by the body's senses —32; X. Whether the body comes from God — 32; XI. Why Christ was born of a woman — 33; XII. The words of a certain wise man —33; XIII. On what evidence it is clear that humans are superior to beasts — 34; XIV. That the body of our Lord Jesus was not a phantasm — 34; XV. On the intellect — 34; XVI. On the Son — 34; XVII. On God's knowledge — 35; XVIII. On the Trinity — 35; XIX. On God and creation — 35; XX. On God's place — 36; XXI. Whether God is not the creator of evil — 36; XXII. That God is not subject to necessity — 37; XXIII. On the Father and the Son — 37; XXIV. Whether both committing sin and acting rightly fall under the will's free choice — 38; XXV. On the cross of Christ — 39; XXVI. On the different kinds of sins — 39; XXVII. On providence — 39; XXVIII. Why God wished to make the world — 40; XXIX. Whether anything is above or below the universe — 40; XXX. Whether everything has been created for the use of human beings — 41; XXXI. The words of a certain person — 43; XXXII. Whether one person can understand a given thing better than another person, and whether the understanding of that thing can thus proceed to infinity —45; XXXIII. On fear — 45; XXXIV. Whether something else should be loved than to lack fear — 46; XXXV. What should be loved — 47; XXXVI. On fostering char-ity — 49; XXXVII. On him who has always been born — 52; XXXVIII. On the conformation of the soul — 52; XXXIX. On foods — 53; XL. Since souls have one nature, where do the different wills of human beings come from? — 53; XLI. Since God made all things, why did he not make them in equal fashion? — 53; XLII. How the Lord Jesus, who is the wisdom of God, was both in his mother's womb and in heaven — 54; XLIII. Why did the Son of God appear in a man and the Holy Spirit in a dove? — 54; XLIV. Why did the Lord Jesus Christ come after such a long time? — 54; XLV. Against mathematicians — 55; XLVI. On ideas — 57; XLVII. Whether we may ever be able to see our thoughts — 59; XLVIII. On

Miscellany of Questions in Response to Simplician

Eight Questions of Dulcitius

General Introduction

Of the three treatises contained in the present volume, part of the second builds on part of the first, and part of the third is a quotation of part of the second. Some themes are shared as well, especially between the first and the second and the second and the third. But the main thing that brings these three works of Augustine of Hippo into a single volume in this series (and that brought them, along with *The Divination of Demons,* into a single volume in the French series Bibliothèque Augustinienne) is the fact that they all have roughly the same format. Each is a collection of topics introduced by other persons and addressed by Augustine. In the case of the *Miscellany of Eighty-three Questions* the topics were introduced by Augustine's monastic confreres and responses were provided by him over the course of about seven years. In the other two works it was Simplician and Dulcitius, the second nearly three decades after the first, each of whom asked a few questions by letter and each of whom received a response within a relatively short period of time. The question-and-answer format that Augustine uses in these three writings is replicated in his *Questions on the Gospels.* This is not a style unique to him, however. It had a pedigree reaching back at least to Philo and Plutarch in the first century, which was to continue on beyond Ambrosiaster and Jerome in the late fourth.

Whereas the *Miscellany of Eighty-three Questions* runs a gamut of topics from philosophy to biblical exegesis, some of them treated in several pages and others disposed of in a few lines, the *Miscellany of Questions in Response to Simplician* and the *Eight Questions of Dulcitius* are exclusively scriptural, and each of their topics is covered with relative amplitude. The *Miscellany* addressed to Simplician is by far the most cohesive of the three. It is also the most important, since it is the document that seems to have seen a major change in Augustine's thinking about the role of divine grace in human activity, which is arguably the area in which he made his greatest theological contribution and helped to shape the western mind until the present day.

Yet, despite the undoubted importance of the *Miscellany of Questions in Response to Simplician,* neither it nor the other two works in this volume belong to the first tier of Augustine's writings or are very well known outside the circle of Augustine scholars. But the first two in particular are illustrative of the early stages of Augustine's thinking and allow a glimpse of its development: while in the *Miscellany of Questions in Response to Simplician* a more comprehensive understanding of grace than had ever previously been expressed by anyone (except perhaps St. Paul) takes shape before our eyes, in the *Miscellany of Eighty-three Questions* Augustine's historic shift from a philosophical to a scriptural perspective is accomplished gradually but in plain view. And in all three works we catch sight of the kinds of philosophical and theological questions that vexed at least some of Augustine's contemporaries and of an Augustine who, despite the numerous claims on his time, treated both questions and questioners with respect. The Latin texts used in the translation of the *Miscellany of Eighty-three Questions* and the *Eight Questions of Dulcitius* are from the critical editions in the Corpus Christianorum, Series Latina, volume 44A, prepared by Almut Mutzenbecher.

The Latin text used in the translation of the *Miscellany of Questions in Response to Simplician* is from the critical edition in volume 44 of the same series, likewise prepared by Dr. Mutzenbecher. Supplementary material, such as the relevant excerpts from the *Revisions,* comes from these two volumes as well. Dr. Mutzenbecher's introductions, along with the introductions and notes by Gustave Bardy and J.-A. Beckaert in the Bibliothèque Augustinienne 1, 10, have been immensely helpful in composing the introductions and notes for this volume.

Translations into English of these three works of Augustine have been sparse. David L. Mosher has translated the *Miscellany of Eighty-three Questions* for the seventieth volume of the Fathers of the Church series (Washington: Catholic University of America Press, 1977). His introduction and notes are valuable aids, especially for English speakers, to understanding both the problems posed by the text and its philosophical and theological content. As for the *Miscellany of Questions in Response to Simplician,* only the first of its two books has been translated by John H. S. Burleigh in *Augustine: Earlier Writings* = Library of Christian Classics 6 (London: SCM Press, 1953) 376-406; there is no English translation of the second book. Finally, the *Eight Questions of Dulcitius* has been translated by Mary E. Deferrari in the Fathers of the Church 16 (New York: The Fathers of the Church, 1952) 423-466.

Miscellany of Eighty-Three Questions

Introduction

The first of the three works presented in this volume is the earliest and by far the longest of them. Augustine tells us in his *Revisions* I,26,1 that it is a mélange of questions and answers collected between the time when he returned from Italy to Africa in 388, when he founded a community at Thagaste, and the time when he was ordained to the episcopate in Hippo in 395. Since the same section of the *Revisions* mentions that his "brothers" were the ones who were asking the questions to which he responded and that they did so when they saw that he had spare time, we may safely assume that reference is being made to the members of Augustine's communities at both Thagaste and Hippo rather than to the members of the Christian family at large.

Augustine does not give any hint in *Revisions* I,26,1 as to whether the eighty-three questions and answers were put into book form in as random a way as they arose, and were then simply numbered "so that whoever wants to read about something may find it easily." It is hard to believe, however, that his monastic brothers approached Augustine with their questions in precisely the same order as those questions now appear, even though, by and large, the order in which the topics are treated reflects the intellectual development that the course of his writings betrays—i.e., beginning with an absorption in philosophy as a study with its own logic, even when used for Christian purposes, and turning increasingly to a reliance on the logic of scripture, always interpreted in the light of faith. Not only is roughly the first half of the questions devoted mainly to philosophical-theological material while roughly the second half focuses primarily on scriptural interpretation. In addition, within each of these two large blocks of questions there are smaller clusters of questions that deal with related topics—e.g., XXXIII-XXXVI (on fear and love) and XLII-XLIV (on the Incarnation) in the first block, and LXI-LXV (on passages from the gospel of John) and LXVI-LXXV (on passages from the epistles of Paul) in the second. The questions that make up these clusters seem to belong together by reason of their very titles. In some cases, on the other hand, questions have been put side by side whose titles do not imply any relationship. Questions XXIII ("On the Father and the Son") and XXIV ("Whether both committing sin and acting rightly fall under the will's free choice") belong within this category; but each develops the notion of participation, albeit in a different context.

15

There is, then, a certain order in the *Miscellany of Eighty-three Questions.*[1] It is far from being comprehensive, however. For instance, a small cluster of questions that have numerological concerns (LV-LVII) is followed by three questions of another sort, and the one following that is, once again, markedly numerological. Question LXXIX, on the miracles performed by Pharaoh's magicians as recorded in Ex 7-8, seems as though it would be better placed next to question LIII, on the Israelites' taking the Egyptians' gold and silver. Other examples, where an obvious order could have been imposed but for some reason was not, could easily be given.

It is the work's incomplete order—not any utter randomness, which is clearly not the case—that constitutes the *Miscellany's* greatest mystery. Perhaps in Augustine's view a hasty and inchoate arrangement was all that this potpourri of questions, some of them among his very earliest writings as a Christian and not representative of his more mature thinking, deserved. Perhaps many of these questions were for him little more than archival material, which he preserved because—as that remarkable work, the *Revisions*, demonstrates—he was careful about preserving nearly everything that he wrote.[2]

Yet the *Miscellany of Eighty-three Questions* is not alone among Augustine's compositions in displaying a lack of what would appear to be due order in a question-and-answer format. His *Questions on the Gospels,* written four or five years after the *Miscellany,* present a similar case. In the prologue of this work Augustine explains that it is a collection of questions and answers resulting from discussions on the gospels that he had had with a disciple of his, and he confesses that there was never any intention of producing something orderly. The *Questions* are divided into two books, the first devoted to Matthew and the second to Luke, but apart from that there is no consistent attempt at systematization.

---

1. It is also worth noting, without implying that it has any bearing whatsoever on the work's intended arrangement, that the questions in the *Miscellany* tend to get longer. Yet question XLII, which is the shortest of them all, is located at the exact center between the first and the eighty-third.
2. Adding to the mystery of the *Miscellany* is the existence of a work composed by Possidius, Augustine's disciple and biographer. His *Indiculus* is a catalogue of Augustine's writings in which there is no mention of the *Miscellany* itself, although the titles of its questions are scattered throughout the catalogue under various headings. For the text of the *Indiculus* see *Miscellanea Agostiniana* 2 (Rome 1931) 161-208.

The questions in the *Miscellany* often have the air of being jottings. Certainly that is true of the shorter ones, in which topics that could benefit from a monograph are addressed in a few sentences and from a very specific perspective. Readers looking for anything remotely approaching comprehensive treatment will be sorely disappointed, for example, by the very narrow focus of question XVIII ("On the Trinity") or by that of the one that follows it ("On God and creation"), both of whose sweeping titles are hugely misleading. Eventually some of the topics, like the Trinity and the scriptural account of creation, did indeed become the subjects of lengthy monographs, while others, like question XXIX's query as to whether there was anything above or below the universe, were never revisited. Some of the questions may also once have been sermons. Question LXIV,7 contains a phrase that seems to have been directed to an audience, which makes no sense if it is not homiletic.

As if to underline the catch-all nature of his work, Augustine includes two questions that are in fact passages quoted verbatim from other authors. Question XII is taken from a treatise entitled On *Purifying the Mind in order to See God* by a certain Fonteius of Carthage, while question XXXI comes from Cicero's *De inventione rhetorica*. Both of these quotations, the *Revisions* tell us, were familiar to Augustine's monastic brothers because he had introduced them to them. The brothers themselves collected them and wanted them placed among Augustine's writings.

The chapters (*capitula*) that precede the body of the text belong to the manuscript tradition and are perhaps alluded to in *Revisions* I,26,1 when Augustine mentions the "numbered sections" that would make it easy for his readers to find what they were looking for.

Revisions I,26

1. Among the things that we have written there is also a certain lengthy work, which is nonetheless counted as a single book, whose title is *A Miscellany of Eighty-three Questions*. They were scattered on numerous pieces of paper because, from the time when I was first converted, after we came to Africa, they were dictated by me in the same random order as the brothers asked me questions, when they saw that I had time to spare. So, when I was already a bishop, I ordered that they be collected and made into a single book, which is in numbered sections so that whoever wants to read something may find it easily.

2. The first of these questions is on whether the soul exists of itself.

The second is on free choice.

The third is on whether it is by God's causality that humankind is evil.

The fourth is on why humankind is evil.

The fifth is on whether an irrational animal can be blessed.

The sixth is on evil.

The seventh is on what the soul should properly be called in an ensouled being.

The eighth is on whether the soul is moved by itself.

The ninth is on whether truth can be grasped by the body's senses. In that question I said: "Everything that a bodily sense has contact with, which is itself referred to as sensible, is subject to continual temporal change." Without doubt this is not at all true of the incorruptible bodies of the resurrection. But now no bodily sense of ours has contact with them unless perhaps something of the sort is divinely revealed.

The tenth is on whether the body comes from God.

The eleventh is on why Christ was born of a woman.

The twelfth, which is entitled "The words of a certain wise man," is not mine, but it was through me that it became known to some of the brothers, who then very carefully compiled the material. They liked it, and they wished to place it among our writings. It comes from the work On *Purifying the Mind in order to See God* by a certain Fonteius of Carthage, which was actually written when he was a pagan, although he died a baptized Christian.

The thirteenth is on by what evidence it is clear that humans are superior to beasts.

The fourteenth is on the fact that the body of our Lord Jesus Christ was not a phantasm.

The fifteenth is on the intellect.

The sixteenth is on the Son.

The seventeenth is on God's knowledge.

The eighteenth is on the Trinity.

The nineteenth is on God and creation.

The twentieth is on God's place.

The twenty-first is on whether God is not the creator of evil. There it must be seen if what I said may be misunderstood: "The creator of all things that exist is not the creator of evil, because to the extent that they exist they are good," and if this could give rise to the idea that the sufferings of the wicked, which are indeed an evil to those who are punished by them, do not come from him. But I said this in the same way that it is said, *God did not make death* (Wis 1:13), although elsewhere it is written: *Death and life are from the Lord God* (Sir 11.14). The sufferings of the wicked, then, which are from God, are indeed an evil to the wicked, but they are among God's good works, because it is just that the wicked be punished, and everything that is just is truly good.

The twenty-second is on the fact that God is not subject to necessity.

The twenty-third is on the Father and the Son, in which I said, "He himself produced the wisdom by which he is called wise." But afterwards I dealt better with this question in a book on the Trinity.

The twenty-fourth is on whether both committing sin and acting rightly fall under the will's free choice. That this is the case is utterly true, but it is by the grace of God that one is free to act rightly.

The twenty-fifth is on the cross of Christ.

The twenty-sixth is on the difference of sins.

The twenty-seventh is on providence.

The twenty-eighth is on why God wished to make the world.

The twenty-ninth is on whether anything is above or below the universe.

The thirtieth is on whether everything has been created for the use of human beings.

The thirty-first is not my own but Cicero's. But because it too became known to the brothers through me, they placed it among the writings that they were collecting, wishing to know how the soul's virtues were differentiated and defined by him.

The thirty-second is on whether one person can understand something better than another person, and whether the understanding of that thing can thus proceed to infinity.

The thirty-third is on fear.

The thirty-fourth is on whether something else should be loved than to lack fear.

The thirty-fifth is on what should be loved. I do not completely concur with what I said there: "That must be loved which to possess is nothing but to know." For they did not possess God to whom it was said, *Did you not know that you are the temple of God and that the Spirit of God dwells in you?* (1 Cor 3:16) Yet they did not know him, or did not know him as he should have been known. Again, when I said, "No one, therefore, knows a blessed life while being wretched," I said "knows" in terms of how it should be known. For who, among those who use their reason in this regard, is completely ignorant of it, since they know that they desire to be blessed?

The thirty-sixth is on fostering charity, where I said, "Thus, when God and the soul are loved it is properly called charity, and it is most refined and most perfect if nothing else is loved." If this is true, why does the Apostle say, *No one ever hates his own flesh* (Eph 5:29), teaching in this way that wives should be loved?[1]

The thirty-seventh is on him who has always been born.

The thirty-eighth is on the conformation of the soul.

The thirty-ninth is on foods.

The fortieth asks, since souls have one nature, where the different wills of human beings come from.

The forty-first asks, since God made all things, why he did not make them in equal fashion.

The forty-second asks how the Lord Jesus, who is the wisdom of God,[2] was both in his mother's womb and in heaven.

The forty-third asks why the Son of God appeared in a man and the Holy Spirit in a dove.[3]

The forty-fourth asks why the Lord Jesus Christ came after such a long time. When we were discussing the ages of the human race as if they were those of an individual person I said, "It was not opportune for the Master, by

---

1. See Eph 5:25. 28.
2. See 1 Cor 1:24.
3. See Mt 3:16.

whose imitation it [i.e., the human race] would be fashioned for the most excellent manner of life, to come from heaven except during the period of its youth." And I added, "In this respect what the Apostle says is apropos—that under the law we were like children under a guardian's tutelage."[4] But it could be confusing that we said elsewhere that Christ came in the sixth age of the human race, in the old age of the old person, so to speak.[5] In the one place, then, what was said of youth refers to the vigor and fervor of faith that works through love,[6] whereas in the other what was said of old age refers to the enumeration of ages. For both can be understood of the whole of human-kind, which cannot be the case in regard to the periods of life of individuals. Thus both youth and old age cannot co-exist in the body, but they can in the soul—the former through vivacity and the latter through gravity.

The forty-fifth is against mathematicians.

The forty-sixth is on ideas.

The forty-seventh is on whether we may ever be able to see our thoughts. There I said, "It must be believed that angelic bodies, such as we hope to possess, are very light and ethereal." If this is understood to preclude the members that we now have or to preclude substance, even though it is that of an incorruptible flesh, it is erroneous. This question on seeing our thoughts was treated much better in the work entitled *The City of God*.[7]

The forty-eighth is on believable things.

The forty-ninth asks why the children of Israel sacrificed oblations of cattle in visible fashion.

The fiftieth is on the equality of the Son.

The fifty-first is on humankind as made to the image and likeness of God. There I said: "Without life one may not correctly (*recte*) be called a human being." Is a human corpse not also referred to as a human being? Consequently I should at least have said that it is not properly (*proprie*) called such instead of saying that it is not correctly called such. I also said: "Neither is this distinction useless—that the image and likeness of God ... is one thing, and being in the image and likeness of God, as we understand

---

4. See Gal 3:23-24.
5. See question LXIV, 2.
6. See Gal 5:6.
7. See XXII, 29.

that humankind was made,[8] is another." This must not be understood as if humankind (*homo*) is not called the image of God, since the Apostle says, *A man* (vir) *indeed should not cover his head, because he is the image and the glory of God* (1 Cor 11:7). But he is also said to be *in* the image of God, which is not the case with the only-begotten [Son of God], who is only the image and not *in* the image.

The fifty-second is on what is said: *I regret having made humankind* (Gn 6:7).

The fifty-third is on the gold and silver that the Israelites took from the Egyptians.[9]

The fifty-fourth is on what is written: *But it is good for me to cling to God* (Ps 73:28). There I said, "But that which is superior to every soul we call God." What should have been said instead was "superior to every created spirit."

The fifty-fifth is on what is written: *There are sixty queens and eighty concubines, and the young maidens are numberless* (Sg 6:8).

The fifty-sixth is on the forty-six years of the building of the Temple.[10]

The fifty-seventh is on the one hundred and fifty-three fish.[11]

The fifty-eighth is on John the Baptist.

The fifty-ninth is on the ten virgins.[12]

The sixtieth is on the words: *But of the day and the hour no one knows, neither the angels of heaven nor the Son of Man but only the Father.* (Mt 24:36)

The sixty-first is on what is written in the gospel, that on the mountain the Lord fed the crowds with five loaves.[13] There I said, "The two fish ... seem to signify two offices ... —namely, a kingship and a priesthood, to which that most holy anointing also belonged." "Especially belonged" should have been said here instead, because we read that the prophets were sometimes anointed.[14] I also said, "Luke, who as it were suggested that Christ the priest ascended after the abolition of our sins, goes in ascending order to David through Nathan, because Nathan was the prophet who was sent at whose reproach David by his repentance obtained the abolition of

---

8. See Gn 1:26.
9. See Ex 3:22; 11:2; 12:35-36.
10. See Jn 2:20.
11. See Jn 21:6-11.
12. See Mt 25:1-13.
13. See Jn 6:3-13.
14. See, e.g., 1 K 19:16.

his sin." This should not be understood as if it were Nathan the prophet who was David's son, because it was not said here that he himself had been sent as a prophet but that "Nathan was the prophet who was sent." Thus the mystery would apply not to the same man but to the same name.

The sixty-second is on that which is written in the gospel: *That Jesus baptized more than John, although it was not he himself who baptized but his disciples* (Jn 4:1-2). There I said, "But that thief to whom it was said, *Amen, I say to you, today you will be with me in paradise* (Lk 23:43), who had not received baptism." In fact we found out that other teachers of the holy Church had also said this in their writings before we did. But I do not know by what testimony it can be adequately shown that that thief was not baptized. This matter has been given careful treatment in some of our later works, especially in that which we addressed to Vincentius Victor on the origin of the soul.[15]

The sixty-third is on the Word.

The sixty-fourth is on the Samaritan woman.[16]

The sixty-fifth is on the resurrection of Lazarus.[17]

The sixty-sixth is on what is written: *Are you unaware, brothers—for I speak to those who know the law—that a person is subject to the law for as long as he lives?* (Rom 7:1) up until the place where it is written: *He will also give life to your mortal bodies through his Spirit dwelling within you* (Rom 8:11). What the Apostle said there, *We know that the law is spiritual, but I am fleshly* (Rom 7:14), I tried to explain by saying, "That is, since I have not yet been liberated by spiritual grace." This should not be understood as if a spiritual person already living under grace could not also say this, as well as what remains, in reference to himself, up until the place where it is said: *Wretched man that I am, who will liberate me from the body of this death?* (Rom 7:24) This I taught later, as I have already previously acknowledged.[18] Again, explaining what the Apostle said, *The body indeed is dead on account of sin* (Rom 8:10), I said, "The body is said to be dead for as long as it disturbs the soul by a lack of temporal things." But later it seemed to me more accurate that the body is referred to as dead because it is already under the necessity of dying, which was not the case before sin.

---

15. See *The Soul and its Origin* I,9,11; III,9,12.
16. See Jn 4:5-29.
17. See Jn 11:17-44.
18. See *Revisions* I,23,2.

The sixty-seventh is on what is written: *For I think that the sufferings of this time are insignificant in comparison to the glory that is to come that will be revealed in us* (Rom 8:18) up until that which is said: *For by hope we have been saved* (Rom 8:24). When I was explaining the words, *Creation itself as well shall be liberated from slavery to destruction* (Rom 8:21), I said, "And creation itself—that is, humanity itself, once the mark of the image was lost because of sin and the creature alone remained." This should not be understood as if humankind lost in its entirety the image of God that it possessed. For if it had not lost anything at all the condition would not have existed on account of which it was said: *Be reformed in the newness of your mind* (Rom 12:2); and: *We are being transformed into the same image* (2 Cor 3:18). But if, on the other hand, all of it were lost, nothing would have remained so that it could be said: *Although man walks in an image, yet he is disturbed in vain* (Ps 39:6). I also said, "The highest angels live spiritually but the lowest live in conformity with the soul." This was said more rashly of the lowest than can be shown either by the holy scriptures or by the facts themselves because, even if it is perhaps the case, it can be shown only with great difficulty.

The sixty-eighth is on what is written: *O man, who are you that you talk back to God?* (Rom 9:20) There I said, "Because even if someone with lighter sins or even with any number of more serious ones has nonetheless, in his great groaning and the pain of his repentance, been accorded the mercy of God, it does not come down to him (who would perish if he were abandoned) but to a merciful God who comes to the aid of his entreaties and distress. For, if God is not merciful, it is not enough to will something, but God, who calls us to peace, is only merciful if the willing is already present." This applies to the period after repentance. For if God's mercy did not also precede the willing, the will would not be prepared by the Lord. Pertaining to that mercy is the calling itself, which also precedes faith. Treating of this a little later I said, "But this calling, which is at work at appropriate times whether in individual persons or in nations and in the human race itself, is of a lofty and profound ordination. Whence these words apply: *In the womb I sanctified you* (Jer 1:5); and, 'When you were in your father's loins I saw you'; and, *I loved Jacob, but I hated Esau* (Rom 9:13)"; and so forth. But how the words "When you were in your father's loins I saw you" struck me as scriptural I do not know.

The sixty-ninth is on what is written: *Then the Son himself will be subjected to the one who has subjected everything to him* (1 Cor 15:28).

The seventieth is on what the Apostle says: *Death has been swallowed up in victory. Where, O death, is your struggle? Where, O death, is your sting? The sting of death is sin, but the strength of sin is the law.* (1 Cor 15:54-56)

The seventy-first is on what is written: *Bear one another's burdens, and thus you will fulfill the law of Christ* (Gal 6:2).

The seventy-second is on the eternal times.

The seventy-third is on what is written: *And found in* habitus *as a man* (Phil 2:7).

The seventy-fourth is on what is written in Paul's letter to the Colossians: *In whom we have redemption, the remission of sins, who is the image of the invisible God* (Col 1:14-15).

The seventy-fifth is on God's inheritance.

The seventy-sixth is on what the apostle James says: *Do you wish to know, O foolish person, that faith without works is useless?* (Jas 2:20)

The seventy-seventh is on whether fear is a sin.

The seventy-eighth is on the beauty of images.

The seventy-ninth asks why Pharaoh's magicians performed certain miracles like Moses, the servant of God.[19]

The eightieth is against the Apollinarians.

The eighty-first is on quadragesima and quinquagesima.

The eighty-second is on what is written: *Whom the Lord loves he corrects; he scourges every son whom he receives* (Heb 12:16).

The eighty-third, on marriage, is on what the Lord says: *If anyone renounces his wife, except because of fornication* (Mt 5:32).

This work begins thus: "Whether the soul exists of itself."

---

19. See Ex 7-8.

Chapters

Miscellany of Eighty-three Questions

I. Whether the soul exists of itself

Everything that is true is true by reason of the truth,[1] and every soul is a soul inasmuch as it is a true soul. Consequently every soul depends upon the truth in order that it may exist as a soul at all. But the soul is one thing and the truth is something else, for the truth never endures error, whereas the soul often errs. Therefore, since the soul depends upon the truth, it does not exist of itself. Now God is the truth. Consequently the soul has God as its creator so that it may exist.

II. On free choice[2]

Nothing that comes into existence can be equal to that from which it comes into existence; otherwise justice, which is obliged to give to each person what is his, would necessarily be removed from affairs.[3] Therefore, when God made humankind, although he made it very good, he nonetheless did not make it what he himself was. But a person who *wills* to be good is better than one who *has* to be good. Free will, then, had to be given to humankind.

III. Whether it is by God's causality that humankind is evil[4]

No person becomes evil by the causality of a wise person. For that is no small crime— indeed, it is a great one—and it could not occur in the case of any wise person. But God is superior to every wise person. Much less, then, does a person become evil by God's causality, for the will of God is far superior to that of a wise person. When someone's causality is spoken of, it is his

---

1. Augustine distinguishes here between "the true" (*verum*) and "the truth" (*veritas*), as in question XXIII he distinguishes between the chaste and chastity, the eternal and eternity, the good and goodness, and so forth. While the true is dependent on the truth, the truth itself is not dependent on anything else. See *Soliloquies* I,15,27 for Augustine's first use of this distinction.
2. Augustine deals extensively with this issue in his treatise entitled *Free Will*.
3. The reasoning here is that, since justice can only be practiced in unequal situations, equality—in this case between the creator and his human creation—would remove the need for justice.
4. The "evil" of this and the following question is a translation of *deterior*, which is comparative in form and hence means "worse." But "worse" is clearly out of place here. In his translation Mosher renders the question as "Is God responsible for human perversity?" He translates the title of question IV in similar fashion. The arguments given in this and the following question are elaborated in dialogue form and at length in *Free Will* I. The discovery of the cause of evil in the human will was one of the major steps in the process of Augustine's conversion. See *Confessions* VII,3,4-5.

31

willing that is meant. It is by a flaw in his will, therefore, that humankind is evil. If this flaw is foreign to the will of God, as reason teaches, where it may be must be inquired after.

IV. Why humankind is evil

The cause as to why humankind is evil is either in itself or in something else or in nothing. If it is in nothing, there is no cause. Or "if it is in nothing" is understood in such a way that humankind was made from nothing or from things that were made from nothing, the cause will then be in it, because nothing is, so to speak, its matter. If it is in something else, we must investigate whether it is in God or in some other human or in what is neither God nor humankind. But it is not in God, for God is the cause of good things. If it is in humankind, it must be so either by force or by persuasion. But it is certainly not so by force, in which case it would be more powerful than God, since in fact God made humankind so very well that, had he wished to remain perfectly good, nothing would have stood in his way. If it is by the persuasion of another human, then we concede that humankind is depraved, and in that case we must investigate by whom the persuader himself was depraved, for a persuader of such things cannot but be depraved. We are left at an impasse, because it is neither God nor humankind. But even this, whatever it is, has either introduced force or been persuasive. The answer to the question of force was given above. As far as persuasion is concerned, inasmuch as persuasion does not compel the unwilling, the cause of depravity goes back to the will of a given person, and he is depraved whether he has been persuaded by someone else or not.

V. Whether an irrational animal can be blessed[5]

An animal that lacks reason lacks knowledge. No animal, however, that lacks knowledge can be blessed. It is not the case, therefore, that animals devoid of reason are blessed.

---

5. "Blessed" (*beatum*) may also be translated as "happy"; these two adjectives are virtually interchangeable in Augustine. The question demonstrates that Augustine's understanding of blessedness, or happiness, is founded first upon the possession of reason (and then upon its proper use). See Etienne Gilson, *The Christian Philosophy of Saint Augustine*, trans. L. E. M. Lynch (New York: Random House, 1960) 3-10.

VI. On evil

Everything that exists is either corporeal or incorporeal. The corporeal is contained within the sensible species, but the incorporeal within the intelligible. Nothing that exists, therefore, exists apart from some species. But where there is a species there is necessarily a modality, and modality is something good. Hence absolute evil has no modality, for it lacks any goodness. Therefore it does not exist because it is contained within no species, and this whole designation of evil is determinable by its lack of a species.[6]

VII. What the soul should properly be called in an ensouled being

The soul is sometimes spoken of in such a way as to be taken for the mind, as when we say that the human person consists of soul and body, and sometimes in such a way that it is referred to apart from the mind. But when it is referred to apart from the mind it is understood with regard to the activities that we have in common with beasts. For beasts lack reason, which is proper to the mind.

VIII. Whether the soul is moved by itself [7]

The person who feels that the soul is moved by itself feels in himself the presence of his will, for, if we will something, there is no one else willing on our behalf. And this motion of the soul is spontaneous, for it was given to it by God. Yet this motion is not from place to place as is the case with the body, for to be moved in regard to place is proper to a body. And even when a soul moves its body in regard to place by way of the will—that is, by a motion that has no reference to place—this does not prove that it itself is moved from one place to another. For example, when we see that something is moved over a considerable space by the action of a hinge, nonetheless the hinge itself does not change its place.

---

6. The discovery that evil is a deficiency in being, while goodness implies being, represented another step along Augustine's path to conversion. See *Confessions* VII,12,18.
7. The question, as becomes apparent, has to do with the possible materiality or corporeality of the soul, which Augustine also discusses in *The Greatness of the Soul* 14,23-24. In the present question the soul is referred to as implying the mind (see question VII). In *The Trinity* XIV,6,8 the exercise of the will is described as one of the mind's three dynamic actions, along with that of the memory and the understanding.

IX. Whether truth can be grasped by the body's senses[8]

Everything that a bodily sense has contact with, which is itself referred to as sensible, is subject to continual temporal change.[9] Thus, when the hairs on our head grow, or the body reaches old age or blossoms into youth, this happens continuously and there is no pause whatsoever in the process. What does not remain the same, however, cannot be grasped, for what is grasped is what is laid hold of by knowledge, but what is continuously changing cannot be laid hold of. Consequently there is no authentic truth to be expected from the body's senses.

But if anyone should say that some sensible objects are always the same and should question us concerning the sun and the stars, about which it is not easy to offer proof, certainly there is no one who would not be compelled to acknowledge that there is nothing sensible which does not have a false likeness such that no difference can be discerned. For, to be brief, we experience images of all the things that we know through the body, even when they are not present to our senses, either in sleep or in a state of high emotion, as though they were really present. And when we experience them, whether we know them through the senses themselves or they are images of sensible objects, we are unable to make a distinction. If, then, the images of sensible objects are false and cannot be verified by the senses themselves, and nothing can be grasped unless it can be distinguished from what is false, the wherewithal to judge the truth does not exist in the senses.

Hence we are very usefully warned to turn away from this world, which is in point of fact corporeal and sensible, and with wholehearted commitment to turn to God—that is, to the truth which is seized upon by the intellect and the mind within, which forever abides and has the same modality, and which has no false image that cannot be distinguished [from the truth].

X. Whether the body comes from God

Everything good is from God. Everything belonging to a species is good insofar as it is specified, and everything contained in a species possesses speci-

---

8. This longest of the initial questions of the *Miscellany* begins by asking whether the senses are able to attain to truth and ends by drawing the conclusion that it is best to turn away from the sensible world in order to grasp the truth that is God. Here the theme of the soul's ascent from the sensible world to God, so frequently employed by Augustine (see, e.g., *Confessions* VII,17,23; IX,10,23-25), is reduced to its bare bones.

9. Augustine qualifies this sentence in the *Revisions* by saying that it does not take into account the incorruptible bodies of the resurrection, even though those bodies are not presently susceptible to contact with our bodily senses apart from a divine revelation.

fications. But every body, in order for it to be a body, is contained in some species. Therefore every body is from God.

XI. Why Christ was born of a woman

When God liberates, he does not liberate a particular part, but he liberates the whole whenever it is endangered. Now the wisdom and power of God,[10] which is called the only-begotten Son, signified the liberation of human beings when he took humanity upon himself.[11] But the liberation of human beings had to be apparent in both sexes. Therefore, since it was right for him to take upon himself the male, which is the more honorable sex,[12] it followed that the liberation of the female sex should appear from the fact that he, as a man, was born of a woman.

XII. The words of a certain wise man[13]

"Act," he says, "O wretched mortals, act in such a way that the wicked spirit never pollutes this dwelling, that he does not intrude himself into your senses and defile the holiness of your soul or becloud the light of your mind. This evil being slithers through all the openings that your senses provide: he assumes different shapes, adapts himself to colors, clings to sounds, lies concealed in anger and in false speech, hides in odors, pours himself into flavors, and by his turbulent and filthy activity casts the senses into the gloom of dark emotions. With certain vapors he fills the pathways of the intellect through which the light of reason, the mind's ray, is accustomed to spread. And since this is a ray of heavenly light, there is in it also a mirror of the divine presence; for God and a blameless will and the reward of deeds well done shine forth in it.

---

10. See 1 Cor 1:24.
11. "When he took humanity upon himself ": *homine suscepto*. This is a reference to Christ as the *homo susceptus* or, in its better-known form, the *homo assumptus*—"the one who took humanity upon himself." The concept also appears in this work under the guise of *hominem gerere* or *gestare* ("to bear humanity"), *hominem induere* ("to clothe oneself in humanity"), and *hominem agere* ("to act in one's humanity"). Although Augustine uses this language in orthodox fashion, it could easily be open to a Nestorian interpretation (according to which Christ's two natures would only be externally joined). See also questions XXV;LVII,3; LXII; LXV; LXIX,1-2.10; LXXI,4; LXXIII,2; LXXV,2; LXXIX,5; LXXX,1-2.
12. Augustine takes it for granted, as did his contemporaries, that the male is the more honorable sex, although elsewhere he does not deny spiritual equality to women, as in Letter 147,2. For a brief overview of this controversial issue, with a bibliography, see Allan D. Fitzgerald, ed., *Augustine through the Ages* (Grand Rapids: Eerdmans, 1999) 887-892.
13. The first of two questions whose text does not come from Augustine, this one, as we know from the *Revisions*, quotes the treatise of a certain Fonteius of Carthage entitled *On Purifying the Mind in order to See God*. Nothing more is known of either Fonteius or his work, written while he was still a pagan (although he would die a Christian). The excerpt is notable not for its depth but rather for its vivid contrast between the flamboyant activity of Satan and the divine presence.

"God is present everywhere. But he is there in his fullness to each one of us when the unsullied purity of our mind is aware of his presence. For as our vision, if it has been damaged, is unaware of the presence of what it cannot see (for in vain does an image of something present have an effect on our vision if our vision is deficient), so also is the never-absent God, whom the world's blindness cannot see, present in vain to polluted souls."

XIII. On what evidence it is clear that humans are superior to beasts[14]

Among the many ways by which it can be shown that, thanks to reason, humankind surpasses the beasts, this one is obvious to all: animals can be tamed and pacified by human beings, but by no means can human beings be treated in such fashion by animals.

XIV. That the body of our Lord Jesus was not a phantasm[15]

If the body of Christ was a phantasm, Christ was a deceiver, and if he is a deceiver there is no truth. But Christ is truth. Hence his body was not a phantasm.

XV. On the intellect

Everything that understands itself comprehends itself. Whatever comprehends itself, however, is limited to itself. The intellect understands itself and therefore it is limited to itself. It does not wish to be without limits, even if it could be, because it wishes to be known for itself, for it loves itself.

XVI. On the Son

God is the cause of everything that is. But, since he is the cause of all things, he is also the cause of his own wisdom, and God is never without wisdom. The cause of his own eternal wisdom, then, is eternal; he is not prior in time to his own wisdom. And so, if to be the eternal Father is intrinsic to God, and he never existed without being a Father, he was never without a Son.[16]

---

14. The same argument offered in this question is advanced in *Free Will* I,7,16; *On Genesis: A Refutation of the Manicheans* I,18,29.
15. The inclination to view Christ's body as a phantasm was widespread in early Christianity, as witness the Docetists, the Gnostics and also the Manicheans, with whom Augustine was acquainted. See the *Answer to Faustus, a Manichean* V,5.
16. The tradition identifying the Son of the Father with wisdom goes back to 1 Cor 1:24 and the gospel of John. Augustine famously develops it in *The Trinity* XIV,6,8ff, where he finds the human analogy to the Son in the *intellectus*, the intellect or the understanding.

XVII. On God's knowledge[17]

Whatever is past no longer exists, and whatever is future does not yet exist. Both the past and the future, therefore, are entirely absent. To God, however, nothing is absent, and hence nothing is either past or future, but everything is present to God.

XVIII. On the Trinity

Everything that exists is one thing in regard to existence, another in regard to differentiation, and still another in regard to suitability. All creation, therefore, if it exists in some way, and if it differs utterly from that which is nothing at all, and if its parts conform to each other, must also have a threefold cause: that by which it exists, that by which it is this particular thing, and that by which it accords with itself. But the cause of creation—that is, its maker—we call God. He must therefore be a trinity, anything more excellent or intelligent or blessed than which is beyond the capacity of human reasoning to find. And therefore also, when truth is sought, there can be no more than three sorts of questions: whether a thing exists at all, whether it is this or something else, and whether it is appropriate or inappropriate.[18]

XIX. On God and creation[19]

Whatever is unchangeable is eternal, for it exists always in the same way. But whatever is changeable is subject to time, for it does not exist always in the same way, and therefore it is not rightly called eternal. For whatever changes does not abide; whatever does not abide is not eternal. And there is this difference between what is immortal and what is eternal: everything that is eternal is immortal, but not everything that is immortal is with sufficient accuracy called eternal, because if something undergoes change, even if it is always alive, it is not properly called eternal because it does not exist always in the same way; yet it can rightly be called immortal because it is always alive. Nonetheless

---

17. The issue of time, which is discussed in this question, is expounded at length in *Confessions* XI. On the non-existence of past and future, see especially ibid. XI,26,33-31,41.
18. This is one of Augustine's earliest attempts to locate analogies to the Trinity in the created order. Indeed, there are two such analogies here: 1) that by which a thing exists, that by which it is this particular thing, and that by which it accords with itself; and (in question form) 2) does a thing exist? is it this or something else? and is it appropriate or inappropriate? Similar analogies from Augustine's early writings can be found in Letter 11,3-4; *True Religion* 7,13.
19. On this question, which is about time and eternity (and which distinguishes between eternity and immortality), see also *Confessions* XI; *Exposition of Psalm* 101 [102],2,10; *The Trinity* IV,18,24. The latter two passages, and arguably the first as well, hold out the hope of human beings' participating in eternity, for which the present question, in all its brevity, seems to make no provision (as is not the case, for example, with question XXIII).

what is immortal can sometimes also be called eternal. But that which both undergoes change and is said to be alive thanks to the presence of a soul, although it is not a soul, can in no way be understood as immortal and much less as eternal. For in what is eternal, as is properly said, there is neither anything past, as if it had ceased, nor anything future, as if it did not yet exist, but it is what simply exists.

XX. On God's place

God is not in a place, for that which is in a place is contained in that place. That which is contained in a place is a body, but God is not a body. Therefore he is not in a place. And yet, since he is and he is not in a place, all things are in him rather than he himself being in some place, although they are not in him as if he himself were a place. For a place is in space because it is defined by the length, breadth and width characteristic of a body. God is not like this. Everything, therefore, is in him, and he is not a place.

Yet in a loose sense God's temple[20] is called God's place—not because he is contained in it but because he is present to it. This, however, is understood to be nothing better than the pure soul.

XXI. Whether God is not the creator of evil

In no way can non-existence be associated with him who is the creator of all things that exist and upon whose goodness it alone depends that all things that exist are in existence. Now everything that is deficient is deficient in regard to existence and tends toward non-existence. But to exist and to be in no respect deficient is good; to be deficient is evil. He, however, who is not associated with non-existence is not the cause of deficiency—that is, of tending toward non-existence—because, as I would assert, he is the cause of existence. He is only the cause of good, therefore, and hence he is the highest good. On that account the creator of all things that exist is not the creator of evil, because to the extent that they exist they are good.[21]

---

20. See 1 Cor 3:16.
21. In his *Revisions* Augustine says that he fears that this final sentence could be misunderstood to mean that God did not create the sufferings of the wicked. Therefore he emphasizes that "the sufferings of the wicked, then, which are from God, are indeed an evil to the wicked, but they are among God's good works, because it is just that the wicked be punished, and everything that is just is truly good."

XXII. That God is not subject to necessity

Where there is no lack there is no necessity; where there is no deficiency there is no lack. But there is no deficiency in God, and therefore no necessity.

XXIII. On the Father and the Son[22]

Everything chaste is chaste by reason of chastity, everything eternal by reason of eternity, everything beautiful by reason of beauty, everything good by reason of goodness; therefore also everything wise by reason of wisdom and everything like by reason of likeness. But what is chaste is said to be so by reason of chastity in two ways—either because it produces it, so that it is chaste by reason of the chastity which it produces and for which it is the source and cause of its existence, but otherwise when something is chaste on account of its participation in chastity, because sometimes it can be unchaste. And so it is to be understood in the other instances. For the soul, too, is understood and believed to acquire eternity, but it becomes eternal on account of its participation in eternity. It is not thus that God is eternal, but because he is the creator of eternity itself. This is clearly evident with regard to both beauty and goodness. Hence when God is called wise and is called wise by reason of that wisdom without which it is wicked to believe that he ever could exist or can exist, he is called wise not on account of his participation in wisdom, as is the case with the soul, which can be both wise and unwise, but because he himself produced the wisdom by which he is called wise.[23] Similarly, those things which, on account of their participation, are chaste or eternal or beautiful or good or wise admit, as it is said, of being able to be not chaste or eternal or beautiful or good or wise. But chastity, eternity, beauty, goodness and wisdom in no way admit of either corruption or, as I might say, temporality or wickedness or malice. Those things, therefore, that are alike on account of participation admit of unlikeness. But likeness itself can in no way be unlike in any regard. Thus it is

---

22. See also question I and note 1. Whereas in question I Augustine had said that the distinction between "the true" and "the truth" was based upon the dependence of the former upon the latter, here he says that the distinction between "the chaste" and "chastity," and so forth, is based upon the participation of the former in the latter. Since chastity and other such qualities are participants they can undergo corruption, whereas that which is participated in cannot be corrupted. "Those things, therefore, that are alike on account of participation admit of unlikeness" on account of corruption. Likeness (*similitudo*) alone cannot be corrupted and become unlike, as is consistent with reason. Hence, when the Son is called the Father's "likeness" (in Col 1:15), the implication is that there is no dissimilarity between the two at all. The topic of participation will be developed in the following question.

23. In citing these words in the *Revisions* Augustine says merely that he dealt better with this question in *The Trinity*, and he is probably referring to VI,2,3 of that treatise.

that when the Son is called the likeness of the Father[24]—because by participation in him whatever is alike is alike either between themselves or with reference to God, for this is the first species by which, as I might say, all things are specified, and the form by which they are formed—he can in no regard be unlike the Father. The Son, then, is like the Father, but in the way that he is the Son and the Father the Father—that is, the former is the likeness and the latter is that whose likeness he is, and from this comes one substance. For, if it is not one, likeness admits of unlikeness, which all completely consistent reasoning denies can be the case.

XXIV. Whether both committing sin and acting rightly fall under the will's free choice[25]

Whatever occurs by chance occurs accidentally; whatever occurs accidentally does not occur by providence. If, then, some things occur by chance in the world, the universe is not governed by providence. But if the universe is not governed by providence, there is some nature and substance that is unrelated to the workings of providence. But everything that exists is good to the extent that it exists. Now in the highest place is that good by participation in which everything else is good. And everything that is changeable is good to the extent that it exists not of itself but on account of its participation in the unchangeable good. Furthermore, that good by participation in which other things are good, whatever they may be, is good by reason not of something else but of itself, and this we call divine providence. Therefore nothing occurs by chance in the world.

Once this has been established it follows that whatever is done in the world is done partly by divine action and partly by our will. Now God is incomparably better and more righteous by far than the best and most righteous human being that one could imagine. But he who rules and governs all things righteously allows no punishment to be inflicted undeservedly and no reward to be bestowed undeservedly on anyone. But sin is deserving of punishment and acting rightly is deserving of reward, and neither sinfulness nor acting rightly can be justly imputed to anyone who has done nothing by his own will. Therefore both committing sin and acting rightly fall under the will's free choice.

---

24. See Col 1:15.
25. Augustine qualifies what he wrote in this question by adding, in the *Revisions*, that it is grace that frees a person so that he is free to act rightly.

XXV. On the cross of Christ

The wisdom of God assumed humanity in order to give us a model of upright living. But not fearing the things that should not be feared is part of an upright life. Now death is not to be feared. Therefore it was appropriate that that very thing be demonstrated by the death of the human being whom the wisdom of God[26] assumed.[27] But there are people who, although they do not fear death itself, are still horrified by a particular kind of death. Yet, however, just as death itself should not be feared, neither should a particular kind of death be feared by a person who leads a good and upright life. No less, then, did this too need to be shown by the cross of that person. For among all the different kinds of death there was none more detestable and frightening than that kind.

XXVI. On the different kinds of sins

Some sins are due to weakness, others to ignorance and still others to wickedness. Weakness is contrary to power, ignorance is contrary to wisdom and wickedness is contrary to goodness. Whoever, therefore, knows what the power and wisdom of God[28] is can understand what sins are pardonable. And whoever knows what the goodness of God is can understand for which sins certain punishment is due both here and in the world to come.[29] An appropriate judgment can be made in the case of those who have acted well, who may not be obliged to a painful and sorrowful penance although they confess their sins, and in the case of those for whom no salvation whatsoever may be hoped for unless through penance they have offered God the sacrifice of an afflicted spirit.[30]

XXVII. On providence

It can happen that by means of a bad person divine providence both punishes and assists. For the wickedness of the Jews both overthrew the Jews and was salvific for the gentiles. Similarly it can happen that by means of a good person divine providence both condemns and helps, as the Apostle says, *For some we are the odor of life unto life, while for others we are the odor of death unto death* (2 Cor 2:16). But since every tribulation is either punishment

---

26. See 1 Cor 1:24.
27. "The human being whom the wisdom of God assumed": *illius hominis quem dei sapientia suscepit*. See note 11.
28. See 1 Cor 1:24.
29. See Mt 12:31-32.
30. See Ps 51:17.

for the wicked or training for the righteous (for the same threshing sledge [*tribula*] both beats the straw and separates the grain from the straw, which is how the word "tribulation" originated), and since peace and repose with respect to bodily annoyances is profitable for the good and corrupting for the wicked, divine providence arranges all these things in accordance with the deserts of souls. But the good do not choose tribulation on their own as a help, nor do the wicked love peace. And so they, by means of whom things are done of which they are unaware, receive recompense not for the righteousness whose source is God but for their own wickedness. In the same way it is not imputed to the good that, when they themselves will to do good, harm befalls someone, but the reward of a good will is bestowed upon the good soul. Likewise also the rest of creation is perceptible or lies hidden, is troublesome or advantageous, in accordance with the deserts of rational souls. For, as the most high God disposes well everything that he has made, there is nothing in the universe that is disordered and nothing that is unjust, whether we know this to be the case or not. Yet for its part the sinful soul suffers loss; still, because it is where it ought to be in accordance with its deserts, and suffers those things which it is right for it to suffer, it does not disfigure any part of God's kingdom by its own deformity.[31]

Hence, because we are not aware of everything that the divine order accomplishes profitably in our regard, we act in accordance with the law solely by good will; but at other moments we are moved in accordance with the law, since the law itself remains immutable and regulates all mutable things by a governance that is most beautiful. *Glory to God in the highest,* therefore, *and peace on earth to men of good will* (Lk 2:14).

XXVIII. Why God wished to make the world

Whoever questions why God wished to make the world is asking a question about the cause of God's will. But every cause is efficient. Every efficient agent, however, is greater than that which is effected. But nothing is greater than the will of God; its cause, therefore, is not subject to question.

XXIX. Whether anything is above or below the universe

Know the things that are above (Col 3:2). We are commanded to know the things that are above—namely, spiritual things, which are to be understood as being above not with reference to places and parts of this world but by reason

---

31. This is an early illustration of Augustine's profound belief in the universe's ineluctable order, which appears in full flower in *The City of God* XIX,12-13.

of their excellence—lest we attach our soul to a part of this world from which we ought to separate ourselves completely. But there is an above and a below in its parts. On the other hand the universe in itself does not have an above and a below, because it is bodily inasmuch as everything visible is bodily, yet there is nothing in this body in its entirety that is above or below. For since the movement that is called linear—that is, which is not circular—seems to exist in six parts, in a front and a back, in a right and a left, and in a higher and a lower, there is no reason at all why there should be nothing before or after in respect to this body in its entirety, or right or left, or above or below. But those who reflect on these things are deceived because there is strong resistance from the senses and from habit. For it is less easy for us to turn our body by lowering our head than by turning from right to left or from front to back. Hence one must lay aside language and delve into one's own soul in order to understand this.

XXX. Whether everything has been created for the use of human beings[32]

Just as there is a difference between the good (*honestum*) and the useful (*utile*), so there is one between what is to be enjoyed and what is to be used. For although the fact that everything good is useful and everything useful is good can be logically defended, nonetheless what is desired for itself is more appropriately and more customarily called *good*, whereas what is to be referred to something else is called *useful*. Hence, we now speak in keeping with this distinction, while maintaining that the good and the useful are in no respect opposed to one another. For they are occasionally thought, in an ignorant and popular way, to be mutually opposed. And so we are said to enjoy a thing from which we derive pleasure, while we use a thing which we refer to that from which pleasure is to be derived. Every human waywardness, then, which we also call vice, comes from wishing to use what should be enjoyed and to enjoy what should be used. Likewise, everything that is rightly ordered, which is also named virtue, comes from enjoying what should be enjoyed and using what should be used. Now good things are to be enjoyed while useful things are to be used.

---

32. This question raises Augustine's famous distinction between use and enjoyment. Augustine begins by suggesting that to use (*uti*) and to enjoy (*frui*) are related to one another as two Ciceronian categories, the useful (*utile*) and the good (*honestum*), are (see Cicero, *De officiis* II,9-10). He builds upon distinctions already made in questions I and XXIII when the true and the truth and the chaste and chastity, and so forth, were being discussed. Thus use is dependent upon usefulness (*utilitas*), which is in fact divine providence, while the good is dependent upon goodness (*honestas*), which is also (the divine) intelligible beauty. The second half of the question in particular anticipates Augustine's better known and more extensive treatment of use and enjoyment in *Teaching Christianity* I.

I call goodness (*honestatem*) an intelligible beauty, which we appropriately say is spiritual, but usefulness (*utilitatem*) I call divine providence. Consequently, although there are many visible things that are beautiful, which are less appropriately denoted as good, nonetheless beauty itself, on account of which whatever is beautiful is beautiful, is in no way visible. Similarly, many visible things are useful, but usefulness itself, on account of which whatever benefits us is beneficial, which we call divine providence, is not visible. It should of course be understood that everything bodily is contained in the term "visible." It is proper, then, to enjoy beautiful things that are invisible— namely, good things; but whether it is proper to enjoy all these things is another matter, although perhaps only what should be enjoyed is rightly called good. But all useful things should be used as each person has need of them. And even the beasts, in fact, do not think it so very absurd to enjoy food and a certain degree of bodily pleasure. But only a being possessed of reason can make use of something, for to know to what a thing is to be referred has not been given to those deprived of reason nor even to reasonable beings that are foolish. Nor can someone use a thing if he does not know to what it should be referred, neither can he know unless he is wise. Hence those who do not use things well are customarily and more precisely said to abuse them, for that which is badly used is of no benefit to a person, and what is of no benefit is not really useful. But whatever is useful is useful in the using, and thus no one uses something unless it is useful. Therefore, whoever uses something badly does not use it.

Consequently a person's reason, which is called virtue once it is perfected, uses itself first of all in order to understand God, so that it may enjoy him by whom also it was created. It uses other rational beings, too, for companionship, and irrational beings for advancement. Its own life, as well, it refers to the enjoyment of God, for that is how it is blessed. And therefore it uses itself. It certainly lays the foundations for unhappiness, by way of pride, if it is referred to itself and not to God. It also uses bodies—some of them to be given life for the sake of kindness (for thus it uses its own body), some to be accepted or rejected for the sake of good health, some to be endured for the sake of patience, some to be regulated for the sake of justice, some to be reflected upon as an instance of truth; even what it abstains from it uses for the sake of temperance. Thus it uses everything, things both tangible and intangible: there is no third possibility. But everything that it uses it judges; God alone it does not judge, because it judges everything else according to God. Neither does it use him, but it enjoys him. For God is not to be referred to anything else, since everything that must be referred to something else is lower than that to which it must be referred, and nothing is higher than God—not in terms of place but on account of the excellence of his nature. Everything that has been created, then, has been created for the use of human beings, because reason uses with judgment everything that has been given to human beings. Before the Fall he did not, to be sure, use things that had to be endured, nor does he use them after the Fall unless he has been converted, and although he uses them before the body's death, he does so nonetheless already as much as possible as God's friend, because he is his willing servant.

XXXI. The words of a certain person[33]

1. "Virtue is a habit of the soul that is in accord with the measure of nature and with reason. Therefore, once it is known in all its parts, its full vigor will have to be considered by sincere and good persons. It has, then, four parts: prudence, justice, fortitude and temperance.

"Prudence is the knowledge of good and bad and neutral things. Its parts are memory, intelligence and foresight. Memory is that by which the mind recalls things that have been; intelligence is that by which it observes things that are; foresight is that by which a thing is seen before it has happened.

"Justice is the habit of soul that, while preserving what benefits the common good, assigns his proper place to each person. Its origin is in nature; then certain things became customary on account of their usefulness; after that, fear of the laws and religion sanctioned things that were derived from nature and that were tested by custom. The law of nature is that which opinion has not produced but which a certain innate power has inserted, like religion, piety, gratitude, vengeance, courtesy and truth. Religion is that which bestows attention and reverence on a superior nature of a certain kind that people call divine. Piety is that by which kindly concern and loving honor are shown to blood relations and to one's fatherland. Gratitude is that in which the remembrance of another's friendliness and good deeds and the desire to repay them are contained. Vengeance is that by which violence, insult and anything what-

---

33. In the *Revisions* Augustine identifies the author of these words as Cicero (106-43 B.C.) and says that the brothers of his monastery had become familiar with them because of him and included them among his writings. They are taken from the treatise *De inventione rhetorica* II,159-167, an important passage in which Cicero, following the Stoic model, divides virtue into its four principal parts, prudence, justice, fortitude and temperance, which are then further subdivided. The passage concludes with some comments on the role of usefulness, which Cicero (unlike Augustine both in the previous question and elsewhere) seems to see as a function of enjoyment. Augustine's inclusion of this excerpt does not necessarily imply his agreement with every aspect of it. He certainly would not, for example, have placed vengeance, at least as Cicero describes it, under justice, and he would have been repelled by the unspoken assumption that virtue was within human reach. For Augustine's somewhat ambivalent relationship to Cicero's writings see Augustine Curley, "Cicero, Marcus Tullius," in Fitzgerald 190-193.

soever that would cause injury is resisted by defending or avenging oneself. Courtesy is that by which persons who stand out by reason of some dignity are accorded respect and honor. Truth is that by which things that exist now or have existed or will exist are spoken of exactly as they are. Customary law is what has condoned something easily drawn from nature and that usage has improved, as we see in the case of religion and of those things that we spoke of previously that are derived from nature and that custom has improved or that long duration has, with the approval of the multitude, transformed into acceptable behavior. Its divisions are the contract, the equal return and the precedent. A contract is that which is acceptable between persons. An equal return is uniform for all persons. A precedent is that about which something has already been established by the words of one or several persons. Statutory law is what is contained in written form, which has been set out to the people for their observance.

"Fortitude is the considered acceptance of dangers and the endurance of labors. Its parts are magnanimity, boldness, patience and perseverance. Magnanimity is the contemplation and administration of great and lofty matters with a certain grandeur of soul and brilliance of purpose. Courage is that by which the soul, in great and good matters, relies greatly upon itself with a certain confident hope. Patience is the voluntary and long-lasting endurance of arduous and difficult things for the sake of what is good and useful. Perseverance is the stable and continuous persistence in a well-considered plan.

"Temperance is the reason's firm and moderate domination over the wantonness and other inordinate impulses of the soul. Its parts are continence, clemency and modesty. Continence is that by which desire is restrained by the governance of counsel. Clemency is that by which souls that are impetuously drawn to and aroused by hatred of someone are restrained by gentleness. Modesty is that by which decency and self-respect establish a precious and lasting reputation.

2. "And all of these are to be sought for themselves alone, without any hope of acquiring some advantage. It does not pertain to this exposition of ours to demonstrate this, nor does it conform to the brevity of instruction. On their account not only are those things to be avoided that are contrary to them, as cowardice is to fortitude and injustice to justice, but even those things that seem to be closely akin but that are far removed. And so the contrary of courage is timidity, and hence it is a vice. Recklessness is not its contrary but is near and related, yet it is a vice. Thus for each virtue there will be found a neighboring vice, either one already given a particular name—like recklessness, which is similar to courage, or stubbornness in the case of perseverance,

or superstition, which is akin to religion—or one without any particular name. All of these will be counted, likewise, among the things that must be avoided and as contrary to good things. And as far as that class of goodness is concerned which is desirable on its own account, enough has been said. Now it seems that something should be said in addition about the role of usefulness, which we nonetheless refer to as good.

3. "Now there are many things that attract us not only by reason of their dignity but also because of their enjoyable qualities. Corresponding to this description are glory, dignity, grandeur and friendship. There is glory when a person is often spoken of with a tone of praise. There is dignity when a person's good reputation stands out by reason of upbringing and honor and modesty. Grandeur is a great abundance of power or majesty or wealth. Friendship is the willing of good things for a person who is loved for his own sake, in conjunction with the same will on his part. Since we are speaking here of the public forum, we add to friendship its enjoyable aspects, so that it may be seen to be sought for that reason as well, lest perhaps those who think that we are speaking about every sort of friendship criticize us. Although there are those who believe that friendship should be sought merely on account of its usefulness, there are others who believe that it should be sought only for itself and still others who believe that it should be sought both for itself and for its usefulness. It will be discussed elsewhere which of these is most correct."

XXXII. Whether one person can understand a given thing better than another person, and whether the understanding of that thing can thus proceed to infinity

Whoever understands a given thing differently than that thing exists is in error, and whoever is in error does not understand that about which he is in error. Whoever, therefore, understands a given thing differently than it exists does not understand it. A thing cannot be understood, then, except as it exists. Now we understand a thing as it exists, just as nothing is understood when it is not understood as it exists. Hence there is no doubt that there is a perfect understanding, which cannot be surpassed, and so the understanding of a given thing does not proceed to infinity, nor is it possible for one person to understand it more than another.

XXXIII. On fear

No one doubts that there is no other cause of fear than losing what we love or have acquired or not acquiring what we have hoped for. Hence what fear will there be of the possibility of losing something if a person loves and possesses this very quality of not fearing? For we fear losing many of the things that we love and possess, and so we hold onto them with fear. But no one can, by fearing, hold onto not fearing. Likewise, whoever loves not fearing and does not yet possess it and hopes that he will possess it— him it does not behoove to fear that he might not acquire it, for by this fear nothing is feared other than that same fear. Furthermore, each fear is fleeing from something, and nothing flees from itself. Hence fear is not feared. But if anyone thinks that it is not correct to say that fear fears something since it is rather the soul that fears because of fear itself, he should be attentive to what is easily ascertainable, which is that there is no fear except that of a future and imminent evil. It is necessarily the case, however, that he who fears is fleeing from something. And so whoever fears to fear is completely absurd, because by fleeing from it he possesses that very thing from which he is fleeing. For since there is no fear unless something evil occurs, to fear lest fear occur is nothing else than to embrace what you detest. Now if this is repugnant, as indeed it is, in no way at all does he fear who loves nothing other than not fearing. And therefore no one can love this alone and not possess it. But whether this alone should be loved is another question. He whom fear has not killed will not be destroyed by lust or distressed by care or disturbed by heedless and empty pleasure. For if he lusts, since lust is nothing but a love for passing things, he will necessarily fear either lest he lose them once he has acquired them or lest he not acquire them. But he does not fear; therefore he does not lust. Likewise, if he is anguished by sorrow of soul he is also necessarily agitated by fear, because anxiety over present evils means fear of imminent ones. But he lacks fear and, therefore, anxiety as well. Likewise, if he is foolishly engaged in pleasure, his pleasure is in things that he can lose, and hence he necessarily fears lest he lose them. But he does not fear at all; therefore he does not at all engage foolishly in pleasure.

XXXIV. Whether something else should be loved than to lack fear

If not fearing is a vice, it must not be loved. But none of those who are completely happy[34] is fearful, and none of those who are completely happy is in vice. Thus not fearing is not a vice. But recklessness is a vice. Not everyone who does not fear is reckless, therefore, although whoever is reckless is not fearful. Likewise, no corpse is fearful. Hence, although not fearing is common to a completely happy person, to a reckless person and to a corpse, a

---

34. "Completely happy": *beatissimus*. The translation could also reasonably be "completely blessed" or "very happy" or "very blessed." The former possibilities suggest eternal bliss, the latter this-worldly happiness. Given Augustine's pessimism about this world, other-worldly happiness seems more likely.

completely happy person possesses it through tranquility of soul, a reckless person through foolhardiness, and a corpse because it lacks all sensibility. And so, because we wish to be happy, we should love not to fear, but, because we do not wish to be reckless or dead, we should not love this not fearing alone.

XXXV. What should be loved

1. Since whatever is not alive does not fear, and no one would persuade us that we should be deprived of life in order to be able to be deprived of fear as well, to live without fear should be loved. But since a life deprived of fear is not to be desired if it is also deprived of understanding, however, what should be loved is to live without fear and with understanding. Should that alone or, rather, should love itself also be loved? Of course, since apart from this those things are not loved. But if love is loved for the sake of other things that should be loved, it is not rightly said to be loved. For to love is nothing other than to desire something for its own sake. Inasmuch as when what is loved is absent there is certain misery, should love, then, be desired for its own sake? And, since love is a kind of motion, and there is no motion unless it be towards something, when we look for what should be loved, we ought to look for the thing towards which the motion is directed. Hence, if love should be loved, by no means should all love be loved. For there is a base love by which the soul pursues things that are beneath it, which is more appropriately called cupidity —namely, the root of all evils.[35] And therefore a thing that can be taken away from the one who loves and enjoys it should not be loved.

What is the thing whose love should be loved if not what cannot disappear while it is being loved? But to possess that is nothing but to know it.[36] To possess gold or any other material object, however, is not to know it, and so it should not be loved. And since a thing can be loved and not possessed, not only from among those things that should not be loved, such as an attractive body, but also of those that *should* be loved, such as the blessed life, and, on the other hand, since something can be possessed and not loved, such as shackles,

---

35. See 1 Tm 6:10. In the Greek text of this scriptural passage it is specifically the love of money that is the root of all evils. In his *Exposition of Psalm* 118 [119],11,6 Augustine indicates that he knows this, but he says that Paul is using the part—the love of money—for the whole—avariciousness (or greed [*cupiditas*]) for anything whatsoever.

36. In the *Revisions* Augustine disagrees with what he says here. For, as he observes, the people to whom it was said, *Do you not know that you are the temple of God and that the Spirit of God dwells in you?* (1 Cor 3:16) did not know God or at least did not know him as he ought to have been known. It is not clear what clarity either this remark or the succeeding one concerning this question brings to the text. See Bibliothèque Augustinienne 1,10,717: "These two remarks, which witness to a concern for precision, do not at all modify the general sense of the thesis."

it is justifiably asked whether, given that possessing is nothing else than knowing, anyone could not love what he possesses when he possesses it—that is, when he knows it. But when we see some people studying mathematics, for example, for no other reason than, by way of that same study, to become rich or to please men, and referring it, once they have learned it, to the same goal that they had set for themselves when they were studying it, or any other discipline that is pursued for the sake of possessing rather than of knowing, it could transpire that someone would possess something whose possession would be its knowledge, and yet he would not love it.[37] Nevertheless no one can perfectly possess or know a good that is not loved. For who can know how good a thing is if he does not enjoy it? But he does not enjoy it if he does not love it. Nor, therefore, does he who does not love what should be loved possess it, even though one can love what one does not possess. No one, therefore, loves a blessed life while being wretched[38] since, if it should be loved just as it is, knowing it means possessing it.

2. This being the case, what does it mean to live blessedly if not to possess something eternal through knowledge of it? For the eternal, as is rightly believed of it alone, is that which cannot be taken away from the one who loves it, and it itself is that state in which possessing is nothing other than knowing. For the most excellent of all things is that which is eternal, and therefore we are not able to possess it except by means of that by which we are more excellent—namely, by the mind. But whatever is possessed by the mind is possessed by knowing, and no good is perfectly known that is not perfectly loved. And as it is not the mind alone that can know, neither can it alone love. For love is a kind of appetite, and we see that in other parts of the soul as well there is an appetite which, if it is in agreement with the mind and with reason, will allow the mind to contemplate what is eternal in exceptional peace and tranquility. Therefore the soul must love with its other parts also this great thing that should be known by the mind. And since it is necessarily the case that what is loved exerts an influence, of itself, upon the lover, it transpires that thus the thing that is loved, when it is eternal, exerts an influence upon the soul by its eternity. Hence this is precisely the way it is with that blessed life which is eternal. But what is eternal that exerts an influence upon the soul by its eternity if not God? But the love (*amor*) of the things that should be loved is better called charity (*caritas*) or *dilectio*. On this account that commandment should

---

37. This sentence betrays some of Augustine's well-known skepticism about formal education, expressed also, e.g., in *Confessions* I,16,25-18,29; *Sermon on Christian Discipline* 11,12.

38. Augustine cites these words in the *Revisions* and adds: "I said 'knows' in terms of how it should be known. For who, among those who use their reason in this regard, is completely ignorant of it, since they know that they desire to be blessed?" See note 36.

be considered with all the force of our mind as most beneficial, *You shall love* (diliges) *the Lord your God with all your heart and with all your soul and with all your mind* (Mt 22:37), along with what the Lord Jesus uttered, *This is eternal life, that they may know you, the one true God, and Jesus Christ, whom you sent* (Jn 17:3).

XXXVI. On fostering charity[39]

1. I call charity that by which those things are loved that should not be despised in comparison with the lover himself—namely, that which is eternal and that which can love the eternal itself. Thus, when God and the soul are loved it is properly called charity, and it is most refined and most perfect if nothing else is loved; it is appropriate for this to be called *dilectio* as well.[40] But when God is loved more than the soul, so that a person prefers to belong to God than to himself, then it is truly of the greatest advantage to the soul, and consequently to the body, since we are indifferent to satisfying our desires but use only what is at hand and offered to us.

But what poisons charity is the hope of acquiring and keeping temporal things. What fosters it is the decrease of greed; its perfection is no greed. The sign of its increase is the decrease of fear; the sign of its perfection is no fear, because greed is also the root of all evils,[41] and perfect *dilectio* casts out fear.[42] Whoever, then, wishes to foster it must pursue the diminishing of his greed. But greed is the love (*amor*) of acquiring or obtaining temporal things. The beginning of diminishing this is to fear God, who alone cannot be feared without love. For this inclines a person toward wisdom, and nothing is more true than what has been said: *The beginning of wisdom is the fear of the Lord* (Sir 1:14). Of course there is no one who would not flee pain more than he

---

39. This question is actually a kind of description—under the rubric of "fostering charity"—of the progressive conversion of the soul, a process divided into two parts, pre-baptismal (1-2) and post-baptismal (3-4). Baptism itself ("the sacraments of regeneration") is mentioned toward the beginning of section 2. The taming of desire, which is encouraged by the fear of the Lord, and a growing awareness of the beauty of virtue characterize the pre-baptismal period. The post-baptismal period is depicted in terms of the instruction that must now be given to the newly baptized. They must first be made aware of the difference between temporal and eternal things, then be inspired by the example of Christ and the saints and finally, once bodily pleasures no longer offer the temptation that they previously had, be warned of the dangers of pleasing human beings and of spiritual pride. The fear of the Lord is as necessary here as at the beginning of the entire process.
40. Augustine comments on this sentence in the *Revisions*, although when quoting it he phrases it slightly differently. By way of qualification he asks why Paul says in Eph 5:29 that *no one hates his own flesh* if it is true that, when charity is perfect, nothing else is loved but God and the soul. *Dilectio*, however, encompasses the flesh—although only on account of the soul.
41. See 1 Tm 6:10.
42. See 1 Jn 4:18.

would long for pleasure. Indeed, we see that even the most savage beasts are deterred from the greatest pleasures because of their fear of pain, and when this has become habitual with them they are said to be subdued and tamed. Now, although reason is innate in the human person, it may by a wretched perversion serve greed, so that human beings are not fearful, and suggest that they can conceal what they have committed and concoct the cleverest falsehoods in order to cover over their hidden sins. Thereupon it transpires that people whom the beauty of virtue does not yet delight are subdued with greater difficulty than the wild beasts, unless they are deterred from sinning by the penalties that are preached with the greatest truth by holy and godly men and they realize that what they hide from human beings cannot be hidden from God. But, so that God may be feared, it must be made clear that divine providence governs all things not so much by reasons (and the one who can grasp these can also understand the beauty of virtue) as by recent examples, however they may occur, or by history—especially by that which, through the administration of divine providence itself, whether in the Old or in the New Testament, has obtained the most excellent authority of religion. But at the same time both the punishments for sin and the rewards for good deeds must be discussed.

2. But when somehow or other a habit of not sinning has demonstrated that what used to be considered burdensome is easy, the sweetness of piety should already begin to be tasted and the beauty of virtue should begin to make itself felt, so that the freedom of charity may prevail over the slavery of fear. It is then that the faithful, now that they have received the sacraments of regeneration,[43] which ought to have made a profound impression upon them, should be shown the difference between the two persons, the old and the new, the outer and the inner, the earthly and the heavenly—that is, between the one who pursues bodily and temporal goods and the one who pursues spiritual and eternal ones—and they should be warned not to look for perishable and transient benefits from God, in which even wicked persons can abound, but rather solid and everlasting ones, for the obtaining of which everything that is considered good in this world should be utterly disdained. At this point that

---

43. The term "sacrament," which appears often in the *Miscellany*, is one with numerous usages in Christian antiquity, as will be apparent as the treatise continues. Although here it is the baptismal ritual that is being referred to, the early Church did not limit the sacraments to a particular number, such as seven. Rather a sacrament was understood to be virtually any event, thing or person that formed part of God's plan and somehow mediated divine grace. The Latin *sacramentum* is frequently (although not in these pages) translated as "mystery." See *Dictionnaire de Théologie Catholique* XIV,1,493-495.

most excellent and singular example of the Lordly Man[44] should be offered, who, when he showed with numerous miracles the great power that he exercised over things, spurned those things which the ignorant consider great goods and endured those things which they consider great evils. Lest a person be less daring to attempt this conduct and discipline the more he honors it, it should be demonstrated from his promises and exhortations and from the multitude of those who have followed after him—apostles, martyrs and countless saints—how much those things are not to be despaired of.

3. But when the enticements of bodily pleasures have been overcome, it is to be feared lest the greed for pleasing men, by way of either some miraculous deeds or an arduous self-control or patience or some act of generosity or through a reputation for knowledge or eloquence, creep in and take their place. Here is also to be found the greed for honor. Against this should be cited all those things that have been written in praise of charity and on the foolishness of pride, and it should be taught how shameful it ought to be to wish to please those whom you do not wish to imitate, for either they are not good, and there is nothing great about being praised by the bad, or they are good and should be imitated. But those who are good are good by reason of virtue, but virtue does not long for what is in the power of other persons. He, then, who imitates the good longs for no one's praise, while he who imitates the bad is unworthy of praise. If you wish to please men, however, so as to help them to love God, you are greedy not for this but for something else. But he who wishes to please [in this way] still possesses the requisite fear—first of all, lest he be counted a hypocrite by the Lord because of his secret sinfulness, and then, if he wishes to please by his good deeds, lest in yearning for this reward he lose it, because it is God who will give it.

4. But once this greed has been conquered, there is pride to be feared. For it is difficult for a person who no longer wishes to please them and who thinks himself full of virtue to deign to be associated with human beings. And so fear is still necessary, lest even that which he seems to possess be taken away from

---

44. "The Lordly Man": *homo dominicus*. Augustine uses this term during a very brief period, from 393 to 395. In *Revisions* I,19,8 he writes: "Who in [Christ's] holy household could not be referred to as a 'lordly man'?" and he regrets, despite its previous broad and orthodox usage in both the Latin West and the Greek East, that he ever employed the phrase in any of his works; for this change of opinion he gives no reason. After the early fifth century the expression became suspect and fell out of fashion. See also questions LVII,3 and LXXV,2. For a study of the term see Aloys Grillmeier, "Ὁ κυριακὸς ἄνθρωπος: Eine Studie zu einer christologischen Bezeichnung der Väterzeit," in *Tradition* 33 (1977) 1-63. It is also discussed more briefly in Tarsicius van Bavel, *Recherches sur la christologie de saint Augustin* (Fribourg, 1954) 15-16.

him[45] and he be bound hand and foot and cast into the outer darkness.[46] Hence the fear of God not only begins but also completes wisdom[47]—that is, in him who loves God most of all and loves his neighbor as himself.[48] But the dangers and difficulties that one must beware of, and the remedies that one must use, are another matter.

XXXVII. On him who has always been born[49]

Better is he who has always been born than he who is always being born, because he who is always being born has not yet been born, and if he is always being born he has never been born and never will be born. For being born is one thing and having been born another. And if he has never been born he is on that account never a son. But he is the Son because he has been born, and he is always the Son. Therefore he has always been born.

XXXVIII. On the conformation of the soul[50]

Since nature is one thing and upbringing (*disciplina*) another and habit still another, and since these things should be understood to exist in a single soul with no diversity of substance; likewise, since natural disposition is one thing and virtue another and tranquility still another, and since they too belong to one and the same substance; and since the soul is of another substance than God, although created by him, and since God himself is that most holy Trinity about which much is said but little understood, what Jesus declared should be most carefully explored: *No one comes to me unless the Father has drawn him*

---

45. See Mt 25:29.
46. See Mt 22:13.
47. See Sir 1:14.
48. See Mt 22:37-39.
49. See *The Trinity* V,5,6: "The one is always Father and the other always Son, yet not 'always' in the sense that the Father ceases to be the Father from the moment when the Son is born, because from that moment the Son never ceases to be the Son, but in the sense that the Son has always been born and never begins to be the Son." Question XXXVII as well as this passage from *The Trinity* perhaps reflect a certain concern over the Latin translation of Origen's *Homily on Jeremiah* 9,4, where the translator, Jerome, renders Origen's Greek text as follows: "If, then, the Savior is always being born, and therefore he says, *Before the hills he begets me* (Prv 8:25), and not, as some incorrectly read, 'begot'—if the Lord is always being born of the Father, you too, having so great a spirit of adoption unto his likeness, are always being begotten of God through each of your understandings and through each of your works, and you are being made a son of God in Christ Jesus."
50. In this question Augustine sets out two human "trinities," each listed in ascending order—1) nature, upbringing and habit; and 2) natural disposition, virtue and tranquility (which may mean either a calming of the passions in this life or, less likely, the eternal calm of the next). He then compares the human person with the divine Trinity and poses the problem, without resolving it, of how the human soul, which is different than God, may be united, or conformed, to him.

(Jn 6:44); and: *No one comes to the Father except through me* (Jn 14:6); and: *He himself shall lead you into all truth* (Jn 16:13).

XXXIX. On foods

What is it that takes in the thing that it changes as an animal does food? What is it that is taken in and changed like that very food? What is it that is taken in and not changed, like light in the case of the eyes and sound in the case of the ears? But these things the soul takes in through the body. On the other hand, what is it that takes a thing into itself and changes it into itself, as in the case of another soul, which it makes similar to itself by receiving it into friendship?[51] And what is it that takes a thing into itself and does not change it, like truth? From this perspective must be understood what was said to Peter: *Slaughter and eat* (Acts 10:13), and what is said in the gospel: *And the life was the light of men* (Jn 1:4).

XL. Since souls have one nature, where do the different wills of human beings come from?

From the difference among things perceived comes the different appetite of souls, from the different appetite comes a different procedure in acquiring, from the different procedure comes a different usage, and from the different usage comes a different will. But it is the order of things—hidden, to be sure, but nonetheless certain under the sway of divine providence—that produces different perceptions. Not because there are different wills, therefore, should it be thought that there are souls of different natures, for the will of even a single soul changes over the course of time, since at one time it wishes to be rich while at another it despises riches and desires to be wise. And, in its very appetite for temporal things, at one time business affairs are attractive to a person and, at another, military matters.

XLI. Since God made all things, why did he not make them in equal fashion?

Because if they were equal they would not all exist. For there would not be the many kinds of things out of which the universe is constructed, with creatures in the first place and in the second, and thence all the way to the last place. And that is what is meant by "all."

---

51. On taking something into oneself, on the other hand, and being changed by it without the thing itself changing—in this case God's truth or God himself—see *Confessions* VII,10,16; *Homilies on the Gospel of John* 41,1. The eucharist would seem to be an obvious illustration of this process, but Augustine does not use it.

XLII. How the Lord Jesus, who is the wisdom of God,[52] was both in his mother's womb and in heaven

In the same way that, even if many hear the word of human beings, each person hears it in its totality.

XLIII. Why did the Son of God appear in a man and the Holy Spirit in a dove?[53]

Because the one came to show people an example of how to live, while the other appeared in order to point out the very gift by which living well may be attained. But each one became visible for the sake of those who are fleshly, that they might be moved step by step by way of the sacraments[54] from these things that are seen by bodily eyes to those that are understood by the mind. For words, too, sound and pass away, yet those things which are pointed out by words, when it is something divine and eternal that is spoken of, do not pass away in that fashion.

XLIV. Why did the Lord Jesus Christ come after such a long time?

Because everything beautiful comes from the highest beauty,[55] which is God, whereas temporal beauty is marked by a succession of dying things. But each individual period of life, from infancy to old age, has its own comeliness in individual persons. Therefore, just as he is foolish who, as a human being subject to the flux of time, would wish only to be a youth, because he looks askance at the other beauties that alternate in orderly fashion at other periods of life, so he is foolish who desires one age for the whole human race. For just like a single human being it has its own ages, and it was not opportune for the Master, by whose imitation [the human race] would be fashioned for the most excellent manner of life, to come from heaven except during the period of its youth. In this respect what the Apostle says is apropos—that under the law we were like children under a guardian's tutelage until he came[56] whom [the guardian] served and who had been promised through the prophets. For it is

---

52. See 1 Cor 1:24.
53. See Mt 3:16.
54. Here the sacraments are understood to be not ecclesiastical rituals but rather (it would appear) moments in the divine plan in the history of the individual Christian. See note 43.
55. This phrase recalls the opening words of question I. See note 1.
56. See Gal 3:23-24. In his *Revisions* Augustine observes that his statement here to the effect that Christ came during the youth of the human race could appear to be in conflict with what he said later in question LXIV,2—namely, that Christ came in the sixth age of the human race, which was its old age. He seeks to reconcile the two statements by asserting that the former refers to the vigor of a new faith working through love, while the latter has chronological meaning. And, although youth and old age cannot co-exist in the body, they can in the

one thing when divine providence acts, so to speak, privately with individuals, and another thing when it has regard, so to speak, publicly for the whole race. For even some individuals have arrived at undoubted wisdom; only they have been enlightened by the same truth individually as their periods of life have provided the opportunity. By this truth a person was raised up at an appropriate age of the human race itself so that the people might become wise.

XLV. Against mathematicians[57]

1. The ancients did not call mathematicians those who are now called such, but rather those who searched out the rhythms (*numeros*) of times by way of the movement of heaven and of the stars. Of these it is very rightly said in holy scripture: *Again, this must not be forgiven them. For if they were able to know so much, so that they could investigate the world, how did they not more easily discern its lord?* (Wis 13:8-9) For the human mind, when judging visible things, can recognize that it itself is better than all visible things. Yet, even though it acknowledges that it is changeable on account of its decreasing and increasing in wisdom, it finds that above itself is unchangeable truth. And thus, clinging to it, as it is written, *My soul has clung to you* (Ps 63:8), it is made blessed, and it also finds within itself the creator and lord of all things visible. It does not seek visible things outside itself, even heavenly ones, which either are not found or are found to no purpose and with great difficulty, unless from the beauty of the things that are exterior their maker is found, who is within and who

---

soul (and hence, by implication, in the spiritual interpretation of events). The relevant note in Bibliothèque Augustinienne 1,10,721 observes: "This explanation gives the strong impression of being a kind of escape. In fact Saint Augustine, like the majority of Christians of his time, thought that Christ had come at the end of the ages." This is a rare if not unique instance of Augustine's saying the opposite. See questions LVIII,2 (and note 124) and LXIV,2.

57. The "mathematicians" (*mathematici*) referred to here are of course better known as astrologers. The word *mathematicus* originally designated someone skilled in the science of numbers (including not only disciplines such as arithmetic and geometry but also geography and optics) but soon came to apply to and then be used almost exclusively for the related field of astrology. Augustine is perhaps the most prominent early Christian polemicist against astrology, and he often uses the hoary example that he adduces here (2) of the diverse histories of twins to prove that astrology is delusory. See *Miscellany of Questions in Response to Simplician* I,2,3; *Confessions* VII,6,8-10; *Teaching Christianity* II,22,33-34; *The City of God* V,16. At the end of the question he inveighs against the random opening of a text ("the dead skins of manuscripts") in order to obtain knowledge of one's future—to which he did not object if it was the biblical text that was being consulted for a spiritual purpose, as he himself records that he did in *Confessions* VIII,12,29. See Letter 55,20,37.

first produces loftier beauties in the soul and then lowlier ones in the body.[58]

2. But against those who are now called mathematicians, who want to subject our activities to the heavenly bodies and to sell us to the stars and get from us the very price of our sale, nothing can be said with more truth and brevity than that they make no utterances unless the constellations are agreeable. Now in the constellations they say that three hundred sixty parts are designated which constitute a zodiac. But the movement of heaven occurs in fifteen parts over the course of one hour, so that within this space of time as many parts develop as an hour contains. These parts are each said to contain sixty minutes each. But smaller parts of the minutes already in the constellations, from which they say that they predict the future, they do not find.

The conception of twins, however, inasmuch as it occurs in a single sexual act (as physicians attest, whose learning is much more certain and evident), happens in such a brief moment that it does not last more than two smaller parts of a minute. Where, then, does such a difference in the behavior, success and choices of twins come from, if they have to have the same constellation under which to be conceived and a single constellation is posited by the mathematicians for both of them as though it were for a single individual? But if they want to insist upon birth constellations, they are not excluded for twins, who for the most part emerge from the womb one after the other in such a way that the interval of time in question is a matter, once again, of the smaller parts of a minute, which they never allow to be brought up in the constellations, nor can they bring it up.

But, although it is said that they have predicted many true things, that is the case because people do not remember their falsehoods and errors and are intent only upon those things that have come to pass in conformity with their utterances, while they forget the things that have not come to pass, and what they recall are things that come about not by that skill, which is nothing, but by a certain obscure chance arrangement of affairs. If they want to attribute this to their expertise, let them say that the dead skins of manuscripts prophesy as well, from which a person's fate often emerges in conformity with one's will. If it is not by skill that a verse foretelling the future frequently emerges from a text, what is so surprising if some prediction of future events also emerges, not by skill but by chance, from a speaker's mind?

---

58. See Rom 1:19-22.

XLVI. On ideas[59]

1. Plato is said to be the first to have used the term "ideas." On the other hand, if this word did not exist before he introduced it, it is either because the things themselves, which he called ideas, did not exist, or because no one understood them. But perhaps they were called by other names by other persons, for it is legitimate to give a name to something that is known which has no common name. For it is unlikely either that there were no wise men before Plato or that they did not understand what Plato, as has been said, calls ideas, whatever the things may be, since there is such meaning in them that no one could be wise without having understood them. It is believable that even outside Greece there were wise men in other races, since even Plato himself not only bears witness to this by his travels abroad for the sake of making progress in wisdom but even mentions it in his writings.[60] It should not be thought, therefore, that these persons, if they existed, were ignorant of ideas, although they may have called them by another name. Let this be sufficient as far as the name is concerned. Let us look at the thing, which should very much be reflected upon and known, now that the terms have been established, so that whoever wishes may refer to the thing that he knows.

2. In Latin, then, we can call ideas either forms or species, so that we seem to use the terms loosely. But if we call them reasons we are in fact departing from the proper interpretation (for reasons are referred to as $\lambda \acute{o} \gamma o \iota$ in Greek and not as ideas), yet whoever wishes to use this term will not be far from the thing itself. For ideas are the principal forms or the fixed and unchangeable reasons of things that have themselves not been formed and consequently are eternal, always constituted in the same way and contained in the divine intelligence. And although these neither come into existence nor perish, nonetheless everything that *can* come into existence and perish and everything that *does* come into existence and perish is said to be formed in accordance with them. But no

---

59. This question is much studied on account of Augustine's definition of ideas and the more controversial topic of how ideas are known. First of all, in section 1, Augustine allows for flexibility in terminology, having credited Plato with inventing the word "idea." He insists, though, because it is impossible for him to imagine otherwise, that wise men everywhere knew of the concept even if they were unaware of the term. Then, in section 2, he provides the definition: "Ideas are the principal forms or the fixed and unchangeable reasons of things that have themselves not been formed and consequently are eternal, always constituted in the same way and contained in the divine intelligence." Every perishable thing, he continues, is formed in accordance with these imperishable patterns. They are visible to the mind and to reason, and so they are known. On this last issue, which is not as clear as Augustine suggests and which touches upon the topic of illumination that is introduced at the end of the question, see Gilson 80-96.

60. See, e.g., *Phaedrus* 274 cd.

soul except a rational one is given the possibility of seeing them in that part of itself by which it excels—that is, in the mind itself and the reason— which is, so to speak, its visage (*facie*) or its interior and intelligible eye. And indeed it is not just any rational soul, but one that is holy and pure, which is said to be suited to that vision—that is, which possesses that eye by which those things are seen and is whole and sound and peaceful and similar to those things that it is intent upon seeing.

But what religious person imbued with true religion, although not yet able to see these things, would nonetheless dare to deny—indeed, would not acknowledge—that everything that exists—that is, whatever is contained just as it is in its own genus by its own nature—was produced by God as its maker; and that, with him as their maker, all living things are alive; and that the universal soundness of things and the very order by which those things that undergo change proclaim that their trajectories through time are subject to a firm control are contained within and governed by the laws of the most high God? Once this has been established and conceded, who would dare to say that God created all things without good reason? If this cannot be rightly said and believed, it remains that all things were created in accordance with reason, but humankind in accordance with a different reason than the horse, for it is absurd to think this [i.e., that they were created in accordance with the same reason]. Individual things, then, have been created in accordance with their own reasons. But where should these reasons be thought to exist if not in the very mind of the creator? For it is sacrilegious to imagine that there was something located outside of himself that he looked at, so that in accordance with it he could create what he created. If the reasons for all the things that will be created and that have been created are contained in the divine mind, and if there can be nothing in the divine mind that is not eternal and unchangeable, and if Plato refers to these principal reasons of things as ideas, then ideas not only exist but are themselves true because they are eternal and remain the same and unchangeable. It is by participation in them that a thing exists, in whatever way it exists.

But the rational soul stands out among all those things that have been created by God and, when it is pure, is very near to God. To the extent that it clings to him in charity it is to a certain degree filled and lit by him with intelligible light and discerns, not with the eyes of the body but by that principle of its very self by which it excels (that is, by its intelligence), those reasons whose vision produces supreme blessedness. As has been said, it is legitimate to refer to these reasons as ideas or forms or species or reasons, and it is granted to the many to call them whatever they please but to the very few to see what is true.

XLVII. Whether we may ever be able to see our thoughts[61]

It is often asked how, after the body has risen and has become immutable,[62] which is promised to the saints, we may be able to see our thoughts. And so a conjecture should be made based upon that part of our body which has more light, since it must be believed that angelic bodies, such as we hope to possess, are very light and ethereal.[63] If, then, the many inclinations of our soul are recognized now in our eyes, it is likely that no inclination of our soul will be hidden when our entire body is ethereal, in comparison with which these eyes are flesh.

XLVIII. On believable things[64]

There are three kinds of believable things. There are those which are always believed and never understood, such as all of history, comprising temporal and human deeds.[65] There are others which are understood as soon as they are believed, such as all the human reasons concerning numbers or certain disciplines. Thirdly, there are those which are believed and later understood, such as what cannot be understood about divine matters except by those whose hearts have been purified,[66] which happens when the commandments that are received concerning right living have been observed.

---

61. In his *Revisions* Augustine says that this subject was better treated in *The City of God* (XXII,29).
62. See 1 Cor 15:52.
63. In the *Revisions* Augustine expresses concern that his words about our hoping to possess light and ethereal bodies like those of the angels could be misconstrued to imply that our resurrection bodies will lack substance, which would be false.
64. This question is in the form of an ascent (a scheme that Augustine greatly favors) from historical mutability to immutable reasons and numbers to divine matters. The first is characterized by belief but never by understanding, the second by simultaneous belief and understanding, the third by belief and subsequent understanding. In this scheme belief is the constant, understanding the variable.
65. Historical matters are believed rather than understood (*intelleguntur*) because they have not been experienced first-hand. See *The Teacher* 11,37; *True Religion* 25,46 ("Faith in temporal things, whether past or future, is more a question of believing than of understanding"); *Confessions* VI,5,7. See also question LIV: "Whatever is true and is cut off from both the senses and the mind can only be believed but not known or understood."
66. See Mt 5:8.

XLIX. Why did the children of Israel sacrifice oblations of cattle in visible fashion? [67]

Because there are also spiritual rites whose images a fleshly people were required to celebrate, so that by the slavery of the old the prefiguration of the new people would occur. It is legitimate to observe the difference between these two peoples in any one of us, since everyone necessarily acts the part of the old person[68] from his mother's womb until he comes to the age of youth, when he need no longer be wise in terms of the flesh but can be converted in his will to spiritual things and be reborn within.[69] What takes place, then, in a single individual who has been properly reared in accordance with the order of nature and with discipline is, in keeping with this analogy, most excellently brought about and perfected by divine providence in the whole human race.

L. On the equality of the Son[70]

Him whom God begot, because he could not beget one better than himself (for nothing is better than God), he begot as his equal. For if he wanted to do so and could not, he is weak; if he could do so and did not want to, he is envious. From this it is clear that he begot his Son as his equal.

LI. On humankind as made to the image and likeness of God

1. Since sacred scripture refers to an inner and an outer person and distinguishes them to such a degree that it is said by the Apostle, *Even if our outer person is decaying, yet our inner person is being renewed from day to day* (2 Cor 4:16), it can be asked whether one of these has been made to the image and likeness of God. Now it is foolish to ask which of these it is. For who hesitates to say that it is the one that is being renewed rather than the one who is decaying? But whether it is both is a great question. For if the outer person is Adam and the inner person Christ, both are rightly understood. But since Adam, as he was created by God, did not remain good and by loving fleshly things became fleshly, it cannot seem absurd that this very thing perished in him and that he lost the image and likeness of God. And on this account he is being renewed and he is also inner. How, then, is he outer as well? Does this

---

67. This subject is also addressed in Letter 102,16-21 and *The City of God* X,5, but in those longer texts the perspective is considerably different and the continuity between the old and the new covenant is stressed. Here Augustine's purpose is to draw an analogy between the two covenants on the one hand and the old and new persons of Col 3:9 on the other.
68. See Col 3:9.
69. The reference is to baptism.
70. The problem raised in this question is similar to one raised in Origen, *On First Principles* I,2,2. See also Gregory Nazianzen, *Oration* 29,6-7.

refer to the body, so that the inner refers to the soul, and are the inner person's the resurrection and the renewal, which now happen after the death of the former life, which is sinful, and after the rebirth of the new life, which is righteous? Thus, once more, he refers to these two persons, speaking of one as old, whom we must put off, and of the other as new, who must be put on.[71] One of these, again, he calls the image of the earthly person because it is brought about as a result of the sin of the first man, who is Adam, while the other he calls the image of the heavenly person[72] because it is brought about as a result of the righteousness of the second man, who is Jesus Christ. But the outer person, who is now decaying, will be renewed at the future resurrection,[73] when it has paid the debt of death that is due to nature in accordance with that law which was given by precept in paradise.[74]

2. But how it is not incongruous to say that the body also has been made according to God's likeness is easily understood by the one who attends carefully to what is written: *And God made all things very good* (Gn 1:31). For no one doubts that God himself is primordially good. For things can be said to be like God in many ways: some have been created in accordance with virtue and wisdom (*sapientia*) because in him are uncreated virtue and wisdom;[75] others are alive only because he is most excellently and primordially alive; still others exist only because he exists most excellently and primordially. And so the things that only exist and yet are not alive or are not wise (*sapiunt*) are not perfectly but tenuously in his likeness, because they are good in their own rank, whereas he is good above all things, and from him their goodness comes. But all the things that are alive and are not wise partake slightly more of his likeness. For whatever is alive also exists, but it is not the case that whatever exists is also alive. On the other hand, those that are wise are so close to that likeness that among creatures there is nothing closer. For what partakes of wisdom is also alive and exists, whereas what is alive must also exist but need not possess wisdom. Hence, when someone can partake of wisdom according to the inner person, he is to such a degree in accordance with his image that no nature may be placed between them, and so there is nothing that is more united to God. For he knows and is alive and exists, and nothing is better than this creature.

3. If the outer person participates in that life by which, through the body, we possess awareness by way of those well-known five senses, which we have in

71. See Col 3:9-10.
72. See 1 Cor 15:47-49.
73. See 2 Cor 4:16.
74. See Gn 3:19.
75. See 1 Cor 1:24.

common with animals (for even they can be destroyed by physical afflictions brought on by adversity), not inappropriately is that person also said to partake of the likeness of God not only because he is alive, which is also the case with the beasts, but even more because he is oriented toward what rules him and what wisdom enlightens—namely, his mind—which is not the case with the beasts that are deprived of reason. The body of human beings, too, alone among the bodies of earthly animals, is not cast upon its belly, since it is able to see and is upright in order to look upon the heavens, which are the origin of visible things. Although the human body is known to live not on its own account but by the presence of a soul, still, not only because it exists and is good to the degree that it exists but also because it is fashioned so that it may more easily contemplate the heavens, it can rightly be seen to have been made more in the likeness of God than the bodies of other animals. Yet, because without life one may not correctly be called a human being,[76] it is not the body alone that constitutes the outer person nor that life alone which is in the body's senses, but probably both are more properly to be taken together.

4. Neither is this distinction useless—that the image and likeness of God, which is also called the Son,[77] is one thing, and being *in* the image and likeness of God, as we understand that humankind was made,[78] is another.[79] There are also those who, not without reason, would understand that two things are said to be in the image and likeness [of God] since, as they assert, if they were one thing, then a single term could have sufficed.[80] But they want to say that the mind was made in the image [of God], which is formed without the interposing of any substance, by the truth itself; it is also called the spirit—not that Holy Spirit who is of the same substance as the Father and the Son are, but the spirit of human beings. This is how the Apostle distinguishes between them: *No one knows what takes place in a human being except the spirit of the human being, and no one knows what takes place in God except the Spirit of God* (1 Cor 2:11).

76. In the *Revisions* Augustine balks at what he says here and observes that a corpse may correctly (*recte*) but not properly (*proprie*) be called a man.
77. See Col 1:15.
78. See Gn 1:26.
79. Augustine warns in his *Revisions* that these words should not be read as if humanity did not qualify on each count—as being both the image and *in* the image of God. As for the Son of God, he is only the image of God and not in his image.
80. The distinction between image and likeness is addressed here, although Augustine professes to see it from the perspective of others rather than from his own. These unnamed others assert that the human mind is made in God's image while other aspects of the human being are made in his likeness. Augustine does not disagree with this position—indeed, he will build on it especially in *The Trinity*—but he says in his concluding words that caution should be exercised lest, through a misunderstanding of what being in God's image and likeness implies, it be thought that God has material substance.

Further, he says of the spirit of the human being: *May your spirit and soul and body be made safe* (1 Thes 5:23). For it too, like the other creatures, was made by God. For it is written this way in Proverbs: *Know that the Lord knows the hearts of all, and he who has fixed the spirit in all himself knows all things* (Prv 12:24 LXX). There is no doubt, then, that this spirit, in which there is understanding of truth, was made in the image of God, for it draws from the truth without the intervention of a creature. They want to say that other aspects of the human person seem to have been made in the likeness [of God], because every image is in fact a likeness, but not everything that is alike is also an image, properly speaking, although perhaps it can be called such in a loose way.

But caution should be exercised in matters such as these lest one be tempted to make too bold an assertion. At least one should rightly maintain that, inasmuch as bodies occupy space, God's own substance must not be believed to be something similar. For something that is less in part than in its entirety is not worthy of the soul's dignity and is that much less worthy of God's majesty.

LII. On what is said: *I regret having made humankind* (Gn 6:7)[81]

The divine scriptures, which have lifted us up from their earthly and human meaning to one that is divine and heavenly, have stooped down to a language that is current even among the most unlearned. And so those men through whom the Holy Spirit spoke did not hesitate to place in the [sacred] books, with great appropriateness, references to those emotions that our souls undergo and that one whose knowledge is better understands are very far removed from God. For example, since it is exceedingly difficult for a human being to take vengeance for something without anger, they decided that the vengeance of God, which occurs entirely without this perturbation, should nonetheless be called anger. Likewise, because men have customarily maintained the chastity of their wives with jealousy, they referred to as God's jealousy that providential activity of God by which he is seized and aroused lest a soul be corrupted and somehow prostituted by following other gods. It is the same with the power by which he works, which they called the hand of God; and with the power by which he continues to maintain and rule all things, which they called the feet of God; and with the power by which he perceives

---

81. This question reflects the concern manifested at the conclusion of the previous question—namely, that God will be understood in anthropomorphic terms, particularly because the Old Testament uses anthropomorphic language when speaking of him. Here, however, that concern is spelled out graphically. It is only at the very end that the actual issue of God's "regret" is discussed. See *Miscellany of Questions in Response to Simplician* II,2, which also deals with divine "regret" and its implications.

and understands all things, which they called the ears of God and the eyes of God; and with the power by which he manifests himself and is discerned, which they called the face of God; and so on in this fashion. They did this because we to whom their words are addressed are accustomed to work with our hands, to walk and come to the place where our soul leads us with our feet, to perceive material objects with our ears and eyes and the other senses of our body, to be known by our faces, and so forth for anything else along those lines. And so, although, to those who contemplate it with an unclouded mind, divine providence appears to administer all things with the most steadfast order, yet, since we are not easily accustomed to change a thing once begun and to transform it into something else, except by regret, things that come into existence but do not endure as long as it was hoped that they would endure are said—in the way that most accommodates our lowly human understanding— to have been removed, so to speak, by God's regret.

LIII. On the gold and silver that the Israelites took from the Egyptians [82]

1. Whoever gives careful consideration to the dispensations of the two covenants, which were arranged in conformity with the times over the course of the ages of the human race, understands well enough, I think, what is appropriate to the earlier age of the human race and what to the later. For, with divine providence governing all things excellently, the whole series of generations from Adam until the end of the world is administered as though it were the life of a single person whose span, from childhood to old age, is marked by defined segments. And so it is also necessary for him who bends his devout soul to the sacred texts to distinguish steps of virtue in behavior, until he comes to the highest and perfect virtue of a human being, lest perhaps, when he discovers that sometimes small things are commanded for those who are young and

---

82. See Ex 3:22; 11:12; 12:35-36. This entire question is devoted to the issue of the morality of the Israelites' act of despoiling the Egyptians, and particularly to the deceit that was employed in obtaining their treasures. Augustine's next treatise after the *Miscellany* was *Lying*, and clearly this theme was on his mind, although he does not mention this example of untruthfulness in that later work. His argument is that the Israelites, at this early stage in their moral maturity, were allowed by God, rather than commanded by him (here Augustine seems to contradict the evidence of Ex 3:22 and 11:12), to punish the Egyptians by taking their property under false pretences. Since God would not do such a thing directly himself, the Israelites are acting as his ministers. See also the *Answer to Faustus, a Manichean* XXII,71-72; *Exposition of Psalm* 104 [105],28. There is no mention here of the famous allegorical interpretation of this episode (according to which the Israelites symbolize the Christians who take from pagan literature whatever might serve their purposes), first propounded by Origen in his *Letter to Gregory* 2 (PG XI,88-89) and also used by Augustine in, e.g., *Confessions* VII,9,15; *Teaching Christianity* II,40,60-61. Irenaeus in *Against Heresies* IV,30,1-3 was the first Christian author to notice the difficulties posed by this unusual event in the Old Testament narrative.

greater things for those who are older, while reckoning that in comparison with greater ones those are lesser sins, he not think that it was appropriate for God to have commanded people to do such things. But now it would be much too time-consuming to expatiate on the steps of virtue; still, this is sufficient for discussion of the question at hand.

As far as deceit is concerned, the highest and perfect virtue is to deceive no one and to be an example of what has been said: *Let this be in your mouth: yes, yes and no, no* (Jas 5:12). But, because this commandment was given to those to whom the kingdom of heaven was already promised (but it is a great virtue to carry out these greater matters, on account of which this reward is owed, for *the kingdom of heaven is suffering violence, and the violent are seizing it* [Mt 11:12]), it should be asked by what steps one may arrive at that height of perfection. On those steps, to be sure, are found those to whom an as yet earthly kingdom was promised and, this having been promised, they would, like little children, play for a while with the earthly joys for which they still longed and which they had obtained from the one God, who is lord of all things, and advancing from there and maturing in spirit, they would dare to hope for heavenly ones as well. Just as the highest and nearly divine virtue, then, is to deceive no one, so the ultimate vice is to deceive someone. For those who are making their way from this ultimate vice to that highest virtue there is a step, which is to deceive no one, to be sure, who is either a friend or a stranger, but occasionally, nonetheless, to deceive an enemy. On that basis the poet's words have acquired very nearly the force of a proverb: "Deceit or courage, what difference does it make in regard to an enemy?"[83] But, inasmuch as even the enemy himself can often be unjustly deceived, as when some agreement is made about a temporary peace, which is called a truce, and it is not kept, and other such things, he is much more excusable and closer to that highest virtue who, although he wishes to deceive the enemy, nonetheless does not deceive him except by divine authority. For God knows, often by himself and certainly more clearly and more justly than men, whoever is worthy of punishment or reward.

2. Hence God in no way deceives anyone by himself, for he is the father of truth, and the Spirit of truth.[84] Yet, as he distributes their deserts to those who deserve them, because this also pertains to justice and truth, he makes use of souls for the merits and deserts that are appropriate to their steps [of virtue], so that, if someone deserves to be deceived, not only does he not deceive him by himself but neither does he deceive him by the type of person who sufficiently

83. Virgil, *Aeneid* II,390.
84. See 1 Jn 5:6.

loves and consistently observes [the words], *Let this be in your mouth: yes, yes
and no, no*, nor by an angel, for whom the role of deception is out of character,
but either by the type of person who has not yet stripped himself of inclinations
of this sort or by the type of angel who, on the lowest rungs of nature because
of the perversity of his will, has been set aside either to punish sins or to discipline and purify those who are being reborn according to God. For we read that
a king was deceived by the false prophecy of pseudo-prophets, and in reading
it we discover that it was not done apart from the divine judgment, because he
was worthy to be deceived in that way, not by an angel for whom it would not
be right to accept the task of deception, but by an angel of error who gladly and
of his own accord requested that such a role be given him.[85] For in certain
places in the scriptures a clearer explanation is given of something that a
careful and devout reader might understand as well in other places where it is
less clear. For our God has, by the Holy Spirit, set up the divine books for the
salvation of souls in such a way that he wishes not only to nourish us with what
is obvious but also to exercise us with what is obscure.[86] From this ineffable
and sublime arrangement of affairs, then, which is accomplished by divine
providence, a natural law is, so to speak, inscribed upon the rational soul,[87] so
that in the very living out of this life and in their earthly activities people might
hold to the tenor of such dispensations. Hence it is that a judge considers it
unworthy and heinous to kill with his own hands someone who has been
sentenced to death; at his command, though, an executioner does it who by
reason of his temperament has been appointed for the task of killing, in conformity with the law, a person who has been sentenced to death; but he could as
well, because of his cruelty, kill an innocent person. For a judge does not do
this by himself or by a bureaucrat or a lawyer or anyone else in his employ
upon whom such a responsibility would be inappropriately imposed. Hence it
is also that we use irrational beings for those things that it would be heinous for
human beings to carry out. For, to be sure, it is right for a thief to be badly
bitten, yet a person does not do this by himself, nor is it done by his son or by a
member of his household or even by his slave but by his dog, which is fitting
for this animal to do because of its nature. When, therefore, it is fitting that
certain persons suffer something that it is not fitting for others to inflict, certain
offices are the vehicles by which appropriate tasks are performed, so that, in its

85. See 1 K 22:6-23. See also *Miscellany of Questions in Response to Simplician* II,6.
86. The idea that scripture was written in such a way that a truth obscurely presented in one place
    would be clearly presented in another, and so that it would not only nourish its readers' souls
    but also exercise their intellects through a providential obscurity, is a favorite one with the
    Fathers and often appears in Augustine. See *Teaching Christianity* II,6,8; Letter 137,18.
87. See Rom 2:15.

use of them, justice itself may not only command a person to suffer such things as it is fitting for him to suffer but also command those doing it, for whom it is no less fitting to do such things.

Therefore, when it was appropriate for the Egyptians to be deceived, and the people of Israel were still situated upon that moral step congruent with the age of the human race [at the time], whereon they would not inappropriately deceive their enemy, it came about that God commanded them—or rather allowed them, in keeping with their inclinations—to ask the Egyptians for the gold and silver vessels which, as persons still longing for an earthly kingdom, they eagerly desired and would not return, although they took them as if they would return them.[88] And the recompense for such lengthy toil and exertion God did not wish to be incommensurate with the step on which these souls were situated, nor did he wish the punishment of those whom he justly caused to lose that which they were obliged to hand over. God is therefore not a deceiver (who would not understand that to believe such a thing is wicked and impious?) but rather the most just overseer of merits and persons. Certain things that are fitting for him alone and appropriate for him alone he accomplishes by himself, such as illuminating wise and blessed souls and manifesting himself to them so that they may enjoy his gifts; other things he does, in accordance with the most wholesome laws and on the basis of merit, by way of a creature at his service who has been chosen for the task, commanding some things and allowing others, to the point of caring for the sparrows, as the Lord says in the gospel,[89] and to the point of the beauty of the grass,[90] and even to the point of the number of our hairs[91]—all under the sway and with the present help of the divine providence of which it is also written: *It stretches forth powerfully from end to end and orders all things pleasantly* (Wis 8.1).

3. But that, by the ministry of souls that observe his laws, God punishes and requites with fitting punishments those who deserve them, although he himself remains completely tranquil, is written most openly as follows: *You consider it foreign to your power to condemn him who should not be punished. For your power is the source of justice, and because you are lord of all you cause yourself to be merciful to all. For you manifest your power when you are not believed to be perfect in power, and you expose their presumption in those who know. But you, the lord of powers, judge with tranquility, and you rule us with great care.* (Wis 12:15-18)

---

88. See Ex 3:22.
89. See Mt 10:29.
90. See Mt 6:30.
91. See Mt 10:30.

4. Likewise, the Lord shows that the first step to heavenly justice, which is already enjoined upon those who are stronger, is taken in earthly affairs, when he says, *If you have not been faithful in another's affairs, who will give you what is yours?* (Lk 16:12) And that souls are taught in accordance with their steps the Lord shows when he says, *I have many things to tell you, but you cannot bear them now* (Jn 16:12). The Apostle, too, when he says, *And I, brothers, have been unable to speak to you as to spiritual persons but as to fleshly persons. I have given you milk to drink, not solid food, for you were unable, but you are still unable, for you are still fleshly.* (1 Cor 3:1-2) What took place, then, in those persons according to their steps we recognize in the whole human race—that, in keeping with the times, some things were enjoined upon a fleshly and others upon a spiritual people. It is not surprising, then, if those who were still worthy of deceiving an enemy were commanded to deceive an enemy who was worthy of being deceived. For they were not yet fit to be counted among those to whom it was said, *Love your enemies* (Mt 5:44), but were such as those to whom it was only required to be said, *You shall love your neighbor and hate your enemy* (Mt 5:43). For there was still not time enough to explain how broadly that *neighbor* was to be understood. A certain start, then, was made under a guardian, while the conclusion was reserved to the teacher, since it was still the same God who gave a guardian (namely the law, by way of his servants)[92] to the little ones and a teacher (namely the gospel, by way of his only Son)[93] to those who were older.

LIV. On what is written: *But it is good for me to cling to God* (Ps 73:28)

Everything that exists exists either in the same way or not. And every soul is superior to every body, for everything that gives life is superior to that which is given life; no one has any doubt, however, that the body is given life by the soul, not the soul by the body. This body, however, is not and yet *is* something; it is either a soul or something better than that. For nothing is inferior to any given body because, even if one should speak of the material out of which the body is made, in fact it is nothing that is being spoken of, since it lacks all specificity. Again, there is nothing between the body and the soul that would be superior to the body and inferior to the soul. If there were something in between, either it would be given life by the soul or would give life to the soul or would do neither, or it would give life to the body or would be given life by the body or would do neither. But whatever is given life by the soul is a body; if, however, something gives life to a soul, it is superior to the soul. Again,

92. See Gal 3:24.
93. See Mt 23:10.

what gives life to a body is a soul; what is given life by a body is nothing. But that which is neither—that is, not lacking life and not bestowing life—is either nothing at all or is some body or is to some degree superior to both body and soul. But whether such a thing exists in reality is another question. Now, however, reason discloses that there is nothing between the body and the soul that would be superior to the body and inferior to the soul. But that which is superior to every soul we call God.[94] Whoever understands him is joined to him. For what is understood is true, but not everything that is believed is true. But whatever is true and is cut off from both the senses and the mind can only be believed but not known or understood. Whatever understands God, then, is joined to God. But the rational soul understands God, for it understands that what always exists in the same way does not undergo any change. But the body undergoes change through time and space, and the rational soul under-goes change as well, since sometimes it is wise and sometimes foolish. But that which always exists in the same way is far superior to that which does not. There is nothing superior to the rational soul except God. When, therefore, something understands that it always exists in the same way, it certainly understands itself. This, however, is truth itself. Since the rational soul is joined to it by understanding it, and this is good for the soul, that which is said to be so—*but it is good for me to cling to God*—is properly grasped.

LV. On what is written: *There are sixty queens and eighty concubines, and the young maidens are numberless* (Sg 6:8)

The number ten can signify knowledge of everything. If this [knowledge] is referred to matters interior and intelligible, which are signified by the number six, ten is as it were multiplied by six, which is sixty. If it is referred to matters earthly and corruptible, which can be signified by the number eight,[95] ten is multiplied by eight, which is eighty. The queens, then, are souls holding sway in matters intelligible and spiritual. The concubines are those that receive a reward in earthly goods; of them it is written: *They have received their reward* (Mt 6:2). The young maidens who are numberless are those that have no specific knowledge and that can be at risk from different dogmas, given that a number, as is said, signifies the certain and indubitable establishment of knowledge.

---

94. Augustine corrects himself here in the *Revisions* and says that he should have written "superior to every created spirit" rather than "superior to every soul."
95. In Augustine's thought the number eight is more usually a symbol of perfection and completion. See *The Lord's Sermon on the Mount* I,4,12; *The City of God* XXII,30. The present usage suggests how arbitrary the science of numerology could be.

LVI. On the forty-six years of the building of the Temple[96]

Six, nine, twelve and eighteen together make forty-five. Add one, then, and they become forty-six. Multiplied by six this becomes two hundred seventy-six. Now human conception is said to follow its course and come to term in such a way that in the first six days there is a resemblance to milk; in the following nine days this is converted to blood; then in twelve days it is solidified; in the next eighteen days the features of the members are perfectly. formed; and in the time that remains, up until the moment of birth, it grows in size. Forty-five days, then, with the addition of one, which represents the sum, because six and nine and twelve and eighteen all together make forty-five—with the addition of one, then, as has been said, this becomes forty-six. When this has been multiplied by the number six, which is the first in our series of numbers, it becomes two hundred seventy-six—that is, nine months and six days, which are computed from the eighth day of the calends of April, the day on which it is believed that the Lord was conceived, because on that same day he also suffered, until the eighth day of the calends of January, the day on which he was born.[97] Not without reason, then, is it said that it took forty-six years to build the Temple, which signified his body,[98] so that there were as many days in the completing of the Lord's body as there were years in the building of the Temple.

LVII. On the one hundred and fifty-three fish[99]

1. *All things are yours, but you are Christ's, and Christ is God's* (1 Cor 3:22-23). If these are numbered from the beginning, they appear as one, two, three and four. Likewise: *The head of woman is man, the head of man is Christ, but the head of Christ is God* (1Cor 11:3). If these are numbered in the same way, they appear similarly as one, two, three and four. Again, one and two and three and four all together make ten. Hence the number ten (*denarius*) appropriately signifies discipline, which points to God the creator and the creation that he established. And when a perfect and immortal body is made subject to a perfect and immortal soul, and that is in turn made subject to Christ and he to

96. See Jn 2:20. This explanation of the number forty-six is also given in *The Trinity* IV,5,9.
97. March 25th and December 25th respectively. At the time that Augustine wrote the *Miscellany*, December 25th was not universally observed as the day of Christ's birth, but it was celebrated as such throughout most of the Christian world. See Bernard Botte, *Les origines de la Noël et de l'Epiphanie* (Louvain, 1932).
98. See Jn 2:20-21.
99. See Jn 21:6-11. This question represents what is probably the most notorious of Augustine's numerological interpretations. See also *Homilies on the Gospel of John* 122,8-9; Sermons 248,4-5; 252,7-8; *Exposition of Psalm* 49 [50],9. The number 153 is also explained in question LXXXI,3, but a somewhat different procedure is followed, with a somewhat different result.

God, not as dissimilar or possessing a different nature but as Son to Father, all of this, which it is hoped will exist eternally after the resurrection of the body, is appropriately signified by the same number ten.[100] And it is perhaps on this account that those who are brought to the vineyard receive a denarius as their pay.[101]

But, as one and two and three and four together make ten, so one and two and three and four multiplied four times make forty.

2. But if the number forty appropriately signifies the body because of the four well-known natures from which it is composed—dry, wet, cold and hot—and because the movement from a point to width, from width to breadth and from breadth to height makes for the solidity of the body, which is in turn included in the number four, not without reason is the number forty understood to signify the temporal dispensation, which was wrought for our salvation, when the Lord assumed a body and deigned to appear in a visible way to human beings. For one and two and three and four, which signify the creator and creation, multiplied four times (that is, as represented by the body in its temporal state), make forty. For between four and four times there is this difference—that four is static, whereas four times implies motion. Hence, as four refers to the body, so four times refers to time, and with that is suggested the sacrament that was enacted in body and in time for the sake of those who were entangled in the love of bodies and under the sway of time.[102] The number forty, then, as has been said, is not unfittingly believed to signify the temporal dispensation. And perhaps this is why the Lord fasted for forty days,[103] exhibiting the neediness of this world, which is symbolized by the motion of bodies and by time, and why he was with his disciples for forty days after his resurrection,[104] suggesting to them (as I believe) this very temporal dispensation that he wrought for our salvation.

But the number forty, totaled in its factors, arrives at the number fifty, demonstrating the very same thing, when indeed those very factors are uniform among themselves, because a bodily and visible action, carried out with uniformity, yields perfection to a man in time. This perfection, as has

---

100. In other words: One = all things / woman / body
                               Two = you / man / soul
                               Three = Christ
                       + Four = God

                       Ten = God the creator and his creation
101. See Mt 20:2.
102. The sacrament enacted in body and in time is the incarnation of Christ. See note 43.
103. See Mt 4:2.
104. See Acts 1:3.

been said, is signified by the number ten, just as the number forty, once its factors have been totaled, yields [an additional] ten in order to arrive at fifty, as has been said above. For the number one, which forty has forty times, and two, which it has twenty times, and four, which it has ten times, and five, which it has eight times, and eight, which it has five times, and ten, which it has four times, and twenty, which it has twice, together add up to fifty. For there is no other part that can, treated uniformly, produce the number forty aside from those that we have enumerated and that, once totaled, we have brought to the number fifty.[105] The Lord, then, having completed forty days with his disciples after the resurrection—that is, commending to them what was accomplished for us in time—ascended into heaven.[106] And after another ten days he sent the Holy Spirit, by whom those who had believed in visible and temporal things are spiritually perfected so that they may lay hold of invisible things, thus alluding to the same perfection that is conferred by the Holy Spirit by way of those very ten days after which he sent the Holy Spirit, for ten is the number that forty produces from its factors, if they are treated uniformly, to make fifty, just as, when temporal affairs are carried out with uniformity, that perfection is arrived at which the number ten signifies and which, added to forty, makes fifty. Therefore, since the perfection that comes about through the Holy Spirit—as long as we still walk in the flesh,[107] although we do not live in the flesh—is joined with the temporal dispensation itself, the number fifty rightly appears to point to the Church, but [to a Church] which has already been cleansed and made perfect and which in charity embraces the faith characteristic of a temporal dispensation and hope in an eternity yet to be; that is, it joins as it were the number forty to the number ten.

But this Church, to which the number fifty points, whether because it is drawn from the three kinds of men, Jews, gentiles and fleshly Christians, or because it is moistened by the sacrament of the Trinity,[108] arrives at the number one hundred and fifty by way of the number that signifies it multiplied three times; for fifty multiplied three times produces one hundred and fifty. When you add to it those very three, because what is washed in the bath of regeneration[109] in the name of the Father and of the Son and of the Holy Spirit must be distinguished and noble, it comes to one hundred and fifty-three. This is the

---

105. This process is reproduced in question LXXXI,1.
106. See Acts 1:2-3.
107. See 2 Cor 10:3.
108. "The sacrament of the Trinity," which moistens the Church, is baptism; the persons of the Trinity are invoked during the celebration of the sacrament at the moment of immersion or infusion. The allusion becomes clearer in the subsequent lines. See note 43.
109. See Tit 3:5.

number of fish that is mentioned,[110] because the nets were cast out on the right side[111] and consequently contain big [fish]—that is, ones that are perfect and suited for the kingdom of heaven. For that parable of the net that was not cast out on the right side included good and bad together, which are separated on the shore.[112] For now, in the nets of the commandments and sacraments of God, good and bad are tossed together in the Church as it presently exists. But their separation occurs at the end of the world[113] as if at the edge of the sea (that is, on the shore), when the righteous reign temporarily at first, as is written in the Apocalypse,[114] and then for eternity in that city which is described there.[115] Then, once the temporal dispensation has ceased, which is signified by the number forty, the ten (*denarius*) will remain, which is the reward that the saints who labor in the vineyard will be given.[116]

3. If this number is closely investigated, it can also refer to the holiness of the Church, which was established by our Lord Jesus Christ. Thus, inasmuch as creation corresponds to the number seven (since three is attributed to the soul and four to the body), the [Lord's] assumption of humanity[117] is valued at three times seven, because the Father sent the Son, and the Father is in the Son, and by the gift of the Holy Spirit he was born of a virgin; so the three are these: the Father and the Son and the Holy Spirit; but the seven times is the human being himself who was assumed into the temporal dispensation so that he might become eternal. The product, then, is twenty-one, which is three times seven. But the Lord's assumption of humanity was beneficial for the liberation of the Church, whose head he is.[118] But the Church itself, because of its soul and body, is discerned in that same number seven. And so let twenty-one likewise be multiplied seven times, on account of those who are liberated by the Lordly Man,[119] and the result is one hundred forty-seven. To this is added the number six, which is a sign of perfection inasmuch as it is the sum of its factors, such that nothing is left over, either smaller or greater. For it is the sum of one, which it has six times, and two, which it has three times, and three,

---

110. See Jn 21:11.
111. See Jn 21:6.
112. See Mt 13:47-48.
113. See Mt13:49.
114. See Rv 20:4-6. Reference is made here to the belief in the actual temporal reign of the saints on earth, known as millenarianism because the reign is said to last for a thousand years (see Rv 20:4). Augustine later rejects this belief (as does the rest of the universal Church) as being too literal. See *The City of God* XX,7-9.
115. See Rv 21:2-22:5.
116. See Mt 20:2.
117. "Assumption of humanity": *susceptio hominis*. See also a few lines further down and note 11.
118. See Eph 1:22.
119. "The Lordly Man": *dominicum hominem*. See note 44.

which it has twice; and when these are taken together they make six. This may also point to that sacrament wherein God brought all his works to perfection on the sixth day.[120]

When you add six, then, which is a sign of perfection, to one hundred and forty-seven, one hundred and fifty-three results. This is the number of the fish that are found[121] after, at the Lord's command, the nets were cast out on the right side,[122] where sinners, who belong on the left,[123] are not found.

LVIII. On John the Baptist[124]

1. John the Baptist, as the texts that are read in the gospel indicate, is reasonably believed, thanks to considerable trustworthy documentation, to be the bearer of prophecy and much more, since the Lord says of him, *More than a prophet* (Mt 11:9). He is such since he serves as an image of all that was prophesied concerning the Lord from the beginning of the human race until the coming of the Lord. Now the Lord himself is the bearer of the gospel who was prophetically foretold. From the time of his coming, the preaching of the gospel spread throughout the entire world, whereas prophesying decreased after what had been foretold had come to pass. And so the Lord says, *The law and the prophets are until John the Baptist; from then on the kingdom of God is preached* (Lk 16:16). And John himself says, *He must increase, but I must decrease* (Jn 3:30). This was symbolized by the days on which they were born and by the deaths that they underwent. For John is born at the point when the days begin to decrease; the Lord is born at the point when the days begin to increase. The former is decreased by his head when he is killed, but the latter is raised up on a cross. Thereupon, when the prophecy that had been embodied in John points its finger at him[125] whose approaching presence had been foretold from the beginning of the human race, he begins to decrease, and from then on

---

120. See Gn 2:2. See note 43.
121. See Jn 21:11.
122. See Jn 21:6.
123. See Mt 25:41.
124. This is one of the numerous places where Augustine speaks of John the Baptist, perhaps most notably in sermons, in which he repeats many of the themes that are found here and that are not unique to him. See Sermons 66; 94A; 191,1; 287-293E; 307-308A; 342,2; 379-380. After introducing John, Augustine goes through a list of Old Testament figures whose stories have a prophetic intent. Then he expounds on the six ages of the human race, John being the dividing point between the fifth and the sixth, which correspond to the six ages of an individual human being—infancy, childhood, adolescence, youth, maturity and old age. See also questions XL; LXIV,2; *On Genesis: A Refutation of the Manicheans* I,23,35-40; *The Instruction of Beginners* 22,39; *The Trinity* IV,7; *The City of God* XXII,30.
125. See Jn 1:29-30.

the preaching of the kingdom of God begins to increase.[126] And so John baptized unto repentance, for the old life comes to an end with repentance,[127] and then the new begins.

2. Not only in those who were rightly called prophets, however, but even in the very historical account of the Old Testament is prophecy found not to be silent by those who seek devoutly and are divinely aided in their searchings into these matters. Yet it is most apparent to them by way of the quite evident figures of things that the righteous Abel is killed by his brother[128] and the Lord by the Jews; that Noah's ark, like the Church, is guided through the floods of this world;[129] that Isaac is led off to be slain and in his place a ram is caught sight of as if crucified in a bush;[130] that in Abraham's two sons, one from the slave woman and the other from the free woman, the two testaments are recognizable;[131] that two peoples are exemplified in the twins Esau and Jacob;[132] that Joseph, having suffered persecution from his brothers, is honored by foreigners,[133] just as the Lord, killed by the persecuting Jews, was glorified among the gentiles. It would take too long to recall every individual instance, since the Apostle himself concludes in this way when he says, *But these things happened to them in figure; but they were written on account of us, upon whom the end of the ages has come* (1 Cor 10:11).

But the end of the ages is like the declining years of an old person, when you conceptualize the whole human race on the model of an individual person, and the sixth age signifies the one during which the Lord came. For there are six ages in an individual person—infancy, childhood, adolescence, youth, maturity and old age. Now the first age of the human race is from Adam to Noah and the second is from Noah to Abraham; these are very obvious and clear divisions of time. The third is from Abraham to David, for thus the evangelist Matthew divides it, the fourth from David to the deportation to Babylon, and the fifth from the deportation to Babylon to the coming of the Lord.[134] The sixth is to be awaited from the coming of the Lord until the end of the age, when the outer person, which is also called the old,[135] is decaying through old

---

126. See Jn 3:30.
127. See Mt 3:11.
128. See Gn 4:8.
129. See Gn 7:1-8:13.
130. See Gn 22:1-14.
131. See Gal 4:22-24.
132. See Gn 25:23.
133. See Gn 37:2-50:26.
134. See Mt 1:17.
135. See Col 3:9.

age and the inner is being renewed from day to day.[136] From then on there is everlasting repose, which is signified by the sabbath.[137] It is in keeping with this scheme that on the sixth day humanity was made in the image and likeness of God.[138]

But no one is unaware that the life of human beings, once it undertakes something, hinges upon knowledge and action.[139] For without knowledge action is hasty, and without action knowledge is listless. But the first stage of a person's life, which no one rightly believes engages in any sort of real undertaking, is given over to the five senses, which are sight, hearing, smell, taste and touch. And so the first two ages of the human race, which are like infancy and childhood, are set at ten generations, which is twice five, since a generation occurs through both sexes. There are, then, ten generations from Adam to Noah, and from then to Abraham another ten;[140] we have said that these two ages are the infancy and the childhood of the human race. But its adolescence and youth and maturity —that is, from Abraham to David, and from then to the deportation to Babylon, and from then to the coming of the Lord—are symbolized by sets of fourteen generations,[141] with the number seven (the result of adding action and knowledge to the number five, which is in the senses of the body) doubled for the sake of the two sexes. Old age, however, usually occupies even as much time as all the other ages. For since old age is said to begin with the sixtieth year, and since human life can attain to one hundred and twenty years, it is obvious that old age alone can last as long as all the previous ages. The final age of the human race, then, which begins with the Lord's coming [and lasts] until the end of the age, is uncertain in terms of the number of generations that it contains. God wishes to keep this hidden for a good reason, as is written in the gospel,[142] and the Apostle attests to this when he says that the day of the Lord will come like a thief in the night.[143]

3. But nonetheless by the different previous generations it is taught that the human race was visited in the sixth age by the humble coming of the Lord. By this visitation the prophecy began to be made clear that had lain hidden during

---

136. See 2 Cor 4:16.
137. See Gn 2:2-3.
138. See Gn 1:27.
139. The idea of the complementarity of knowledge and action, briefly developed here, can perhaps be traced to Aristotle, *Metaphysics* I,2, where truth and action are referred to as the objects of two different kinds of knowledge, the contemplative and the practical respectively.
140. See Lk 3:34-38.
141. See Mt 1:17.
142. See Mt 24:36.
143. See 1 Thes 5:2.

the five previous ages. Since John was the bearer of this prophecy, as was said before, he is born of elderly parents,[144] just as that prophecy begins to become known in a dying age, and for five months his mother hides herself, as is written: *Elizabeth hid herself for five months* (Lk 1:24). But in the sixth month she is visited by Mary, the mother of the Lord, and her infant leaps in the womb,[145] just as at the Lord's first coming, when he deigned to appear in humility, prophecy begins to be made clear, but as though in the womb—that is, not yet so openly—so that all may confess that it has been, so to speak, brought out into the light, which we believe will be the case at the Lord's second coming, when he will come in splendor[146] and his coming will be preceded by the longed-for Elijah,[147] just as John preceded this [first coming].[148] And so it is said by the Lord: *Elijah has already come, and men did many things to him* (Mt 17:12). *And if you wish to know, John the Baptist is the very one who is to come* (Mt 11:14), because the latter *has* come and the former *will* come in the same spirit and in the same power, as well as in the same office of forerunner and herald.[149] For this reason, also, it is said through the Spirit with whom his father the prophet was filled[150] that this John will be the forerunner of the Lord in the spirit and power of Elijah.[151] But when Mary had spent three months with Elizabeth she departed.[152] This number seems to me to signify faith in the Trinity and baptism in the name of the Father and of the Son and of the Holy Spirit, with which the human race is imbued[153] at the humble coming of the Lord and perfected at his future coming in glory.

LIX. On the ten virgins[154]

1. Among the parables told by the Lord, the one that was proposed with respect to the ten virgins usually exercises inquirers a great deal. And indeed many persons have thought many things in regard to it that are not alien to the

---

144. See Lk 1:7.
145. See Lk 1:39-56.
146. See Mt 16:27.
147. See Mt 17:10.
148. See Lk 1:17.
149. See Lk 1:17.
150. See Lk 1:67.
151. See Lk 1:76.
152. See Lk 1:56.
153. "Is imbued": *imbuitur*, which can also be translated "is moistened," which would emphasize the connection with baptism.
154. See Mt 25:1-13. Augustine also treats of this parable in Letter 140,31-35; Sermon 93; *Exposition of Psalm* 147,2,10-11.

faith,[155] but how an explanation might take into account all its parts is what must still be elaborated. I have even read in a certain writing from among those that are referred to as apocryphal something that is not contrary to Catholic belief, but it has seemed to me, when I consider all the parts of this allegory, that they make little sense in regard to the [whole] passage. Yet I dare come to no rash conclusion regarding an explanation not because its inappropriateness would perhaps cause me difficulty but rather because my dullness might not discover its appropriateness. But what seems to me to be reasonably acceptable regarding this passage I shall, to the extent possible, explain briefly and carefully.

2. When our Lord was asked in secret by his disciples, then, about the end of the world,[156] among the many other things that he said he also said this: *Then the kingdom of heaven will be considered similar to ten virgins who took their lamps and went to meet the bridegroom. Five of them were foolish, however, and five were prudent. But the five foolish ones, having taken their lamps, did not bring oil with them; the wise ones, however, took oil with them in their vessels along with the lamps. As the bridegroom was delayed, though, they all fell asleep. But at midnight there was a loud cry: Behold, the bridegroom is coming; get up to meet him. Then those virgins got up and prepared their lamps. And those foolish ones said to the wise ones, Give us some of your oil because our lamps are going out. The wise ones, however, responded and said, There may not be enough for us and you; go instead to the vendors and purchase some for yourselves. And while they went off to make their purchase the bridegroom came, and those who were prepared went in with him to the wedding, and the door was closed. Much later, however, the other virgins came and said, Lord, lord, open to us. But he responded and said, Amen, I say to you, I do not know you. Stay awake, therefore, because you do not know the day or the hour.* (Mt 25:1-13)

That five of the virgins are let in and five are shut out signifies the separation of the good and the bad.[157] If the title of virginity is an honorable one, why is it common to those who were admitted and to those who were shut out? And then what does it mean that there are five in each category? What does the oil signify? It seems odd that the wise do not share with those who ask them, since not only is envy not proper for those who are so perfect that they are received by the bridegroom, by which designation there is no doubt that the Lord Jesus Christ is signi-

---

155. The scriptures are to be read in light of Catholic faith (and not the other way around), which is a principle mentioned in *Teaching Christianity* III,10,14. See also section 4 of the present question and questions LXIV,1 and LXVII,7, as well as *Miscellany of Questions in Response to Simplician* II,3,3; *Eight Questions of Dulcitius* 3,4; 6,4 (= *Miscellany of Questions in Response to Simplician* II,3,3).
156. See Mt 24:3.
157. See Mt 25:31-46.

fied, but it is also necessary for them to be merciful by offering from what they possess, as those words of the same Lord demand when he says, *Give to everyone who asks you* (Lk 6:30). But how is it possible that there would not have been enough for both if something had been given? All of this adds greatly to the complexity of the matter. Even after other things have been carefully considered, so that everything combines in a cohesive whole and no one factor is emphasized to the detriment of another, great caution must be exercised.

3. And so five virgins seem to me to signify a fivefold restraint in regard to the allurements of the flesh. For the appetite of the soul must be restrained in the face of the pleasure of the eyes, the pleasure of the ears, the pleasure of smelling, tasting and touching. But because this restraint is practiced some-times before God, so as to be pleasing to him in the inner joy of one's conscience, and sometimes before human beings, solely that renown might be acquired, five are referred to as wise and five as foolish, yet both are virgins because both are restrained, although for different reasons. But the lamps, inasmuch as they are held in the hand, are the works that are accomplished in keeping with that restraint. It is said: *Let your works shine before men* (Mt 5:16). But they all *took their lamps and went to meet the bridegroom* (Mt 25:1). It must be understood, therefore, that this relates to persons who are marked by the name of Christ, for those who are not Christians cannot go to meet the bridegroom, who is Christ. *But the foolish ones, having taken their lamps, did not bring oil with them* (Mt 25:3). For there are many who, although they hope very much in Christ's goodness, nonetheless, while living with restraint, have no joy except in the praises of human beings. They have no oil with them, therefore. For in my opinion gladness itself is signified by oil. *Therefore God, your God,* it says, *has anointed you with the oil of exultation* (Ps 45:7). But the one who does not rejoice because he is pleasing God within has no oil with him. *The wise ones, however, took oil with them in vessels along with their lamps* (Mt 25:4) — that is, they set the gladness of good works in their heart and conscience. Thus also the Apostle warns: *Let a person test himself,* he says, *and then he will boast in himself and not in another* (Gal 6:4). *As the bridegroom was delayed, though, they all fell asleep* (Mt 25:5), because from each kind of persons who exercise this restraint, whether of those who exult before the Lord or of those who rejoice in the praise of human beings, they die for this space of time, until, at the coming of the Lord, the resurrection of the dead occurs. *But at midnight* (Mt 25:6)—that is, when no one is aware or in expectation, since indeed the Lord himself says, *Of that day and hour no one knows* (Mt 24:36), and the Apostle, *The day of the Lord will come like a thief in the night* (1 Thes 5:2), which means that he will be completely

concealed when he comes—there *was a loud cry: Behold, the bridegroom is coming; get up to meet him* (Mt 25:6). In the twinkling of an eye, we shall all rise up at the last trumpet.[158] Therefore *all those virgins got up and prepared their lamps* (Mt 25:7)—that is, the account that they would give of their works. For we must be presented before the tribunal of Christ, so that each one may receive there [the recompense for] what he did in the body, whether good or bad.[159] *And the foolish ones said to the wise ones, Give us some of your oil because our lamps are going out* (Mt 25:8). For the deeds of those who are buoyed up by others' praise come to naught when that has been removed, and out of habit they always ask for what their soul is accustomed to rejoice in. And thus in the presence of God, who is the searcher of the heart,[160] they wish to have the testimony of human beings, who do not see hearts. But what did the wise ones respond? *There may not be enough for us and you* (Mt 25:9). For each one renders an account for himself,[161] and in the presence of God, to whom the secrets of the heart are clear,[162] no one is helped by another's testimony; indeed, a person is hardly able to do this on his own, and his conscience must testify for him.[163] For who will boast that he possesses a pure heart?[164] For this reason the Apostle says, *It is nothing to me that I should be judged by you or by a human tribunal, but neither do I judge myself* (1 Cor 4:3). Hence, since a person cannot at all or only barely make a true judgment in his own case, how can he judge someone else, since *no one knows what takes place in a person except the spirit of the person* (1 Cor 2:11). *Go rather to the vendors and purchase some for yourselves* (Mt 25:9). They should not be considered as having given them advice but as having referred to their misdeed in an oblique way. For oil is sold to flatterers, who by praising what is false or mistaken lead souls into error, and for providing vain delights for them, as if for silly persons who do not understand what is said, *Those who call you happy are leading you into error* (Is 3:12), and they receive from them payment in food or money or honor or some other temporal benefit. But it is better to be reproached by a righteous person than to be praised by a sinner. *The righteous person,* it says, *will correct me in mercy and rebuke me, but the sinner's oil shall never anoint my head* (Ps 141:5). *Go,* therefore, *to the vendors and purchase some for yourselves* (Mt 25:9)—that is, let us see now what helps you, you who have been

---

158. See 1 Cor 15:51.
159. See 2 Cor 5:10.
160. See Prv 24:12.
161. See Rom 14:12.
162. See 1 Cor 14:25.
163. See Rom 2:15.
164. See Prv 20:9.

accustomed to purchasing praise for yourselves and leading yourselves into error, so that you seek glory not before God but from human beings. *But while going off to make their purchase the bridegroom came* (Mt 25:10)—that is, while pursuing things outside themselves and seeking after accustomed joys, because they knew nothing of inner joys, he who judges comes—*and those who were prepared* (Mt 25:10)—that is, those whose conscience offered a good testimony before God on their behalf—*went in with him to the wedding* (Mt 25:10)—that is, where a pure soul that is to become pregnant is joined to the eternal Word of God—*and the door was closed* (Mt 25:10)—that is, once those whose life had been changed into an angelic one had been let in (for *we shall all arise,* it says, *but we shall not all be changed* [1 Cor 15:51])—access to the kingdom of heaven was barred. For after judgment there is no place for entreaties or merits. *Much later, however, the other virgins came and said, Lord, lord, open to us* (Mt 25:11). It is not said that they had purchased this oil, and so they are to be understood as returning to beseech God now that they no longer have any joy from others' praise and are in distress and great affliction; but after judgment his severity is great—he whose ineffable mercy had been implored before judgment. And so he responds and says, *Amen, I say to you that I do not know you* (Mt 25:12)—namely, on the basis of that rule according to which God's practice, which is God's wisdom, does not allow to enter into his joy those who seemed to act in keeping with his precepts not in order to be seen by God but in order to please human beings. And thus he concludes: *Stay awake, therefore, because you do not know the day or the hour* (Mt 25:13) not only of that final time when the bridegroom will come; no one even knows the day and the hour of his own falling asleep. But whoever is prepared for sleep—that is, for the death that is everyone's due—will also be found prepared when that voice sounds at midnight, when all will be roused.

4. But when it said that the virgins went to meet the bridegroom, I think that it should be understood as follows—that she who is called the bride is constituted by those very virgins just as, when all Christians hasten to church, they are said to be like children hastening to their mother, since she who is called mother is constituted by those very children who are gathered together. For now the Church has been betrothed, and she is a virgin about to be given away in marriage—that is, when she restrains herself from worldly corruption. But he whom she marries in time makes her pregnant, when all dying has finished, by a deathless coupling. *I have betrothed you,* it says, *to one man, to show you as a chaste virgin to Christ* (2 Cor 11:2). It says *you* in the plural and concludes with *virgin* in the singular. Therefore they can be called both many virgins and one virgin. Why, however, they are referred to as five has been explained as

best I could. But we see now obscurely, but then face to face; and now partly, but then entirely.[165] But to catch some obscure and partial glimpse of this in the scriptures, which should in any event be in conformity with Catholic belief, depends upon that pledge which the virgin Church received at the lowly coming of her bridegroom, to whom she will be wedded at that final coming, when he will come in splendor,[166] when she will see him face to face. For, as the Apostle says, *he has given us the Spirit as a pledge* (2 Cor 5:5). And therefore this explanation holds no certitude unless it is in accord with faith, and it does not pass sentence on others that could just as well be in accord with faith.

LX. *But of the day and the hour no one knows, neither the angels of heaven nor the Son of Man but only the Father* (Mt 24:36)[167]

God is said to know also when he causes someone to know. As it is written: *The Lord your God puts you to the test so that he may know whether you love him* (Dt 13:4). For this is not said as though God does not know but so that they themselves may know to what extent they have made progress in the love of God, which is not fully realized by human beings except through the trials that befall them; and it is said of him that he puts a person to the test because he allows him to be put to the test. It is the same when he is said not to know or when it is said of him that he does not approve—that he does not recognize what is his in someone's discipline or doctrine, as when it is said, *I do not know you* (Mt 25:13)—or when it is said of him that with good reason he causes someone not to know what it would not be worthwhile to know. Hence both things are well understood: when it is said that the Father alone is said to know in this way because he causes the Son to know, and when it is said that the Son is said not to know in this way because he causes human beings not to

---

165. See 1 Cor 13:12.
166. See Mt 16:27.
167. The ignorance of Christ to which this text and others (Mk 13:32 and Lk 2:52) seemed to point was a problem for which the Fathers had different solutions. See *Dictionnaire de Théologie Catholique* VIII.1,1259-1260 for a comprehensive summary of the views of Augustine's contemporaries. Augustine's own position, presented here and repeated in *The Trinity* I,12,23, is that Christ's ignorance is not intrinsic to him but causative of ignorance in others. In *The Merits and Forgiveness of Sins and the Baptism of Infants* II,29,48 he denies the possibility of ignorance even in the infant Christ (although see question LXXV,2, where there seems to be a willingness on his part to accept that others might hold for Christ's boyhood ignorance). On this issue Augustine does not display the nuance that Athanasius (see, e.g., *Discourses against the Arians* 3,26.28) does in distinguishing between the ignorance displayed by Christ in his human nature and the omniscience characteristic of his divine nature—a distinction that is followed by a large number of Greek Fathers and a few Latin ones. But see André-Marie Dubarle, "La connaissance humaine du Christ d'après saint Augustin," in *Ephemerides Theologicae Lovaniensis* 18 (1949) 5-25, who argues that Augustine does not hold for Christ's human omniscience.

know—that is, he does not give them what it would not be worthwhile for them to know.

LXI. On what is written in the gospel, that on the mountain the Lord fed the crowds with five loaves[168]

1. The five barley loaves, with which the Lord fed the crowds on the mountain,[169] signify the old law either because it was given to those who were not yet spiritual but still fleshly[170]—that is, devoted to the five senses of the body, for the crowds themselves numbered five thousand men[171]—or because the law was given through Moses, for Moses wrote five books. And the fact that the loaves were barley signifies well either the law itself, which was given in such a way that in it the soul's life-giving food was concealed by bodily sacraments,[172] for kernels of barley are covered by very tenacious husks, or the people themselves, who were not yet stripped of fleshly desire because it clung like husks to their hearts—that is, their hearts were not yet circumcised[173] so that, when they were being led through the desert for forty years, the threshing of tribulation did not remove their fleshly coverings and unveil their understanding, just as the barley on the threshing floor is not stripped by threshing of its husky covering; and so such a law was appropriately given to that people.

2. But the two fish,[174] which lent the bread a pleasant taste, seem to signify those two offices by which that people was ruled, so that thanks to them they would be subject to the government of wise counsel—namely, a kingship and a priesthood—to which that most holy anointing also belonged.[175] It was their responsibility never to be hurt and brought to naught by the tempests and commotion of the masses, often to break through the

---

168. See Jn 6:3-13. This is in fact an interpretation of the miracle of the loaves and fishes as recorded not only in Jn 6:3-13 but also in Mt 15:32-38, which are treated here as two separate events. Although Augustine makes brief reference to the eucharist twice in section 2, this is by no means a eucharistic exegesis such as he gives in Sermon 130, which comments on the Johannine text. Instead it focuses upon the numerological meaning of the two miracle stories and concludes, with an analysis of the seven baskets of leftovers, on an eschatological note.
169. See Jn 6:9-12.
170. See I Cor 3:1, 3.
171. See Jn 6:10.
172. See note 43.
173. See Dt 10:16.
174. See Jn 6:9.
175. See 1 S 10:1; Ex 30:30. In his *Revisions* Augustine writes that he should have said that the "holy anointing" in question belonged "especially" but not exclusively to the kingship and the priesthood, since prophets were also sometimes anointed.

violent disputes of the crowds as though they were crashing waves, occasionally to make concessions while maintaining their own integrity, and to be tossed about in the turbulent rule of the people just as though they were fish in a stormy sea. Yet these two offices foreshadowed our Lord, for he alone maintained both of them and he alone—not figuratively but in actual fact—carried them out. For our king is Jesus Christ, who gave us an example of struggling and overcoming, taking on our sins in his mortal flesh,[176] conceding to neither the pleasurable nor the frightening temptations of the enemy,[177] and finally putting off his flesh, confidently despoiling the principalities and powers and triumphing over them in himself.[178] And so, under his leadership we are liberated from the burdens and travails of this pilgrimage of ours as though from Egypt, and during our escape the sins that are in pursuit of us are overwhelmed by the sacrament of baptism,[179] and while we hope in his promise, which we do not yet see,[180] it is as though we are being led through the desert, with the Word of God consoling us in the holy scriptures just as the manna from heaven consoled them.[181] And still under his leadership we have trusted that we can be led into the heavenly Jerusalem[182] as into the promised land, and under his rule and guardianship to dwell there forever. Thus our Lord Jesus Christ is shown to be our king. He is also our priest forever according to the order of Melchizedek,[183] who offered himself as a holocaust for our sins[184] and established the likeness of his sacrifice to be celebrated as a memorial of his passion,[185] so that what Melchizedek offered God we may see is now offered throughout the world in the Church of Christ.

---

176. See 1 Pt 2:24.
177. See Mt 4:1-11.
178. See Col 2:15.
179. See 14:5-31. The Israelites' crossing of the Red Sea, during which their Egyptian pursuers were drowned, was a classic symbol of baptism for the early Christians. See Jean Daniélou, *The Bible and the Liturgy* (Notre Dame, Ind.: University of Notre Dame Press, 1956) 86-98.
180. See Rom 8:24.
181. See Ex 16:13-35. It is surprising that, after comparing the crossing of the Red Sea with baptism, Augustine compares the manna in the desert with the scriptures rather than with the eucharist, not only because baptism and eucharist represented the single rite of initiation but also because the manna was almost universally seen as a symbol of the eucharist. See Daniélou 147-152. The eucharist is, however, mentioned a few lines later in connection with Melchizedek, whose offering was a widely accepted ancient symbol of that sacrament. See ibid. 144-147.
182. See Heb 12:22.
183. See Heb 6:20.
184. See Heb 10:12.
185. See 1 Cor 11:23-26.

Therefore, since our king took up our sins[186] in order to show us an example of struggling and overcoming, the evangelist Matthew,[187] signifying the taking up of those same sins and the character of the king, set down his lineage according to the flesh beginning with Abraham, who is the father of the people of faith, listing his offspring one after the other in descending order as far as David, in whom the stability of the kingship was most manifest, and from him by way of Solomon, born of the woman with whom his father had sinned,[188] he followed the royal line and brought it to the birth of the Lord. But the other evangelist, Luke,[189] because he also set out to explain the lineage of the Lord according to the flesh, albeit in his priestly role, which pertains to the cleansing and abolition of sin, starts not at the beginning of his book, as Matthew does, but at the place where Jesus was baptized,[190] when he foreshadowed the cleansing of our own sins, and he follows the line of his ancestors step by step not in descending order, as did he who showed him lowering himself, so to speak, so as to take up our sins, but in ascending order as though, after abolishing our sins, he were hinting at our ascent, and he does not name the same ancestors that the other one does. For priestly lineage was of another sort, showing (as is customary) the wives coming from the priestly tribe through one of David's sons, so that Mary is related to both tribes, royal and priestly. For also, when Joseph and Mary went to be registered, it is written that they were of the house—that is, the family—of David.[191] And Elizabeth, who it is written was likewise related to Mary,[192] was of the priestly tribe. Just as Matthew, who suggests that Christ the king lowered himself, so to speak, in order to take up our sins, goes in descending order from David through Solomon[193] because Solomon was born of the woman with whom David had sinned,[194] so Luke, who suggests that Christ the priest ascended after the wiping away of our sins, goes in ascending order to David through Nathan,[195] because Nathan was the prophet who was sent at whose reproach David by his repentance obtained the wiping away of his sin.[196] And so after Luke has finished with the person of David he does not differ from Matthew in naming

---

186. See 1 Pt 2:24.
187. See Mt 1:1-17.
188. See 2 S 12:24.
189. See Lk 3:23-38.
190. See Lk 3:21-22.
191. See Lk 2:4.
192. See Lk 1:36.
193. See Mt 1:6.
194. See 2 S 12:24.
195. See Lk 3:31.
196. See 2 S 12:1-13. In his *Revisions* Augustine excuses himself for having given the impression here that David's son Nathan and the prophet Nathan were the same person. In *Revisions*

the generations. For the ones whom [Luke] names while ascending from David to Abraham[197] are those whom [Matthew] names while descending from Abraham to David.[198] For from David that ancestry is divided into two families, royal and priestly, and of those two families, as was said, Matthew followed the royal line in descending order and Luke the priestly line in ascending order, so that our Lord Jesus Christ, our king and priest, might have a priestly lineage and yet not be from the priestly tribe (that is, from the tribe of Levi) but from the tribe of Judah (that is, from the tribe of David), from which tribe no one was intended for the altar.[199] And therefore he is very rightly called the son of David according to the flesh, because both Luke in ascending order and Matthew in descending order agreed with each other in David.[200] For it was fitting that he who was going to make void the sacrifices that took place according to the order of Aaron in the Levitical priesthood should not be of the tribe of Levi, lest the cleansing of sins, which the Lord accomplished by the offering of the holocaust of himself that was prefigured in the old priesthood, should seem to be the prerogative of that tribe and of that priesthood which for a time was a foreshadowing of the one that was to come.[201] And he gave the representation of his holocaust to be celebrated in the Church as a memorial of his suffering,[202] so that he might be a priest forever not according to the order of Aaron but according to the order of Melchizedek.[203] The sacrament[204] that this is can be studied more carefully and at greater length, but as far as the two fish are concerned, in which we have said that two offices—the royal and the priestly—are prefigured, let what has been discussed up to this point suffice.

3. But that the crowd reclined upon the grass[205] signifies that those who had accepted the Old Testament relied upon a fleshly hope because a temporal kingdom and a temporal Jerusalem had been promised them, for *all flesh is grass, and human glory is like the flower of the grass* (1 Pt 1:24). And that twelve baskets of bread were filled with the remaining fragments[206] signifies that the Lord's disciples, among whom the number twelve enjoys pre-eminence, were filled with the revelation and reasoning of the very law that the Jews had left

---

II,16 he makes a correction of the same misleading impression in the *Agreement among the Evangelists* II,4,12.
197. See Lk 3:32-34.
198. See Mt 1:2-6.
199. See Heb 7:11-14.
200. See Lk 3:31; Mt 1:6.
201. See Heb 10:1.
202. See 1 Cor 11:23-26.
203. See Heb 6:20.
204. See note 43.
205. See Jn 6:10.
206. See Jn 6:13.

behind and abandoned. For the New Testament did not exist when the Lord filled his disciples by as it were breaking and opening what was hard and closed in the law, when after his resurrection he opened to them the Old Testament, *beginning with Moses and all the prophets, interpreting for them in all the scriptures the things that touched upon himself* (Lk 24:27). And then the two of them recognized him in the breaking of the bread.[207]

4. And so the second feeding of the people, which was accomplished with seven loaves,[208] is rightly understood to refer to the preaching of the New Testament. For it is not said by any evangelist that these were barley loaves, as John said of those five.[209] This feeding with seven loaves, then, refers to the grace of the Church, which is recognized in that most remarkable sevenfold working of the Holy Spirit.[210] And so two fish are not written of here as in the old law, where only two persons were anointed, the king and the priest,[211] but a few fish[212]—that is, those who first believed in the Lord Jesus Christ and were anointed in his name and set out to preach the gospel and to withstand the turbulent sea of this world so that, as the apostle Paul says,[213] they might serve as ambassadors for the great fish himself, who is Christ.[214] Nor were there five thousand men in this crowd as there were in the other,[215] where the fleshly acceptors of the law—that is, those who are given over to the senses of the flesh—are signified, but rather four thousand;[216] this number signifies spiritual persons on account of the four virtues of the soul—prudence, temperance, fortitude and justice—by which a person lives spiritually in this life. The first of these is the recognition of the things that should be desired and of those that should be shunned; the second is refraining from taking pleasure in those things that provide temporary delight; the third is strength of soul in the face of temporal afflictions; the fourth is that which is diffused through all the others—the love of God and of neighbor.[217]

---

207. See Lk 24:35.
208. See Mt 15:32-38.
209. See Jn 6:9.
210. See Is 11:2.
211. See 1 S 10:1; Ex 30:30.
212. See Mt 15:34.
213. See 2 Cor 5:20.
214. The image of Christ as a fish was a commonplace in ancient Christian imagery and can be attested as early as the late second century. See the inscriptions of Abercius and Pectorius and also Tertullian, *On Baptism* 1.
215. See in 6:10.
216. See Mt 15:38.
217. Note that among the four cardinal virtues, which are dealt with at length in the excerpt from Cicero that constitutes question XXXI, justice is identified with love. See also *True Religion*

5. It seems to me that five thousand are spoken of in one place[218] and four thousand in another, with the exception of women and children,[219] so that we may understand that among the people of the Old Testament there were some persons who were weak in carrying out the righteousness which is according to the law and in which the apostle Paul says that he lived without reproach,[220] and likewise there were others who were easily led astray into the worship of idols. These two conditions—namely, weakness and error—are symbolized by the mention of women and children. For the female sex is weak when it comes to action and childhood is marked by love of play.[221] But what resembles children's play as much as worshiping idols? The Apostle himself referred to this form of superstition when he said, *Let us not serve idols as some of them did, as it is written: The people sat down to eat and drink and got up to play* (1 Cor 10:7). They were like women, therefore, who, while anxiously waiting to attain to God's promises, did not persevere in manly fashion but tempted God,[222] and they were like children who sat down to eat and drink and got up to play.[223] Not only there, however, but also among the people of the New Testament are found those who do not hold out in attaining to perfect manhood[224] and, because of either the weakness of their resources or the levity of their minds, must be compared to women and children. For to the ones it is said, *Yet let us hold on to the firm beginning of his substance until the end* (Heb 3:14), while to the others, *Do not be children in your minds, but be infants in terms of wickedness so that you may be perfect in your minds* (1 Cor 14:20). And so neither in the Old nor in the New Testament are such persons included in the count, but there are said to have been either five thousand in the one instance[225] or four thousand in the other, with the exception of women and children.[226]

48,93. In *The Catholic Way of Life* 15,25 Augustine famously identifies each of these virtues with some form of love. In *The City of God* XIX,4 he views the cardinal virtues in a pessimistic way as continually struggling against the vices and hence as a proof of the misery of life on earth.

218. See Jn 6:10.
219. See Mt 15:38.
220. See Phil 3:6.
221. Although Augustine often finds symbolic meaning in the female sex, as here, his perspective on children is less frequently stated. On children and play see especially *Confessions* I,9,15-10,16; 18,30.
222. See Ex 32:1-4.
223. See Ex 32:6.
224. See Eph 4:13.
225. See Jn 6:10.
226. See Mt 15:38.

6. But although in both the one instance and the other the two groups of people are fittingly fed on a mountain by Christ himself,[227] who is constantly referred to as a mountain in the scriptures,[228] nonetheless in one of them they reclined not on the grass but on the ground.[229] For in the former the loftiness of Christ is concealed by fleshly hope and desire because of fleshly men and the earthly Jerusalem, whereas in the latter all fleshly desire is far removed and the firmness of enduring hope, like the solidity of the mountain itself with no intervening layer of grass, supported those who were together at the New Testament feast.

7. And since the Apostle very rightly says, *Before faith came we were under the custody of the law* (Gal 3:23), the Lord also seems to mean this when he says of those whom he was about to feed with the five loaves: *They do not need to go away, but give them something to eat yourselves* (Mt 14:16). For under these words those who, so to speak, had to be kept in custody were figuratively detained, since his disciples had advised him to send them away.[230] But, in the account of the seven loaves, he says for his part that he feels sorry for this crowd because it was already the third day that they had clung to him without eating.[231] For in the whole span of human existence this is the third age, in which the grace of the Christian faith has been given. The first is before the law, the second under the law, the third under grace. And since the fourth is yet to come, when we shall attain to the fullness of peace of the heavenly Jerusalem[232] to which everyone who rightly believes in Christ is directed, the Lord therefore says that he will feed the crowd lest they faint on the way.[233] For this dispensation, in which the Lord deigned to appear in time and in visible form as a human being and gave us the pledge of the Holy Spirit,[234] by whose seven-fold working we are quickened, with the apostolic authority being as it were the added flavor of the two fish[235]—what does this dispensation accomplish, then, but to make it possible for us to attain to the palm of our heavenly calling

---

227. See Jn 6:3; Mt 15:29.
228. It is Augustine and other Fathers who, of course, understand certain scriptural texts about mountains in reference to Christ. See *Expositions of Psalms* 3,4 (Dn 2:35); 10[11],1; 45[46],6 (Is 2:2).
229. See Jn 6:10; Mt 15:35.
230. See Mt 14:15.
231. See Mt 15:32.
232. See Heb 12:22.
233. See Mt 15:32. Time is divided here into three periods, with a fourth category representing eternity—1) before the law (from Adam until Moses), 2) under the law (from Moses until Christ), 3) under grace (from Christ until the end of time), and 4) the fullness of peace (eternity). Question LXVI,3-7 expatiates considerably upon these periods as they are experienced in the individual. See also the *Commentary on Some Statements in the Letter to the Romans* 13-18.
234. See 2 Cor 5:5.
235. See Mt 15:34.

without succumbing to weakness? *For we walk by faith, not by sight* (2 Cor 5:7). And the apostle Paul himself says that he has not yet attained to the kingdom of God *but, forgetting those things that are behind me and stretching out to those things that are before me,* he says, *I am intent upon the palm of a heavenly calling. But let us walk where we have arrived* (Phil 3:13-14, 16), because those who cling to the Lord on the third day and have been fed by him shall not faint on the way.[236]

8. Even here it was impossible to arrive at the end of eating, for there was food left over.[237] For not without reason is it said of the future: *Do you think that the Son of Man will come and will find faith upon the earth?* (Lk 18:8) And I believe that it will be this way because of the women and children.[238] But nonetheless they filled seven baskets with the remaining fragments,[239] which refers to the sevenfold Church that is described in the Apocalypse,[240] meaning everyone who perseveres until the end.[241] For he who said, *Do you think that the Son of Man will come and will find faith upon the earth?* (Lk 18:8) was in fact indicating that at the end of the meal his food could be abandoned and left behind. But because he also said, *He who perseveres until the end will be saved* (Mt 24:13), he indicated the Church that will not fall away, which, because of the number seven, would receive the same seven loaves in more abundant fashion and hold them in the largeness of its heart, which seems to be the meaning of their being kept in baskets.

LXII. On that which is written in the gospel: *That Jesus baptized more than John, although it was not he himself who baptized but his disciples* **(Jn 4:12)**[242]

The question is whether those who were baptized at that time, when it is written that the Lord baptized more through his disciples than John did,[243] received the Holy Spirit, for in another place in the gospel it is said, *The Spirit had not yet been given because Jesus had not yet been glorified* (Jn 7:39).

---

236. See Mt 15:32.
237. See Mt 15:37.
238. See Mt 15:38.
239. See Mt 15:37.
240. See Rv 1:4.
241. See Mt 24:13.
242. The question at issue is actually formulated in the first sentence: Did those who were baptized by Jesus and John the Baptist receive the Holy Spirit when, according to Jn 7:39, the Spirit had not yet been given? In answer Augustine distinguishes between the hidden pre-resurrection workings of the Spirit in certain holy persons and his visible workings after Christ's glorification.
243. See Jn 4:1-2.

And indeed the simplest answer is that the Lord Jesus, who even raised the dead,[244] could have seen to it that none of them died until they received the Holy Spirit after his glorification—that is, after his resurrection from the dead and his ascension into heaven. But that thief comes to mind to whom it was said, *Amen, I say to you, today you will be with me in paradise* (Lk 23:43), who had not received baptism,[245] although Cornelius and the gentiles who believed with him received the Holy Spirit even before they were baptized.[246] Yet I do not see how that thief was able, apart from the Holy Spirit, to say, *Lord, remember me when you come into your kingdom* (Lk 23:42), for *no one says that Jesus is Lord,* declares the Apostle, *except in the Holy Spirit* (1 Cor 12:3). The Lord himself made clear the fruit of this faith when he said, *Amen, I say to you, today you shall be with me in paradise* (Lk 23:43).

Just as by the ineffable power and justice of an absolute God, then, baptism was credited to the believing thief, and what could not be received in a crucified body was rendered acceptable in an unshackled soul, so likewise the Holy Spirit was given in a hidden way before the Lord's glorification but more openly after the manifestation of his divinity. And this is how it was said that *the Spirit had not yet been given* (Jn 7:39)—namely, that he had not yet appeared in such a way that all could acknowledge that he was given, just as the Lord himself was not yet glorified in the presence of men, although his eternal glorification never ceased, and just as, likewise, his appearance in mortal flesh is referred to as his coming, for he came to the place where he [already] was, because *he came to his own* (Jn 1:11) and *he was in the world, and the world was made by him* (Jn 1:10). Just as the Lord's bodily appearance, then, is understood as his coming, although even before this appearance he himself, as the Word of God and

---

244. See Mk 5:35-43; Lk 7:11-16; Jn 11:38-44.
245. Regarding his statement here that the thief was not baptized, Augustine writes in the *Revisions* that he was not the first to say this but that in any event there is no proof that the thief was not baptized. He says as well that he has investigated this issue in several places and especially in *The Nature and Origin of the Soul* (I,9,11), where he postulates that the thief may have been baptized in his own blood or in the water flowing from Christ's side. An analogous question, frequently asked in the early Church, concerned the baptism of the apostles, first raised in Tertullian, *On Baptism* 12. See H. A. Echle, "The Baptism of the Apostles," in *Traditio* 3 (1945) 365-368. All of this testifies to the ancient Church's belief in the absolute necessity of some form of baptism for salvation.
246. See Acts 10:44-47.

the wisdom of God,[247] spoke in all the holy prophets, so likewise the coming of the Holy Spirit is the Holy Spirit's appearance to mortal eyes, when he was seen as fire dividing itself over them and they began to speak in tongues.[248] For if the Holy Spirit was not in human beings before the Lord's visible glorification, how could David say, *Do not remove your holy spirit from me* (Ps 51:11)? Or how were Elizabeth and her husband Zechariah filled so that they could prophesy,[249] and also Anna and Simeon,[250] concerning all of whom it is written that they were filled with the Holy Spirit and spoke those things which we read in the gospel? But that God does some things in a hidden way but others in a visible way by means of a visible creature is a matter of the governance of providence, by which all divine actions are accomplished with order[251] and with the most splendid refinement in regard to times and places, inasmuch as divinity itself is neither confined to a place nor changes place, nor does it bend or fluctuate with respect to time. But just as the Lord himself really possessed the Holy Spirit in the very humanity that he bore[252] when he came to John to be baptized,[253] so must it be understood that, before the evident and visible coming of the Holy Spirit, some holy persons were able to possess him in a hidden way. We have said this so that we may understand that by the visible appearance of the Holy Spirit, which[254] is called his coming, his fullness has been poured more abundantly into the hearts of human beings in an ineffable and even incomprehensible way.

LXIII. On the Word

In the beginning was the Word (Jn 1:1). What is referred to as *logos* in Greek means both "reason" and "word" in Latin. But in this place "word" is the better translation, signifying not only a relationship to the Father but also the operative power in regard to those things that have been made by the Word. But reason, even if nothing comes into existence through it, is correctly called reason.

---

247. See 1 Cor 1:24.
248. See Acts 2:3-4.
249. See Lk 1:41-45.67-79.
250. See Lk 2:36-38.25-35.
251. Reading *ordines* instead of *ordine*.
252. "In the very humanity that he bore": *in ipso homine quem gerebat*. See note 11.
253. See Mt 3:16.
254. Reading *quae* instead of *qui*.

LXIV. On the Samaritan woman[255]

1. The gospel sacraments[256] that have their expression in the words and deeds of our Lord Jesus Christ are not clear to all, and there are some people who, by interpreting them less carefully and less seriously, often introduce ruin in place of salvation and error in place of knowledge of the truth. Among these sacraments is that where it is written that at the sixth hour of the day the Lord came to Jacob's well and, tired from his journey, sat down and asked for a drink from a Samaritan woman, along with the other things that are spoken of in the same place in the scriptures and that are to be discussed and investigated. In this matter the first thing to be maintained is that the greatest care must be taken in regard to all the scriptures so that any explanation of the divine sacrament may be in accordance with faith.[257]

2. Our Lord came to the well, then, at the sixth hour of the day.[258] I see in the well a dark depth. I am alerted, then, to understand the lowest—namely, the earthly—parts of this world, to which the Lord Jesus came at the sixth hour—that is, in the sixth age of the human race, in the old age of the old person, so to speak, whom we are commanded to put off so that we may be clothed in the new, who was created according to God.[259] For the sixth age is old age, because the first is infancy, the second childhood, the third adolescence, the fourth youth and the fifth maturity.[260] And so the life of the old person, which is lived according to the flesh in a temporal condition, concludes with the sixth age, which is old age. In this old age, as I have said, our Lord, the creator and restorer of the human race, came to us, so that when the old person died he might establish in himself the new one, whom he would transport, stripped of earthly imperfection, to heavenly realms. The well, therefore, as has been said, signifies by its dark depth the earthly travail and error of this world. And since the old person is within and the new one is without—for the Apostle is completely right when he says, *Even if our outer person is decaying, yet our inner person is being renewed from day to*

---

255. See Jn 4:5-29. There is a much longer treatment of this gospel narrative in the *Homilies on the Gospel of John* 15,5-31, where some of the same themes are reprised. Roughly the whole second half of the present question is preoccupied with the possible interpretation of the Samaritan woman's five husbands, who correspond to the five bodily senses. In section 7 Augustine interjects a sentence—"May it [i.e., the spirit by which a person understands spiritual things] be present as I speak to you so that you can receive the spiritual water" —which he does not seem to be putting into the mouth of Christ. He must, then, be speaking in his own person, which suggests that this question was originally a sermon.
256. On the term "sacrament" here and in the following lines see note 43.
257. See note 155.
258. See Jn 4:6.
259. See Eph 4:22, 24.
260. See questions XLIV (and note 56) and LVIII,2 (and note 124).

day (2 Cor 4:16), because everything visible, which Christian discipline renounces, pertains to the outer person—the Lord came to the well at the sixth hour.[261] This is the middle of the day, at which point the visible sun is already beginning its descent toward its setting, because in us too, who have been called by Christ, the pleasure of visible things diminishes, so that by love of invisible things the inner person, once recreated for the inner light that never sets, may return and, in accordance with apostolic discipline, seek not the things that are seen but those that are not seen; for the things that are seen are temporal, whereas those that are not seen are eternal.[262]

3. That he came weary to the well signifies the weakness of the flesh, and that he sat down signifies humility,[263] because he took on even the frailty of the flesh for our sake and humbly deigned to appear as a man to men. Of this weakness of the flesh the prophet says, *A man placed in affliction and able to endure frailty* (Is 53:3), and of his humility the Apostle declares, *He humbled himself, having become submissive even unto death* (Phil 2:8). But the fact that he sat down can, by another interpretation, indicate not the modesty of humility but the role of a teacher, since teachers are accustomed to sitting down.[264]

4. But it can be asked why he requested a drink from the Samaritan woman who had come for the sake of filling her jug with water[265] when he himself predicted later that he was able to supply an abundant spiritual spring for those who asked him.[266] But the Lord thirsted for the faith of that woman because she was a Samaritan and Samaria usually symbolizes idolatry. For they were set apart from the people of the Jews and had consigned the dignity of their souls to the images of dumb animals—that is, to golden cows;[267] but our Lord Jesus came to lead the multitude of the nations, which served images, to the shelter of Christian faith and uncorrupt religion for, he said, *there is need of a doctor not for the healthy but for those who are ill* (Mt 9:12). Therefore he thirsts for the faith of those for whom he poured out his blood. Consequently *Jesus said to her, Woman, give me something to drink* (Jn 4:7). And so that you may know what our Lord was thirsting for, after a short while his disciples, who had gone

---

261. See Jn 4:6.
262. See 2 Cor 4:18.
263. See Jn 4:6.
264. See *The Lord's Sermon on the Mount* I,1,2.
265. See Jn 4:7.
266. See Jn 4:14.
267. Scripture, which would ordinarily have been Augustine's source for such a statement, says no such thing of the Samaritans, and he must have been thinking of the episode of the golden calf in Ex 32:1-24.

off to the city to buy food,[268] *came and said to him, Rabbi, eat. But he said to them, I have food to eat that you do not know. His disciples then said to one another, Did anyone bring him something to eat? Jesus said to them, My food is to do the will of him who sent me and to bring his work to completion.* (Jn 4:31-34) Is any will of the Father who sent him or any work of his, which he declared that he wanted to bring to completion, to be understood here other than that he might convert us from the ruinous error of the world to his faith? His drink, then, is the same thing that his food is. And so he thirsted for this in that woman—that he might do the Father's will in her and bring his work to completion. But she understands in a fleshly way and replies, *Since you are a Jew, why do you ask me for something to drink, since I am a Samaritan woman? For Jews have nothing to do with Samaritans.* (Jn 4:9) To this our Lord said, *If you knew the gift of God and who it is that says to you, Give me something to drink, you would instead have asked of him, and he would have given you living water* (Jn 4:10). Here he shows her that he did not ask for such water as she understood but, because he thirsted for her faith, he desired to give the Holy Spirit to her in her thirst. For we are right to understand this as living water because it is the gift of God, as he himself said, *If you knew the gift of God* (Jn 4:10), and as the same evangelist John testifies in another place when he says that *Jesus stood and cried out, If anyone thirsts, let him come and drink. He who believes in me, as scripture says, streams of living water will flow from his breast.* (Jn 7:37-38) He says with complete consistency, *He who believes in me, streams of living water will flow from his breast*, because we believe first so that [then] we may merit these gifts. These streams of living water, then, which he wanted to give to that woman, are the recompense of the faith that he first thirsted for in her. [Scripture] supplies the interpretation of this living water when it says, *He said this of the Spirit, whom they who would believe in him would receive. But the Spirit had not yet been given because Jesus had not yet been glorified* (Jn 7:39). This is the gift, then, of the Holy Spirit, which he gave to the Church after his glorification, as another scripture says, *Ascending on high he led captivity captive, he gave gifts to men* (Eph 4:8).

5. But that woman still understood in a fleshly way, for she replied thus: *Sir, you do not have a bucket and the well is deep. How can you give me living water? Are you greater than our father Jacob, who gave us this well, and he himself drank from it, with his sons and his cattle?* (Jn 4:11-12) But at this point the Lord explained what he had said: *Everyone*, he declared, *who drinks of that water will thirst again, but whoever drinks of the water that I will give*

---

268. See Jn 4:8.

shall never thirst, but the water that I will give shall become in him a source of water springing up into eternal life (Jn 4:13-14). Yet still the woman held onto the wisdom of the flesh. For what did she respond? *Sir, give me this water so that I may not thirst or come here again to draw water. Jesus said to her, Go, call your husband and come back here.* (Jn 4:15-16) Since he knew that she did not have a husband, it may be asked why he said this. For when the woman said, *I do not have a husband, Jesus said to her, You said well that you have no husband, for you have had five husbands, and the one whom you have now is not your husband; you spoke the truth* (Jn 4:17-18). But these things are not to be taken in a fleshly way, lest we seem to be like this Samaritan woman as she was up to that time. But if we have tasted anything of that gift of God, we would approach the question in a spiritual way.

6. There are some who say that the five husbands are the five books that were given through Moses. And the words *and the one whom you have now is not your husband* (Jn 4:18) they understand that the Lord said of himself. Thus the meaning is as follows: At first you were subject to the five books of Moses as though they were five husbands, but the one whom you have now—that is, whom you listen to—is not your husband because you have not yet believed in him. But inasmuch as she who did not yet believe in Christ was still in fact bound by her relationship to those five husbands (that is, to the five books), one may be puzzled as to how it could be said, *You have had five husbands* (Jn 4:18), as though she now no longer had them, since she actually still lived in subjection to them. Moreover, since the five books of Moses speak of nothing other than Christ, as he himself says, *If you believed Moses you would probably believe me as well, for he wrote of me* (Jn 5:46), how is it thinkable that a person would abandon those five books in order to go over to Christ when one who believes in Christ embraces those books, which are not to be put aside but to be understood spiritually, all the more ardently?

7. There is, then, another meaning, according to which the five husbands are understood as the five senses of the body—one belonging to the eyes, by which we perceive this visible light and the colors and forms of bodies; a second to the ears, by which we discern the movements of voices and of all sounds; the third to the nose, by which we take pleasure in the varying agreeableness of odors; the fourth to taste in the mouth, which senses what is sweet and what is bitter and explores every flavor; while the fifth determines, on account of the feeling that is spread throughout the body, what is hot and what is cold, what is soft and what is hard, what is smooth and what is rough, and anything else that we feel by touching. The first age of humankind is subject to the tutelage of these five fleshly senses, due to the constraints of mortal nature under which we were born after the sin of the first human being, to such a

degree that, at the disposal of the fleshly senses and with our mind's light not yet restored, we live our fleshly life without any awareness of the truth. Infants and small children, who cannot yet reason, are necessarily this way. And since those senses, which govern the first age and were bestowed on us by God the creator, are natural, they are rightly called husbands—that is, lawfully married men, so to speak—because it was not error, by its own perniciousness, but nature, by God's working, that furnished them. But when a person arrives at the age when she is capable of reasoning and is immediately able to grasp the truth, she will no longer yield to those senses as her masters but will have a reasoning spirit as her husband, under whose sway she can bring those senses, subjecting her body to servitude. Then the soul, no longer at the disposal of her five husbands (that is, the five senses of the body), will have the divine Word as her lawful husband, to whom she will be united and bound, and when a man's very spirit has clung to Christ with a spiritual embrace, because Christ is the head of a man,[269] he will enjoy eternal life without any fear of separation. For *who will be able to separate us from the love of Christ?* (Rom 8:35) But because that woman, who signified the vast number in the world who are subjugated to empty superstitions, was bound by error, after the period of the five fleshly senses by which the first age is governed, as we have said, the Word of God did not take her in marriage, but the devil laid hold of her by an adulterous embrace. And so, seeing that she was fleshly, which means that she understood in a fleshly way, the Lord said to her, *Go, call your husband and come back here* (Jn 4:16)—that is, remove yourself from the fleshly affection in which you now find yourself, on account of which you are unable to understand what I am saying. And *call your husband*—that is, be present to the spirit of understanding. For, in a manner of speaking, a person's spirit is like the soul's husband, which rules the soul's affections as though it were his wife. This is not the Holy Spirit, who remains unchangeable with the Father and the Son and who is given unchangeably to worthy souls, but the spirit of a human being, about which the Apostle says, *No one knows what is in a person except the spirit of the person* (1 Cor 2:11). For the former spirit is the Holy Spirit of God, of which he says once again, *So also no one knows the things that are of God except the Spirit of God* (1 Cor 2:11). When this person's spirit, then, is present—that is, when it is within—and piously submits to God, the person understands things that are said spiritually. But when the devil's error dominates in a soul and understanding is absent, as it were, he is adulterous. Therefore, he says, *call your husband*—that is, the spirit which is in you, by which a person can understand spiritual things if the light of truth shines upon him.

---

269. See 1 Cor 11:3.

May it [i.e., the spirit] be present as I speak to you so that you can receive the spiritual water. And when she said, *I do not have a husband,* he replied, *You said well, for you have had five husbands* (Jn 4:17-18)—that is, the five senses of the flesh governed you in the first age—*and the one whom you have now is not your husband* (Jn 4:18), because there is not in you the spirit that understands God, with which you can have a lawful marriage, but rather it is the error of the devil that dominates and that is ruining you by adulterous contamination.

8. And perhaps in order to show those who understand that the five senses of the body which have been spoken of are signified by the reference to the five husbands, that woman, after her five fleshly responses, names Christ in her sixth response. For her first response is: *Since you are a Jew, why do you ask me for something to drink?* (Jn 4:9) Her second: *Sir, you do not have a bucket and the well is deep* (Jn 4:11). Her third: *Sir, give me this water so that I may not thirst or come here again to draw water* (Jn 4:15). Her fourth: *I do not have a husband* (Jn 4:17). Her fifth: *I see that you are a prophet. Our ancestors worshiped on this mountain.* (Jn 4:19-20) For this response is fleshly too, for an earthly place had been given to fleshly persons where they could worship, but the Lord said that spiritual persons would worship in spirit and in truth.[270] After he said that, the woman acknowledges in her sixth response that Christ is the teacher of all these things, for she said, *I know that the Messiah will come, who is called the Christ. When he comes, he will tell us everything.* (Jn 4:25) But still she erred, because she did not see that he whom she hoped would come *had* come. But now by the Lord's mercy this error is cast out as though it were an adulterer. For Jesus said to her, *I who speak to you am he* (Jn 4:26). Upon hearing this she did not respond but immediately left her jug and went quickly into the town, so that she might not just believe the gospel and the Lord's coming but even make it known.[271] Nor is the fact that she left her jug and went off something to be negligently passed over. For a jug perhaps signifies the love of this world—that is, desire—by which people draw pleasure out of the dark depth which the well calls to mind—namely, out of an earthly way of life. And once this [pleasure] has been tasted they flare up once again in their longing for it, just as he says, *Whoever drinks of that water will thirst again* (Jn 4:13). But she who believed in Christ had to renounce the world and, by leaving her jug, show that she had left worldly desire, not only believing with her heart unto righ-

270. See Jn 4:23.
271. See Jn 4:28-29.

teousness but also ready with her mouth to confess and preach unto salvation what she believed.[272]

LXV. On the resurrection of Lazarus[273]

Although we hold with complete faith to the resurrection of Lazarus in accordance with the gospel account,[274] yet I have no doubt that there is an allegorical meaning as well. When deeds are allegorized they do not do away with faith in the actual thing; such is the case when Paul explains that the two sons of Abraham are an allegory of the two covenants.[275] Did Abraham not exist, then, or did he not have two sons? Therefore let us see Lazarus in the tomb as an allegory of the soul buried in earthly sins—that is, the whole human race—to which the Lord refers in another place as the lost sheep that, he says, he came down to set free after leaving behind the other ninety-nine in the mountains.[276]

That he asks, *Where did you put him?* (Jn 11:34) signifies, I think, our calling, which occurs in secret, for the predestination of our calling is something secret. The sign of this secret is the question that the Lord asks as though he did not know the answer, when it is we ourselves who do not know it. As the Apostle says, *That I may know as I am known* (1 Cor 13:12), or as the Lord shows in another place when he says that he does not know sinners, *I do not know you* (Mt 7:23). The entombed Lazarus signified this because in [the Lord's] instruction and precepts there are no sins. Similar to this question is the one in Genesis, *Adam, where are you?* (Gn 3:9) because he had sinned and hidden himself from the face of God.[277] The tomb here signifies this hiding, so that a dying person resembles a sinner and a buried person resembles someone hidden from the face of God. I think that his words, *Take away the stone* (Jn 11:39), signify either those who wished to impose the burden of circumcision upon those entering the Church from the nations, against whom the Apostle frequently writes,[278] or those who live corruptly in the Church and are a stumbling block to those who wish to believe. *Martha said to him, It is*

---

272. See Rom 10:10.
273. See Jn 11:17-44. Augustine begins this question by noting carefully that allegorization does not eliminate faith in the reality of the thing or event being allegorized—a position that does not take into account the possibility that a scriptural text may be susceptible only of an allegorical and not of a literal or historical understanding, which he allows for in *Teaching Christianity* III,10,14. The narrative of Lazarus' resurrection is treated at much greater length in the *Homilies on the Gospel of John* 49.
274. See Jn 11:44.
275. See Gal 4:22-24.
276. See Mt 18:12.
277. See Gn 3:6.8.
278. See, e.g., 1 Cor 7:17-20; Gal 5:11-12.

already the fourth day and he stinks (Jn 11:39). Earth is the last of the four elements,[279] and therefore it signifies the stench of earthly sins—that is, greed for fleshly things. For *you are earth,* the Lord said to Adam when he sinned, *and you shall return to the earth* (Gn 3:19). And once the stone was removed[280] he came out from the tomb with his hands and feet bound, and his face was covered with a cloth.[281] His leaving the tomb signifies the soul's withdrawal from fleshly vices. His being wrapped in bandages means that, even though we withdraw from fleshly things and observe the law of God in our minds,[282] we still live in the body and cannot be removed from the distractions of the flesh. As the Apostle says, *In my mind I observe the law of God, but in my flesh the law of sin* (Rom 7:25). That his face had been covered with a cloth means that in this life we cannot have complete knowledge. As the Apostle says, *Now we see through a mirror in obscurity, but then face to face* (1 Cor 13:12). And that Jesus said, *Unbind him and let him go* (Jn 11:44), means that after this life all veils are removed[283] so that we may see face to face.

How great the difference is between the human being whom the wisdom of God[284] bore,[285] by whom we have been set free, and other people is clear from the fact that Lazarus is not unbound until he leaves the tomb. This means that, even when the soul has been reborn, as long as it sees through a mirror in obscurity[286] it cannot be completely free from sin and ignorance until the body has been released. But the wrapping and face-cloth of the Lord, who committed no sin[287] and was ignorant of nothing,[288] were found in the tomb.[289] For [among those who are] in the flesh he alone was not only not overcome by the tomb, so that some sin might be found in him,[290] but he was not wrapped in cloths, as if something were concealing him or hindering his movement.

---

279. The other elements were fire, air and water. This list of four was first assembled by Empedocles (fl. c. 444 B.C.) and was eventually taken up by the Stoics and became commonly accepted.
280. See Jn 11:41.
281. See Jn 11:44.
282. See Rom 7:25.
283. See 2 Cor 3:16.
284. See 1 Cor 1:24.
285. "The human being whom the wisdom of God bore": *hominem quem Dei sapientia gestabat.* See note 11.
286. See 1 Cor 13:12.
287. See Pt 2:22.
288. On Christ's lack of ignorance of any kind in Augustine's thought see note 167.
289. See Jn 20:6-7.
290. See 1 Pt 2:22.

LXVI. On what is written: *Are you unaware, brothers—for I speak to those who know the law—that a person is subject to the law for as long as he lives?* **(Rom 7:1) up until the place where it is written:** *He will also give life to your mortal bodies through his Spirit dwelling within you* **(Rom 8:11)**[291]

1. In the analogy in which the Apostle speaks of a husband and wife, he observes that three things must be considered, given that a wife is bound by the law of her husband: the wife, the husband and the law—the wife, in other words, subjected to her husband by the bond of the law, from which bond she is liberated upon the death of her husband, when she may marry whom she wills.[292] For this is what he says: *A wife under a living husband is bound to the law; but if her husband dies, she is free of her husband's law. She will be called an adulteress, then, if, while her husband is alive, she is with another man, but if her husband dies, she is liberated from the law, so that she is not an adulteress if she is with another man.* (Rom 7:2-3) The analogy goes as far as that. Then he begins to speak of the topic for the explanation and examination of which he introduced the analogy.

Regarding this topic as well there are three things that must be attended to: man, sin and the law.[293] For, he says, as long as man is under the law he lives in sin,[294] just as a wife is under the law of her husband as long as her husband is alive.[295] But sin is to be understood here as gaining its access through the law.[296] He says that this sin is without limit[297] because, when sin appears, it is augmented by transgression; *for where there is no law there is no transgression* (Rom 4:15). And this is what he says: *That the sinner or the sin may be, thanks to the commandment, without limit* (Rom 7:13).[298] Hence he says that the law, although it forbids sin, was not given in order to liberate from sin but

---

291. This first of three questions on the Epistle to the Romans offers an early view of Augustine's theology of grace, which he constructs in reference not only to the scriptural text but also to the four possible phases or periods of an individual's life—before the law, under the law, under grace and in peace. See question LXI,7 and note 233. Augustine acknowledges the effects of Adam's sin in his descendents, although he does not yet use the expression "original sin," and he recognizes, in section 5, that a person overwhelmed by sin should know that "it was his doing when he fell and that it is not his when he arises." But at this point he does not understand that grace is necessary not only to rescue a person from original sin and from subsequent sins but also to enable him or her to accomplish any good whatsoever. That insight would have to wait perhaps a few months until the composition of the *Miscellany of Questions in Response to Simplician* I,2.

292. See Rom 7:2-3.

293. See Rom 7:4-6.

294. See Rom 7:1.

295. See 1 Cor 7:39.

296. See Rom 7:7.

297. See Rom 7:13.

298. Augustine's Latin text for these words is: *Ut fiat supra modum peccator aut peccatum* (*delinquens* [as in section 5]) *per mandatum.* This is not a precise rendering of the Greek, which

in order to bring sin out into the open,[299] and the soul that serves it must turn to the grace of the liberator in order to be liberated from sin, *for knowledge of sin is through the law* (Rom 3:20). And in another place he says, *But sin, in order to appear as sin, worked death in me through what was good* (Rom 7:13). Where the grace of the liberator is not present, then, the prohibition of sin increases the desire of sinning.[300] This is useful, to be sure, so that the soul may be aware that on its own it cannot extract itself from slavery to sin and that, once pride has completely subsided and been extinguished in this way, it may submit to its liberator and a person may sincerely say, *My soul has clung to you* (Ps 63:8), which means that it is no longer under the law of sin but in the law of righteousness.

Now this is called a law of sin[301] not because the law itself is sin[302] but because it is imposed upon sinners; and so it is also a law of death[303] because death is the wages of sin;[304] the sting of death is sin, but the power of sin is the law.[305] For when we sin we sink into death. But we sin the more vehemently because the law forbids it than if we were not forbidden by any law. At the onset of grace, however, we now fulfill most willingly and without any burden the very thing that the law had burdensomely commanded. The law of sin and death,[306] therefore, which is so called because it has been imposed upon sinful and dying persons, commands only that we not covet, and still we covet.[307] But the law of the spirit of life,[308] which belongs to grace and liberates from the law of sin and death,[309] causes us not to covet but to fulfill the commandments of the law—no longer as slaves of the law through fear but as friends through charity and as slaves of the righteousness[310] that was the source of the law's promulgation. Righteousness, however, must not be served slavishly but willingly—that is, in charity rather than fear. Consequently it is most truly said, *Do we, then, nullify the law on account of faith? By no means. But we have established the law.* (Rom 3:31) For it is faith that makes the law command. The

---

says, "That sin may be sinful without limit," or, as in one of the more accurate Latin versions, *Ut fiat supra modum peccans peccatum.* Augustine's text necessitated the adding of *delinquens* ("criminal") for it to make sense, which for some reason appears in section 5 but not here.

299. See Rom 7:7.
300. See Rom 7:8.
301. See Rom 8:2.
302. See Rom 7:7.
303. See Rom 8:2.
304. See Rom 6:23.
305. See 1 Cor 15:56.
306. See Rom 8:2.
307. See Rom 7:7.
308. See Rom 8:2.
309. See Rom 8:2.
310. See Rom 6:18.

law, therefore, is established by faith. If this faith does not exist, the law merely commands and accuses those who do not fulfill its injunctions, so that it eventually converts to the grace of the liberator those who groan in their inability to fulfill what has been commanded.

2. We see three things in that analogy—a wife, a husband and the law—and another three things in the topic that prompted the analogy—the soul, sin and the law of sin. This alone, then, is the difference: in the analogy the husband dies, and thus his wife may marry whom she wills and is absolved from the law of her husband; in the latter case, however, the soul dies to sin so that it may marry Christ.[311] But when it dies to sin, it dies also to the law of sin. *And so,* he says, *my brothers, you too have died to the law through the body of Christ, so that you may belong to another, who has risen from the dead, so that we may be fruitful for God. For when we were in the flesh,* he says, meaning that we were held bound by fleshly desires, *the passions of sin, which are through the law, were at work in our members, so that they bore fruit for death.* (Rom 7:4-5) He says that, when grace was lacking, there was an increase in the covetousness that the law forbids, and the crime of transgression was added to the accumulation of sins because *where there is no law there is no transgression* (Rom 4:15). [He says that] these passions, *which are through the law, were at work in our members, so that they bore fruit for death* (Rom 7:5). Before grace came through faith, the soul acted under these passions as though under a husband's rule. Whoever, therefore, serves the law of God in his mind dies to these passions, although the passions themselves have not yet died as long as he serves the law of sin in his flesh.[312] Something still remains in him, therefore, who is under grace, which neither overcomes him nor takes him captive, until everything that has been propped up by wicked habits is put to death, and for that reason the body is even now said to be dead[313] as long as it does not properly serve the spirit. But it will come to pass that it serves it perfectly when the mortal body itself is brought to life.[314]

3. From this we understand that there are four phases even in a single person and, when they have been experienced in sequence, eternal life will be attained. For inasmuch as it was necessary and just that, after our nature fell into sin and the spiritual blessedness which is signified by the term "paradise" was lost, we should be born as animals and fleshly beings, there is a first period that is before the law, a second that is under the law, a third that is under grace, and a fourth that is in peace. The period before the law occurs when we do not

---

311. See Rom 7:2-6.
312. See Rom 7:25.
313. See Rom 8:10.
314. See Rom 8:11.

know the law[315] and pursue fleshly desires. The period under the law occurs when we are forbidden to sin and still we commit sin, having been overcome by the habit of it, because faith does not yet help us. The third period occurs when we believe utterly in our liberator and attribute nothing to our own merits but, loving his mercy, are no longer overcome by the pleasure of wicked habits when they strive to lead us to sin, yet we still allow them to disturb us even though we do not give in to them. The fourth period occurs when there is nothing whatsoever in a person that resists the spirit, but all things, harmoniously joined and linked together, preserve the unity of the person in an enduring peace, which will happen when the mortal body has been restored to life,[316] this corruptible thing has put on incorruptibility and this mortal thing has put on immortality.[317]

4. These texts come to mind at the moment as testimonies to the first period: *Sin entered this world through one man, and through sin, death; and thus it passed into all, so that all have sinned. For sin was in the world up until the law, but sin was not imputed, since there was no law.* (Rom 5:12-13) And again: *For without the law sin was dead, but once I lived without the law* (Rom 7:8-9). What is said here—it *was dead* (Rom 7:8)—is what was said before— it *was not imputed* (Rom 5:13)—that is, it was concealed. This is clear from what follows, where it says, *But sin, in order to appear as sin, worked death in me through what was good* (Rom 7:13)—that is, through the law, *because the law is good if a person uses it lawfully* (1 Tm 1:8). If, then, it says, *in order to appear as sin* (Rom 7:8), it is clear that it previously said, *was dead* (Rom 7:8) and *was not imputed* (Rom 5:13), because it was not manifest before it was made manifest by the law that prohibited it.

5. These texts are appropriate in reference to the second period: *But the law entered in so that wrongdoing might abound* (Rom 5:20), for transgression also came, which was not there before. And what has already been mentioned: *For when we were in the flesh, the passions of sins, which are through the law, were at work in our members, so that they bore fruit for death.* And this: *What, then, shall we say? That the law is sin? Of course not. But I did not know sin except through the law, for I did not know about covetousness except that the law said, You shall not covet. But, having seized the occasion, sin brought about every kind of covetousness in me through the commandment.* (Rom 7:7-8) And shortly after: *With the coming of the commandment sin came back to life. But I died, and the commandment, which was for life, turned out to be death for me. For, having seized the occasion, sin deceived me through the*

315. See Rom 7:7.
316. See Rom 8:11.
317. See 1 Cor 15:53-54.

commandment, and in this way it killed me. (Rom 7:9-11) When it says, *I died* (Rom 7:10), it means that I know that I died, because a person sins by way of transgression when through the law he sees what he should not do and still does it. But when it says, *Sin, having seized the occasion, deceived me through the commandment* (Rom 7:11), it means either that the yearning for pleasure inclines a person more strongly to sin where there is a prohibition or that, even if a person does something in accordance with the law's commands, if there is still not that faith which is in grace, he wishes to attribute it to himself rather than to God, and in his pride he sins all the more. Therefore it says as follows, *And so, to be sure, the law is holy, and the commandment is holy and righteous and good. Has, then, what is good become death for me? Of course not. But sin, in order to appear as sin, worked death in me through what was good, so that the sinner or the sin might, thanks to the commandment, be criminal without limit. We know that the law is spiritual, but I am fleshly* (Rom 7:12-14) (that is, since I have not yet been liberated by spiritual grace[318] I yield to the flesh), *sold under sin* (Rom 7:14) (that is, sinning for the price of temporal pleasures), *for I know not what I do* (Rom 7:15) (that is, I do not know whether I am in the precepts of truth, where there is true knowledge). The Lord speaks to sinners in these words: *I do not know you* (Mt 7:23). For nothing is concealed from him but, because there are no sins in the rules of the precepts that the truth has, the Truth itself says to sinners, *I do not know you.* For just as darkness is sensed by the eyes when they do not see, so sins are sensed by the mind when it does not know. On the basis of this idea, I believe, it is said in the Psalms, *Who knows his faults?* (Ps 19:12) *For I do not do what I want, but I do what I hate. But if I do what I do not want, I consent to the law because it is good. But now it is no longer I that do it but the sin that dwells in me. For I know that good does not dwell in me—that is, in my flesh. For to will the good is close at hand, but I find that the doing of it is not. For I do not do the good that I want, but I do the evil that I do not want. But if I do what I do not want, it is no longer I that do it but the sin that dwells in me. I find it, therefore, to be a law that, when I want to do good, evil is close at hand. For I am delighted with the law of God according to the inner person, but I see another law in my members, opposing the law of my mind and making me captive to the law of sin that is in my members.* (Rom 7:15-23) Thus far the words of a man living under

---

318. Augustine qualifies this short phrase in his *Revisions* by commenting that it "should not be understood as though a spiritual person already living under grace could not also say this . . . in reference to himself" regarding all of Rom 7:14-24. In other words the struggle with interior sinfulness consumes not only those not yet set free by grace but even those who have been set free. When he adds that he taught this later, as he had previously acknowledged, he is referring to *Revisions* I,3,2, where he corrects some assertions made in his *Commentary on Some Statements in the Letter to the Romans.*

the law and not yet under grace,[319] who is overcome by sin even if he does not want to sin. For fleshly habit and the natural fetters of mortality, in which we were begotten from Adam, have gained the upper hand. Let the one who is in such a position beg for help, then, and know that it was his doing when he fell and that it is not his when he arises. For when he has been liberated and recognizes the grace of his liberator he says, *Wretched man that I am, who will liberate me from the body of this death? The grace of God through Jesus Christ our Lord.* (Rom 7:24-25)

6. And now here are texts touching upon the person who lives in the period under grace, which we have indicated is the third. It resists the mortality of the flesh, to be sure, but does not overcome and make captive the inclination to sin. Thus it says, *Therefore in my mind I serve the law of God but in my flesh the law of sin. There is, then, no condemnation now for those who are in Christ Jesus. For the law of the spirit of life in Christ Jesus has liberated me from the law of sin and death. For what was impossible to the law, because it was weakened by the flesh* (Rom 7:25-8:3)—that is, by fleshly desires: for the reason the law was not fulfilled was that the love of righteousness itself was not yet present, which would hold the mind by an inner attraction so that it would not be drawn to sin by an attraction to temporal things. Therefore the law was weakened by the flesh—that is, it did not make righteous those who were devoted to the flesh. But *God sent his Son in the likeness of the flesh of sin* (Rom 8:3). For it was not a flesh of sin, not having been born from fleshly pleasure, but there was in it, nonetheless, a likeness of the flesh of sin, because it was mortal flesh. Adam, however, would not have merited death if he had not sinned.[320] But what did the Lord do? *From sin he condemned sin in the flesh* (Rom 8:3)—that is, by taking on the flesh of sinful human beings and teaching how we should live, he condemned sin in the flesh itself, so that the spirit, aflame with the love of eternal things, would not be taken captive by yielding to lust. *So that the righteousness of the law,* [Paul] says, *may be fulfilled in us who walk not according to the flesh but according to the spirit* (Rom 8:4). And so the precepts of the law, which could not be fulfilled through fear, have been fulfilled through love. *For those who live according to the flesh know the things that are of the flesh* (Rom 8:5)—that is, they yearn for fleshly goods as for the highest goods. *But those who live according to the spirit understand the things that are of the spirit. For the wisdom of the flesh is death, but the wisdom of the spirit is life and peace, because the wisdom of the flesh is opposed to God.* (Rom 8:5-7) [Paul] shows what *opposed to* means, lest

---

319. See Rom 6:14.
320. See Gn 2:17.

anyone think that another principle is being introduced from elsewhere, for he adds these words: *For it is not subject to the law of God, for it cannot be* (Rom 8:7). Hence, to act against the law is to be opposed to God, not in the sense that something can harm God but because whoever resists the will of God is harmful to himself. For this is pushing against the goad, as was said to the apostle Paul from on high, when he was still persecuting the Church.[321] But this was said—*For it is not subject to the law of God, for it cannot be*—in the same way as it would be said that snow does not warm, for it cannot, since as long as there is snow there is no warmth; but it can be dissolved and boil, so that it *does* warm, but when it does this it is no longer snow. Thus also wisdom is said to be *of the flesh* when the soul yearns for temporal goods as though they were noble goods. For, as long as such an inclination is in the soul, it cannot be subject to the law of God—that is, it cannot fulfill what the law commands. But when it begins to desire spiritual goods and to disdain temporal ones, the wisdom of the flesh ceases to exist and does not resist the spirit. For when the same soul yearns for baser things it is said to have the wisdom of the flesh, but the wisdom of the spirit in the case of loftier things, not because the wisdom of the flesh is a substance that the soul puts on or takes off; it is, rather, a desire of the soul itself that completely ceases to exist when it turns itself totally to heavenly things. *But those who are in the flesh,* it says, *cannot please God* (Rom 8:8)—that is, those who give in to the extravagances of the flesh. Now, lest anyone think that this was said with reference to those who have not yet departed this life, it was very opportunely added: *But you are not in the flesh but in the spirit* (Rom 8:9). Up to this point, clearly, those who are in this life are being spoken of, for they were in the spirit because in faith and hope and love they acquiesced in the desire for spiritual things. *But if the Spirit of God dwells in you. But if someone does not have the Spirit of Christ, he does not belong to him. But if Christ is in you, the body indeed is dead on account of sin, but the spirit is life on account of righteousness.* (Rom 8:9-10) The body is said to be dead for as long as it disturbs the soul by a lack of bodily things[322] and troubles it with various impulses arising out of that very lack, which cause it to yearn for earthly things. Yet, even though this may be the case, the mind, which already serves the law of God and is established under grace, does not yield to doing what is unlawful. In this regard what was said previously applies

---

321. See Acts 9:5 (not in the original Greek).
322. Augustine corrects this phrase in his *Revisions* by observing that it seemed more accurate to him to say "that the body is referred to as dead because it is already under the necessity of dying, which was not the case before sin." The body's death, therefore, is dependent not on whether or not it disturbs the soul by its desires, which is a relative situation, but on the necessity of its dying, which is absolute.

here: *In my mind I serve the law of God but in my flesh the law of sin* (Rom 7:25). And the person who does not yet have the perfect peace that will come with the resurrection and transformation of the body is described as being presently under grace.

7. It remains, then, to speak of precisely the peace of the resurrection of the body, which is the fourth period—if it can even be called a period—and which is the highest repose. For the next thing that it says is: *If, therefore, his Spirit, which raised Jesus from the dead, dwells in you, he who raised Jesus from the dead will also bring to life your mortal bodies through his Spirit dwelling in you* (Rom 8:11). Here too there is a very clear testimony to the resurrection of the body, and it is quite evident that, as long as we are in this life, neither disturbances coming from this mortal flesh nor some of the titillations of fleshly pleasures will be absent. For, although a person who has been established under grace and serves the law of God in his mind may not give in, nonetheless he serves the law of sin in his flesh. [323]

Once a person has become perfect by way of these stages, evil is found to be of no substance. Neither is the law evil, which shows a person the chains of sin in which he lies so that, having by faith implored the liberator's help, he may deserve to be set free and lifted up and most firmly established. In the first period, then, which is before the law, there is no struggle with the pleasures of this world. In the second, which is under the law, we struggle but are overcome. In the third we struggle and overcome. In the fourth we do not struggle but rest in perfect and eternal peace, for what is beneath us is subjected to us; at one time it was not so subjected because we had abandoned God who is above us.

LXVII. On what is written: *For I think that the sufferings of this time are insignificant in comparison to the glory that is to come that will be revealed in us* **(Rom 8:18) up until that which is said:** *For by hope we have been saved* **(Rom 8:24)** [324]

---

323. See Rom 7:25.
324. This discussion of a second passage from the Epistle to the Romans, in this series of three such discussions, has an almost entirely different thrust than the other two. Here Augustine concerns himself mainly with the significance of the term *creation* as it is used in Rom 8:18-24. From the category of creation, which he defines at the very beginning of the question in Trinitarian terms as "whatever God the Father made and established through his only-begotten Son in the unity of the Holy Spirit," Augustine excludes the Son of God (as distinct from the *sons of God* of Rom 8:19, 21). But he does not exclude the angels, although they are free of the pain and groaning that afflict the rest of creation. Since the problem that Augustine poses himself is what appears to be Paul's distinction between the sons of God

1. This passage is obscure because it is not sufficiently apparent here which creation is indicated. Now in accordance with Catholic teaching it is said that creation is whatever God the Father made and established through his only-begotten Son in the unity of the Holy Spirit. Hence not only our bodies but also our souls and spirits are implied in the word *creation*. Now it is said, *Creation itself shall be liberated from slavery to destruction for the freedom of the glory of the sons of God* (Rom 8:21), as though we were not creatures but sons of God, for the freedom of whose glory creation will be liberated from slavery. Similarly it says, *For we know that all creation groans and is in pain until the present, and not only it but we ourselves as well* (Rom 8:22-23), as though we were one thing and creation were something else. This whole passage, then, must be considered in detail.

2. *For I think,* it says, *that the sufferings of this time are insignificant in comparison to the glory that is to come that will be revealed in us* (Rom 8:18). This is obvious, for he had said previously, *But if by the spirit you put to death the deeds of the flesh, you shall live* (Rom 8:13); this cannot happen without difficulty, which requires patience. What he said shortly before also pertains to this: *But if we suffer, so that we may also be glorified* (Rom 8:17). Hence, when he says, *For the expectation of creation awaits the revelation of the sons of God* (Rom 8:19), I think that he means the same thing. For the very thing that pains us when we put to death the deeds of the flesh—that is, when through self-restraint we are hungry or thirsty, when through chastity we keep in check the pleasure of sexual activity, when through patience we endure the lacerations of insults and the stings of abuse, when by neglecting and renouncing our desires we labor for the good of mother Church: whatever pains us in these and other such distresses is part of creation. For the body and the soul, which are creatures, suffer pain, and they await the revelation of the sons of God—that is, they await the moment when what they have been called to will appear in that glory to which they have been called. For, inasmuch as the only-begotten Son of God cannot be referred to as a creature when everything that God made was made through him,[325] we ourselves are rightly referred to as creatures before that manifestation of glory and rightly referred to as sons of God, although we merit this by adoption, for he is the only-begotten Son by nature. Hence *the expectation of creation*—that is, our

---

and even human beings *tout court* on the one hand and creation on the other, he arrives at a solution that envisages the human being as, microcosmically, containing all creation in himself, because he, like the whole of creation itself, "is composed partly of spirit, partly of soul and partly of body" (5). Human creation, in turn, includes persons on either end of the spiritual spectrum—those who are not yet called *sons of God* because they do not believe along with those who possess the first fruits of the Spirit and are thus aflame with charity.

325. See Jn 1:3.

expectation—*awaits the revelation of the sons of God*—that is, it awaits the moment when what has been promised will appear, when what we now are in hope is manifested in very fact. For *we are the sons of God, and what we shall be has not yet appeared. We know that when it appears we shall be like him, because we shall see him as he is.* (1 Jn 3:2) This itself is the revelation of the sons of God, which the expectation of creation now awaits—not that creation awaits the revelation of some other nature, which would not be creation; rather it awaits, as it now is, the moment when it will be what it is to be. By way of analogy, when a painter is engaged in his craft and has arranged his colors and prepared them for his work, the expectation of the colors awaits the display of the picture—not that they will then be something else or no longer be colors, but only that they will possess a further beauty.

3. *For creation,* it says, *has been subjected to vanity* (Rom 8:20). This means: *Vanity of vanities, and all is vanity! What abundance is there for a man in all the toil of his that he toils under the sun?* (Qo 1:2-3) Apropos of this it is said, *In toil you shall eat your bread* (Gn 3:19). *Creation,* then, *has been subjected to vanity not of its own will* (Rom 8:20). With good reason was *not of its own will* added. Humankind sinned, to be sure, of its own will, but it was not condemned of his own will. And so the commission of sin was a willful act against the precept of truth, but to be subjected to error was the punishment of the sin. Not of its own will, then, was creation subjected to vanity, *but because of him who subjected it in hope* (Rom 8:20)—that is, because of the justice and mercy of him who neither leaves a sin unpunished nor wishes a sinner to go unhealed.

4. *Because creation itself as well* (Rom 8:20)—that is, humankind itself, once the mark of the image was lost because of sin and the creature alone remained:[326] and so *creation itself*—that is, the very thing that is not yet referred to as the finished form of *sons* but is referred to merely as *creation*—*shall be liberated from slavery to destruction.* And so the fact that it says that *it itself as well shall be liberated* (Rom 8:21) means that *it itself as well* is just like us. In other words, there is to be no despair even concerning those who are not yet referred to as *sons of God,* because they have not yet believed, but only as *creation,* because they too shall believe and be liberated from slavery to destruction just like us, who are already sons of God, although *what we shall be has not yet appeared.* They shall be liberated from slavery to destruction, then, *for the freedom of the glory of the sons of God* (Rom 8:21)—that is, they

---

326. In the *Revisions* Augustine writes that he did not intend to say that human beings lost the image of God entirely. Had they not lost any of it, scripture would not call them to conversion. Had they lost all of it, scripture would make no reference to their possessing it.

too shall go from being slaves to being free and from being dead to being glorious in that perfect life which the sons of God will possess.

5. *For we know that all creation groans and is in pain until the present* (Rom 8:22). All creation is contained in humankind, not because all the angels and supereminent virtues and powers are in it, or heaven and earth and the sea and everything that is in them, but because all creation is composed partly of spirit, partly of soul and partly of body. Beginning with the least, we see that bodily creation occupies space, that the soul gives life to what is bodily, that the spirit governs what is bodily and governs it well when it submits itself to be governed by God, but, when his precepts are transgressed, it is caught up in toils and burdens through those very things that it had once been able to govern. Whoever, then, lives in accordance with his body is referred to as a fleshly or animal person—fleshly because he pursues fleshly things, animal because he is carried along by the dissolute wantonness of his soul (*anima*), which the spirit does not govern or confine within the bounds of the natural order, because neither does it itself submit itself to be governed by God. But the person who governs his soul by his spirit and his body by his soul—which he is unable to do unless he himself allows God to govern him because, just as the head of woman is man, so the head of man is Christ[327]—is referred to as spiritual. This life is lived now with some difficulty, but afterwards it will not endure any. And, since the highest angels live spiritually but the lowest live in conformity with the soul,[328] whereas the beasts and all the cattle live in fleshly fashion, while the body does not live but is given life, all creation is in humankind, because it understands with its spirit and senses with its soul and moves about with its body. And so *all creation groans and is in pain* in humankind. It did not say "the entire" (*totam*) but *all* (*omnem*), as though it said: All people who are unimpaired see the sun, but they do not see it in their entirety, because they see it only with their eyes. It is thus that all creation is in humankind, in that it understands and lives and has a body. But creation in its entirety is not in it, because outside of it are the angels, who understand and live and exist, and the cattle, which live and exist, and bodies, which only exist, since to live is itself greater than not to live, and to understand is itself greater than to live without understanding. Since, then, humankind in its wretchedness groans and is in pain, *all creation groans and is in pain until the present.* Rightly did

---

327. See 1 Cor 11:3.
328. In the *Revisions* Augustine calls this a rash assertion and finds that neither scripture nor the facts themselves demonstrate that the lowest angels "live in conformity with the soul."

it say *until the present* because, even if there are some who are already in Abraham's bosom,[329] and that thief was with the Lord in paradise and ceased to be in pain on the very day when he believed,[330] nonetheless until the present *all creation groans and is in pain* because, by reason of the spirit and the soul and the body, all of it is in those who have not yet been liberated.

6. *And not only,* it says, *all creation groans and is in pain, but we ourselves as well* (Rom 8:23.22)—that is, not only in humankind are the body and the soul and the spirit in pain together on account of the body's troubles, but we ourselves as well, apart from our bodies, *having the first fruits of the spirit, groan within ourselves* (Rom 8:23). And well did it say *the first fruits of the spirit*—that is, the spirit of those who have already been offered to God as a sacrifice, so to speak, and who have been seized by the divine fire of charity. These are a person's first fruits, because truth touches our spirit first so that everything else might be grasped by it. He, then, already has first fruits offered to God who says, *In my mind I serve the law of God but in my flesh the law of sin* (Rom 7:25); and who says, *God, whom I serve in my spirit* (Rom 1:9); and of whom it is said, *The spirit indeed is willing, but the flesh is weak* (Mt 26:41). But when he says, *Unhappy man that I am, who will liberate me from the body of this death?* (Rom 7:24) and it is said in words like these, *He will also bring to life your mortal bodies because of the Spirit remaining in you* (Rom 8:11), there is as yet no holocaust. But there will be when death is swallowed up in victory,[331] when it is said to it, *Death, where is your strife? Death, where is your sting?* (1 Cor 15:55) Now, therefore, it says, not only *all creation*—that is, with the body—*but we ourselves as well, having the first fruits of the spirit*—that is, we souls, who have already offered the first fruits of our minds to God—*groan within ourselves*—that is, apart from the body—*awaiting the adoption, the redemption of our body* (Rom 8:23)—that is, so that the body itself, receiving the privilege of the adoption of sons to which we have been called, might show us forth in every respect as sons of God, liberated in our entirety, once all our troubles are over. *For by hope we have been saved, but hope that is seen is not hope* (Rom 8:24). Then, therefore, shall be the thing that at present is our hope, when what we shall be will appear—that is, we shall be like him, because we shall see him as he is.[332]

7. When this passage is explained in the way it has been dealt with here, we do not fall into those difficulties by which many people are forced to say that all the angels and heavenly virtues are beset with pain and groaning before we

329. See Lk 16:23.
330. See Lk 23:43.
331. See 1 Cor 15:54.
332. See 1 Jn 3:2.

are completely liberated, because it is said, *All creation groans and is in pain.* For although they help us in conformity with their elevated state by being obedient to God, who deigned even to send his only Son for our sake, nonetheless they must be believed to do so without groaning and pain, lest they be considered wretched, and Lazarus, who is one of us and who already rests in Abraham's bosom,[333] be considered happier [than they], especially because it said that the same creation that groans and is in pain is subject to vanity, which it is wicked to believe of the most high and noble creatures that are virtues and powers. Then it is said that it had to be liberated from slavery to destruction, into which we cannot believe that they, who live the most blessed life in heaven, have fallen. Yet nothing must be asserted rashly, and the divine text must always be treated with devout attentiveness—lest perchance what groans and is in pain and is subject to vanity be understood in some other way—so that there be no impious thoughts concerning the most high angels, inasmuch as they come to the aid of our weakness at the command of our Lord. But whether the explanation of this passage that we have concluded or some other one be proposed, the only thing that must be heeded is that it not dishonor or damage Catholic faith.[334] For I know that foolish heretics have uttered many impious and absurd things about this passage.[335]

LXVIII. On what is written: *O man, who are you that you talk back to God?* (Rom 9:20)[336]

1. Since the Apostle seems to have reproached the curious when he said, *O man, who are you that you talk back to God?* (Rom 9:20) they ignore the question and do not cease to be curious in their reaction to the very words by which their curiosity was rebuked, and in their abusive irreverence they say that the

---

333. See Lk 16:23.
334. See note 155.
335. These heretics were perhaps the Manicheans, or at least persons with Manichean tendencies, since the passage from Romans has to do with the nature of creation, toward which they had a negative view.
336. In this final question of the three devoted to passages from the Epistle to the Romans, Augustine returns to the topic of grace that had been broached in the first question. It is viewed here from the perspective of God's mysterious plan, about which human beings complain in vain. As in question LXVI, Augustine still does not understand the completely gratuitous nature of grace, which leads him to seek a humanly comprehensible underpinning in the present question for God's choice of some and rejection of others. He postulates in section 3 that merit follows upon belief, although he adds: "But grace itself, which is given through faith, is given when no merits of our own have preceded it." And in section 4 he uses the famous example of Pharaoh to demonstrate that, whether God is merciful to someone or hardens him, his mercy or hardening "springs from the most hidden merits" of the object of his mercy or hardening. In this light, his theology of calling (*vocatio*), elaborated in sections 5-6, is necessarily incomplete.

Apostle, in answering the question, was deficient and rebuked those who were seeking to learn because he was unable to respond to what was being asked of him. Besides, some heretics and adversaries of the law and the prophets,[337] who practice deception only in that they pretend to a knowledge that they do not display, accuse as being untrue and as having been interpolated by falsifiers whatever the Apostle inserted into his writings about them, and they have also decided to include this among the things that they say were interpolated and to deny that Paul said, *O man, who are you that you talk back to God?* For, if it is spoken of those who utter calumnies in order to deceive human beings, they will doubtless be silent, nor will they dare to pretend to the naïve, whom they desire to deceive, that they possess knowledge about the will of almighty God. There are some, however, who, on reading the scriptures, seek to learn with a good and devout mind what reply can be made here to slanderers and false accusers. But we, who cling for salvation's sake to apostolic authority and consider the books that Catholic teaching maintains not to have been falsified in any regard, hold that this is true: that those to whom these things are closed are too unfit and weak to understand the divine secrets. And to those who complain and are indignant because they are not apprised of God's designs, when they begin to say, *On whom he will, then, he has mercy, and whom he wills he hardens. What is there to lament? For who resists his will?* (Rom 9:18-19)—when with these words, then, they begin to disparage the scriptures or to look for an excuse for their own sins, while disdaining the precepts by which they are invited to a good life, let us respond with utmost confidence: *O man, who are you that you talk back to God?* And let us not, because we are afraid of them, give what is holy to dogs or cast our pearls before swine,[338] as long as we ourselves are not dogs and swine. And, at the Holy Spirit's revelation, let us come to a conclusion that is sublime and far removed from vulgar conjecture concerning the merits of souls, even if it is partial and obscure.[339]

2. For in this passage it was not the saints that the Apostle prohibited from seeking to learn but rather those who are not yet rooted and grounded in charity so as to be able to grasp with all the saints the breadth, length, height and depth and the other things that he speaks of in the same place.[340] He did not, then, prohibit from seeking to learn those of whom he says, *The spiritual person*

---

337. Both the Marcionites and the Manicheans took issue with the Old Testament, but since Augustine was particularly familiar with the latter and wrote extensively against them, it seems likely that they are being aimed at here.

338. See Mt 7:6.

339. See 1 Cor 13:12.

340. See Eph 5:17-18.

judges all things, but he himself is judged by no one (1 Cor 2:15), and especially, *But we have not received the spirit of this world but the spirit that is from God, so that we may know what has been given us by God* (1 Cor 2:12). Whom did he prohibit, then, but the clayey and the earthly, who have not yet been reborn and brought up and who bear the image of that man who, having been created first, is of the earth and earthly,[341] and, because he did not want to obey [God] by whom he was created, fell back into that out of which he was created, and after his sin he deserved to hear: *You are earth, and to the earth you shall go* (Gn 3:19)? To persons such as these the Apostle says, *O man, who are you that you talk back to God? Does what was made say to him who made it, Why did you make me thus?* (Rom 9:20) As long as you are a made thing, then, you are not yet a perfect son, because you have not yet taken in the fullness of grace by which we have been given the power to become sons of God,[342] so that you may be able to hear: *I no longer call you slaves but sons* (Jn 15:15). *Who are you that you talk back to God* and wish to know God's designs? Who are you who, if you wished to know those of a person who was your equal, would be acting foolishly if you were not first his friend? Just as we have borne the image of the earthly man, then, let us also bear the image of the heavenly man,[343] taking off the old person and putting on the new,[344] so that it may not be said to us as to a thing made of clay: *Does what was made say to him who made it, Why did you make me thus?*

3. And, so that it may be clear that this is not being said to a sanctified spirit but to fleshly clay, look at what follows: *Or does not the potter have the power to make one vessel for honor and another for shame out of the same lump?* (Rom 9:21) Inasmuch as our nature sinned in paradise,[345] then, we are formed by mortal generation by the same divine providence not along the lines of heaven but along those of earth (that is, not in accordance with the spirit but in accordance with the flesh), and we have all been made from one mass of clay, which is a mass of sin.[346] Since by sinning, therefore, we have lost what was coming to us and God's mercy is far off, and there is nothing else due to sinners apart from eternal damnation, what does a person who belongs to this

---

341. See 1 Cor 15:49.47.
342. See Jn 1:12.
343. See 1 Cor 15:49.
344. See Col 3:9-10.
345. See Gn 3:6.
346. "Mass of sin": *massa peccati*. This is Augustine's first use of an expression that, in one form or other (e.g., *massa damnata, massa peccatorum* or simply *massa*, as in the rest of the present question), would constantly reappear in his writings and be considered particularly characteristic of his pessimistic view of the human condition. See Paula Fredriksen, "Massa," in Fitzgerald 545-547.

mass light upon but to talk back to God and say, *Why did you make me thus?* If you want to know these things, do not be clay but become a son of God through the mercy of him who gave the power to become sons of God to those who believe in his name[347] but not (which you wish) to those who wish to know divine things before they believe. For the reward of knowledge is furnished to those who have merited it, but merit is bestowed on those who believe. But grace itself, which is given through faith, is given when no merits of our own have preceded it. For what merit do the sinner and the impious have? Christ died for the impious and for sinners,[348] however, so that we may be called to believe not by merit but by grace, but may obtain merit by believing. Sinners are commanded to believe, then, so that they may be cleansed of their sins by believing. For they do not know what they will see if they live uprightly. Hence, since they cannot see unless they live uprightly, it is clear that they must begin with faith so that the precepts whereby those who believe are turned from this world may make their hearts pure, whereupon God can be seen. For *blessed are the pure of heart, for they shall see God* (Mt 5:8); and it is announced through the prophet: *Seek him in simplicity of heart* (Wis 1:1). Hence it is justifiably said to persons who are in the twilight of life and whose soul's eye is dimmed for that reason: *O man, who are you that you talk back to God? Does what was made say to him who made it, Why did you make me thus? Or does not the potter have the power to make one vessel for honor and another for shame out of the same lump?* (Rom 9:20-21) *Throw out the old yeast so that you may be a new lump of dough* (1 Cor 5:7) and in it [i.e., that new lump of dough] no longer a child in Christ, so that you must be given milk to drink,[349] but come to the perfect man,[350] so that you may be among those of whom it is said, *We speak wisdom among the perfect* (1 Cor 2:6). Then indeed you shall hear properly and not distortedly, if there are any secrets of almighty God concerning the most hidden merits of souls and concerning grace or justice.

4. In Pharaoh's case the response is easy: because he oppressed the sojourners in his kingdom[351] he had already acquired demerits, the appropriate result of which was that his heart was hardened and he did not believe even the most obvious signs of God's decrees.[352] From that same mass, therefore (that is, of sinners), [God] produced both vessels of mercy by which he came to their aid when the children of Israel beseeched him

---

347. See Jn 1:12.
348. See Rom 5:6.8.
349. See 1 Cor 3:1-2.
350. See Eph 4:13.
351. See Ex 1:8-22.
352. See Ex 9:12.

and vessels of wrath by whose torments he trained them—that is, Pharaoh and his people, because, although both were sinners and for that reason belonged to the one mass, there was nonetheless one way for those who had groaned to the one God for help to be dealt with, and another way for those whose unjust burdens had made them groan. *With great patience, then, he has borne the vessels of wrath that have been produced for destruction* (Rom 9:22). And, for that very reason, when he said *with great patience* he was alluding to their former sins, in which he tolerated them, so that he might opportunely punish them when their punishment would be of use to those who were going to be liberated. *And so that he may make known the riches of his glory to the vessels of mercy, which he has prepared for glory* (Rom 9:23).

Perhaps you are confused at this point and you return to the question: *If he has mercy on whom he will and hardens whom he will, what is there to lament? For who resists his will?* Certainly he has mercy on whom he will and hardens whom he will, but this will of God cannot be unjust. For this springs from most hidden merits, because even though sinners themselves form a single mass on account of the universal sin,[353] there is nonetheless a degree of diversity among them. There is something, then, that is already present in [some] sinners, by which they are made worthy of righteousness even though they have not yet been made righteous, and in the same way something is already present in other sinners that makes them worthy of punishment. You have the same Apostle saying elsewhere: *Because they did not try to keep God in their awareness, God gave them over to a reprobate way of thinking* (Rom 1:28). His having given them over to a reprobate way of thinking is the same as his having hardened Pharaoh's heart, and their not having tried to retain a knowledge of God is the same as their having been worthy to be given over to a reprobate way of thinking.

5. Yet it is true that *it is not a matter of willing or running but of a merciful God* (Rom 9:16), because even if someone with lighter sins or even with any number of more serious ones has nonetheless, in his great groaning and the pain of his repentance, been accorded the mercy of God, it does not come down to him (who would perish if he were abandoned) but to a merciful God who comes to the aid of his entreaties and distress. For, if God is not merciful, it is not enough to will something, but God, who calls us to peace,

---

353. "Universal sin": *generale peccatum.* Augustine does not use the term "original sin" until *Miscellany of Questions in Response to Simplician* I,1,10, but "universal sin" points to the same thing.

is only merciful if the willing is already present,[354] because peace on earth is for persons of good will.[355] And since a person cannot will unless he has been alerted and called, either interiorly where no one sees or exteriorly by audible words or some visible signs, it happens that God works in us even this very willing.[356] For not all of those who were called willed to come to that supper which the Lord says in the gospel had been prepared, and those who did come would have been unable to come unless they had been called.[357] And so those who came must not attribute it to themselves that, having been called, they came; and those who chose not to come must attribute it to no one but themselves, since they had been called to come in free will. A calling, therefore, occurs before the will is deserving. Hence, even if someone attributes it to himself that he came *because* he was called, he cannot attribute it to himself *that* he was called. The person who was called and did not come, who did not possess the merit for having done something worthy in order to be called, begins to merit punishment when he has neglected to come after having been called. And so there shall be those two: *Mercy and judgment I will sing to you, Lord* (Ps 101:1). Calling pertains to mercy, while to judgment pertains the blessedness of those who were called and have come and the punishment of those who chose not to come. Was it hidden from Pharaoh how much good accrued to that land [i.e., Egypt] by Joseph's coming?[358] The acknowledgement of what [Joseph] accomplished, therefore, was [Pharaoh's] calling to treat the people of Israel mercifully and not to be ungrateful. But his unwillingness to hearken to this calling and his display of cruelty to those to whom hospitality and mercy were owed merited the punishment that his heart be hardened and that he suffer such blindness of mind that he did not believe so many and such clear signs from God.[359] By this punishment inflicted on him—be it his obstinacy or the final physical drowning[360]—the people were able to be instructed, and on account of their affliction he merited both the hidden obstinacy and the open drowning.

6. But this calling, which occurs at appropriate times whether in individual persons or in nations and in the human race itself, is part of a lofty and

---

354. Commenting on this passage in his *Revisions*, Augustine says that the divine mercy must precede the willing in order for it to be prepared by the Lord (so as to be able to will correctly).
355. See Lk 2:14.
356. See Phil 2:13.
357. See Lk 14:16-24.
358. See Gn 41.
359. See Ex 7:14-12:30.
360. See Ex 14:23-28.

profound plan. Whence these words apply, *In the womb I sanctified you* (Jer 1:5), and, "When you were in your father's loins I saw you,"[361] and, *I loved Jacob, but I hated Esau* (Rom 9:13), since it was said before they were born. It cannot be comprehended except perhaps by those who love the Lord their God with all their heart and with all their soul and with all their mind, and love their neighbor as themselves.[362] Those who have been established in such great charity can perhaps understand even now, along with the saints, the length, the width, the height and the depth.[363] But this must be grasped with the steadiest faith: God does not do anything unjustly,[364] nor does any nature exist that is not indebted to God for its existence, because to God is owed all its dignity and beauty and the harmony of its parts, and if you have analyzed this [i.e., the dignity, beauty and harmony of a given nature] and removed every element of it down to its final traces, there is nothing that remains.

LXIX. On what is written: *Then the Son himself will be subjected to the one who has subjected everything to him* (1 Cor 15:28)[365]

1. Those who insist that the Son of God is not equal to the Father are in the habit of usurping, with over-familiarity, this text in which the Apostle says, *But when everything has been subjected to him, then the Son himself will be subjected to the one who has subjected everything to him, so that God may be all in all* (1 Cor 15:28). For an error disguised by the name "Christian" could not spring up in them were it not for a misunderstanding of the scriptures, for

---

361. In his *Revisions* Augustine acknowledges that these words are not scriptural and wonders why he thought that they were. As Raymond Canning has pointed out to the translator, they may be a reworking of Heb 7:10.
362. See Mt 22:37, 39.
363. See Eph 3:17-18.
364. See Rom 9:14.
365. This difficult verse, to which Augustine returns in *The Trinity* I,8,15-10,21, had been used at least since the time of Origen (see *On First Principles* III,5,6-8) in the early third century to prove that Christ was subordinate to the Father. Augustine is undoubtedly alluding to the subordinationist Arians, without naming them, at the very beginning of the question, and a few lines later he invokes the rule for interpreting scripture that Athanasius was the first to enunciate against the Arians (see his *Letter to Serapion* 2,8), which subsequently became a commonplace of patristic theology: when in some passages scripture says that the Son is less than the Father they are to be referred to his humanity, whereas when in others it says that the Son is equal to the Father they are to be referred to his divinity. Understanding the verse in question to refer to Christ's humanity, Augustine places it within its context (1 Cor 15:21-28) and interprets it at length, concentrating especially on the notion of Christ's reign in 1 Cor 15:24. Among orthodox Latin writers who commented on 1 Cor 15:21-28 immediately before Augustine were Hilary, *On the Trinity* XI,21-49; Ambrose, *On the Faith* V,2,147-15,187; Jerome, Letter 55,5 (where Hilary's work is mentioned).

they say, "If he is equal, how is he subjected?" This of course is like that gospel question: If he is equal, how is his Father greater? For the Lord himself said, *For the Father is greater than I* (Jn 14:28). But the rule of Catholic faith holds that, when it is said in some places in scripture that the Son is less than the Father, they are to be referred to his assumption of humanity,[366] whereas, when it is clearly said in other places that he is equal, they are to be accepted as referring to the fact that he is God. It is evident, then, how it is said that *the Father is greater than I*, and, *I and the Father are one* (Jn 10:30), and *the Word was God* (Jn 1:1), and *the Word was made flesh* (Jn 1:14), and *he did not think it robbery to be equal to God* (Phil 2:6), and *he emptied himself, taking on the form of a slave* (Phil 2:7). But inasmuch as many things are said of him according to the special character of his personhood, except for what pertains to his assumption of humanity, in such a way that the Father may not be understood as other than the Father and the Son as other than the Son, the heretics think in these instances that what is said and understood thus cannot mean equality. For it is written: *Everything was made through him* (Jn 1:3)—in other words, of course, *through* the Son, the Word of God. But *by* whom if not by the Father? But it was never written that the Son made any creature by the Father. Likewise it is written that the Son is the image of the Father,[367] but it was never written that the Father was the image of the Son. Then there is the matter of one being the begetter and the other being the begotten, and other things of that sort, which have to do not with an inequality of substance but with the special character of their personhood, in which, when they say that there can be no equality, because they use duller minds to penetrate these things, they must be persuaded by the weight of authority. For if there cannot be seen in these cases the equality of him through whom everything was made and of him by whom it was made, of the image and of him whose image he is, of the begotten and the begetter, never would the Apostle have shut the mouths of those contentious persons by saying of the Word himself: *He did not think it robbery to be equal to God.*

2. Since, therefore, those things that were written about the distinction between the Father and the Son were written partly with reference to the properties of the persons and partly with reference to the assumption of humanity, as long as the godhead and the unity and the equality of the divine substance of the Father and the Son remains, it is right to inquire whether the

---

366. "His assumption of humanity": *susceptionem hominis*. The expression is used again further along in section 1 and in sections 2 and 10. See note 11. Here it is contrasted, a few lines later, with Christ's personhood (*proprietatem personae*), by which Augustine clearly understands his divinity.
367. See Col 1:15.

Apostle was speaking in regard to the properties of the persons or in regard to the assumption of humanity in this text: *Then the Son himself will be subjected to the one who has subjected everything to him.* The context of the scriptures customarily illuminates a given passage, when the words adjacent to the text in question are carefully examined. And so we find that we have arrived at this text, as cited above, in this way: *But now Christ has risen from the dead, the first fruits of those who have fallen asleep* (1 Cor 15:20), for it was a question of the resurrection of the dead. This happened in the Lord in regard to his assumption of humanity. In fact it says very clearly in the following lines: *Since indeed death came through a man, and through a man resurrection from the dead. For just as in Adam all die, so also in Christ all shall be restored to life. But each one in his order: first Christ, then those who belong to Christ in his presence, then the end, when he will hand over his reign to God the Father, when he has nullified every principality and every power and virtue. For he must reign until he puts all his enemies under his feet. As the last enemy, death will be destroyed. For he has subjected everything under his feet. But when he said that everything was subjected, it is clear that that does not mean him who subjected everything to him. But when everything has been subjected to him, then also the Son himself will be subjected to the one who subjected everything to him, so that God may be all in all.* (1 Cor 15:21-28) It is clear, then, that this is said in regard to his assumption of humanity.

3. But other things in this passage, the text of which I have quoted in its entirety, customarily raise questions: First these words, *When he will hand over his reign to God the Father* (1 Cor 15:24), as if the Father does not possess his reign now. Then these words, *For he must reign until he puts all his enemies under his feet* (1 Cor 15:25), as though he would not reign after that. And relative to that the words previously cited, *Then the end* (1 Cor 15:24). Their sacrilegious understanding of this is that *the end* is the termination of his reign, although it is written in the gospel: *And of his reign there shall be no end* (Lk 1:33). Finally these words, *But when everything has been subjected to him, then also the Son himself will be subjected to the one who subjected everything to him*, which they choose to understand as if now either something has not been subjected to the Son or he himself has not been subjected to the Father.

4. The question is answered, then, by the particular rhetorical style. For scripture often speaks in such a way as to say that what always exists comes into existence in a given person at the moment when it begins to be known by him. For this is what we say in the prayer, *Hallowed be thy name* (Mt 6:9), as if there were a time when it was not hallowed. Therefore, just as *hallowed be*

means that it should be recognized as hallowed,[368] so also *when he will hand over his reign to God the Father* means that at a given moment he will manifest that his Father reigns, so that by his appearance and manifestation what is believed by the faithful and has not entered the minds of unbelievers may be evident. But he will nullify every principality and power[369] by manifesting the reign of his Father, so that it may be known to all that none of the princes and powers—whether heavenly or earthly—possesses any principality or power of himself but has it from him from whom all things are—not only in terms of their existence but also in terms of their orderly arrangement. For at that manifestation there will be no hope for anyone in any prince or any man. Even now this is announced prophetically: *It is good to hope in the Lord rather than to hope in man, it is good to hope in the Lord rather than to hope in princes* (Ps 118:8-9). Thus, by meditating on this, the soul may already rise to the Father's reign, neither promoting the power of anyone who is great apart from him nor flattering itself ruinously because of its own [power]. He will hand over his reign, then, to God the Father when the Father is known through him through his appearance in glory. For those in whom he now reigns through faith belong to his reign. For in one way the reign is said to belong to Christ by reason of the power of divinity, because all creation is subject to him. In another way his reign is called the Church because of the faith in him that it has, in accordance with which he prays who says, *Possess us* (Is 26:13), for it is not as though he himself does not possess everything. In this respect this is also said, *When you were slaves of sin you were bereft of righteousness* (Rom 6:20). He will nullify, then, every principality and every power and virtue, so that it will not be necessary for or permitted to anyone who sees the Father through the Son to find rest in the power of any creature or in his own.

5. *For he must reign until he puts all his enemies under his feet*—that is, his reign must be manifested until all his enemies confess that he reigns, for that is what it means that his enemies will be under his feet. In case we understand this to refer to the righteous, *enemies* was said, because from being unrighteous they are made righteous and, by believing, are made subject to him. But this must be understood of the unrighteous, who have nothing to do with the coming beatitude of the righteous, because they too will confess in their consternation at the very manifestation of his reign that he reigns. Therefore these words, *He must reign until he puts all his enemies under his feet*, are not said as though, when he put his enemies under his feet, he would not reign after

368. This is a classic interpretation of this petition of the Lord's Prayer, which appears already in Tertullian, *On Prayer* 3 and is used elsewhere by Augustine. See Letter 130,11,21; *The Lord's Sermon on the Mount* II,5,19.
369. See 1 Cor 15:24.

that. But *he must reign until he puts all his enemies under his feet*: he must, it says, make his reign so evident until his enemies in no way dare to deny that he reigns. For it is also written: *Our eyes are on the Lord our God until he has mercy on us* (Ps 123:2); yet, when he has had mercy on us, we ought not therefore to turn our eyes from him, for our beatitude exists to the degree that we enjoy contemplating him. This is also said, then, with this meaning: our eyes are directed to the Lord only until we obtain his mercy, not that they may be turned away after that but that from then on they may ask for nothing more. *Until* means, therefore, that you should not look for more. For why would there be more beyond the moment when all his enemies confess that he reigns? In other words, until which greater manifestation will the reign of Christ be manifested? It is one thing, then, for something not to be manifested more and another thing for it not to remain any longer. Not to be manifested more means not to become more manifest; not to remain any longer means not to continue further. But when will the reign of Christ be more manifest than when it has become evident to all his enemies?

6. *As the last enemy, death will be destroyed* (1 Cor 15:26). For there will be nothing else to be destroyed after this mortal form has put on immortality.[370] *For he has subjected everything under his feet* (1 Cor 15:26), which means that he will also destroy death. *But when he said that everything was subjected*—in fact the prophet said this in the Psalms[371] —*it is clear that that does not mean the one who subjected everything to him* (1 Cor 15:26-27). [Paul] wishes the Father to be understood as having subjected everything to the Son, as the same Lord calls to our attention and announces in many places in the gospel,[372] not only with respect to the form of a slave[373] but also with respect to the source from whom he takes his existence and on account of whom he is equal to him from whom he takes his existence. For, as his image[374] (but in whom dwells all the fullness of divinity[375]), he loves to refer everything to this one source.

7. *But when everything has been subjected to him, then also the Son himself will be subjected to the one who subjected everything to him*—not as if this were not the case now, but then it will be manifest, in accordance with the manner of speaking that was previously discussed—*so that God*

---

370. See 1 Cor 15:54.
371. See Ps 8:6.
372. See, e.g., Jn 17:10.
373. See Phil 2:7.
374. See Col 1:15.
375. See Col 2:9.

may be all in all. He himself is the end,[376] as [Paul] mentioned before, although he wanted to express everything briefly at first and then to explain and expound it in short sections, for he was speaking of the resurrection when he said, *First Christ, then those who belong to Christ in his presence, then the end* (1 Cor 15:23-24). He himself, namely, is the end, *so that God may be all in all*. For it is one thing to speak of an end that means completion and another to speak of an end that means destruction; for a tunic, on the one hand, is finished by sewing, while, on the other, food is finished by eating. But God is said to be *all in all* so that none of those who cling to him may love their own will in contrast to his, and so that what the Apostle says in another place may be clear to everyone: *What do you have that you have not received?* (1 Cor 4:7)

8. There are those, again, who understand this passage—*He must reign until he puts all his enemies under his feet*—in such a way that they say that the verb *reign* was used here with another meaning than that used for the noun *reign*, of which it is said: *When he will hand over his reign to God the Father*. Thus he referred to the noun *reign* as that by which God rules over all creation, but he referred to the verb *reign* in such a way as to allow it to be understood as leading an army against an enemy or defending a city, so that he says, *He must reign until he puts all his enemies under his feet*, because there is no reason for such a reign, which has commanders of armed men, once the enemy has been conquered and cannot stage an uprising. For thus it is said in the gospel, *And of his reign there shall be no end* (Lk 1:33), which means that he reigns forever. But in accordance with the meaning that war is being waged under him against the devil, that warfare will continue only *until he puts all his enemies under his feet*, but it will not continue after that, when we shall enjoy perpetual peace.

9. But these things have been said so that we may know with greater clarity that this too must be considered—namely, that the Lord reigns now by his sacramental dispensation through his incarnation and passion.[377] For, inasmuch as he is the Word of God, his reign is equally without beginning or end or intermission. But inasmuch as he is the Word made flesh, he has begun to reign in believers through faith in his incarnation. This is the reason for the words: *The Lord has reigned from a tree* (Ps 96:6). Hence he has nullified every principality and every power and virtue, although he

---

376. See 1 Cor 15:24.
377. See note 43.

saves those who believe in him not by his glory but by his humility. This has been hidden from the wise and clever and revealed to little ones,[378] because it has pleased God to save believers through the foolishness of preaching.[379] Nor does the Apostle say, when he is with the little ones, that he knows anything except Christ Jesus and him crucified.[380] His humility (which I believe is signified by the word *feet*) has need of this preaching until all enemies are put under his feet, until all worldly pride surrenders and is subdued, as we see for the most part has already happened and is happening every day. But for what purpose do these things occur? So that he may hand over his reign to God the Father—that is, so that by faith in his incarnation he may lead those whom he has fostered to the glory by which he is equal to the Father. For he already stated and said to those who had believed in him, *If you remain in my word, you are truly my disciples, and you shall know the truth, and the truth shall set you free* (Jn 8:31-32). For he will hand over his reign to his Father when he reigns in those who contemplate the truth of his equality with the Father and allows the Father to be seen through himself, the only-begotten Son, in his glory. For he reigns now in his believers, because *he emptied himself, taking on the form of a slave.* But then he will hand over his reign to God the Father, *when he has nullified every principality and power and virtue* (1 Cor 15:24). How will he carry out this nullification except by humility, patience and weakness? For which principality will not be nullified when the Son of God reigns in believers for the very reason that the princes of this world have judged him? Which power will not be nullified when he through whom everything was made[381] reigns in believers for the very reason that he was so subjected to the powers that he said to a man, *You would have no power over me unless it were given you from above* (Jn 19:11)? Which virtue will not be nullified when he through whom the heavens were established[382] reigns in believers for the reason that he was made weak unto the cross and death? It is in this way that the Son properly reigns in the faith of believers. For the Father cannot be said or be believed to have become incarnate or to have been judged or to have been crucified. Through his appearance in glory, however, by which he is equal to the Father, he reigns with the

---

378. See Mt 11:25.
379. See 1 Cor 1:21.
380. See 1 Cor 2:2.
381. See Jn 1:3.
382. See Ps 33:6.

Father in those who contemplate the truth. And he will lose nothing in handing over his reign to God the Father and in leading those who believe in him from faith in his incarnation to the glory of the divinity, but he will manifest himself in both respects as a single object for the enjoyment of those who contemplate him. But it is necessary that Christ reign for so long in this way in persons who are not yet able to perceive by the clear light of their minds the equality of the Father and the Son because such persons can grasp—and because he himself really took upon himself—the humility of the incarnation *until he puts all enemies under his feet*—that is, until all worldly pride yields to the humility of his incarnation.

10. *Then also the Son himself will be subjected to the one who subjected everything to him.* Clearly, although this is said in reference to his assumption of humanity, since the question arose in regard to the resurrection of the dead, yet it is right to ask whether it was said of him alone, in that he is the head of the Church,[383] or of the full Christ, including his body and its members. For when it says to the Galatians, *It does not say, and to your seeds, as though there were many, but as though to one, and to your seed, which is Christ* (Gal 3:16). Lest in this place we understand Christ by himself, who was born of the virgin Mary, it says afterwards, *For you are all one in Christ Jesus. But if you belong to Christ, then you are the seed of Abraham.* (Gal 3:28-29) And when [Paul] was speaking to the Corinthians about charity and was introducing the simile of the members of the body—*For just as the body is one,* he says, *and has many members, although all the members of the body are many, the body is one, and so is Christ* (1 Cor 12:12)—he did not say that they belonged to Christ but that they *were* Christ, indicating that Christ could be referred to in his fullness as the head with the body, which is the Church. And in many places in Scripture we find Christ referred to in this way, so that he is understood in the context of all his members, to whom it is said, *You are the body of Christ and his members* (1 Cor 12:27). It is not unreasonable, then, if we understand *then also the Son himself will be subjected to the one who subjected everything to him* as pertaining not only to the Son who is the head of the Church but to all the saints with him, who are one in Christ, one seed of Abraham,[384] subjected, however, to the contemplation of eternal truth so as to attain to beatitude, while no inclination of the soul and no part of the body offer any resistance. Thus, inasmuch as no one loves his own power in that life, *God will be all in all.*

---

383. See Eph 1:22.
384. See Gal 3:28-29.

LXX. On what the Apostle says: *Death has been swallowed up in victory. Where, O death, is your struggle? Where, O death, is your sting? The sting of death is sin, but the strength of sin is the law* (**1 Cor 15:54-56**)

It is frequently asked what this means: *Then shall come to pass what is written: Death has been swallowed up in victory. Where, O death, is your struggle? Where, O death, is your sting? The sting of death is sin, but the strength of sin is the law.* (1 Cor 15:54-56) I think that in this passage death signifies fleshly habit, which resists a good will through pleasure in enjoyable temporal things. For it would not be said, *Where, O death, is your struggle?* (1 Cor 15:55) if it had not been resisted and opposed. Its struggle is described as well in another passage: *The flesh lusts against the spirit, the spirit against the flesh. For they are opposed to each other, so that you do not do what you want.* (Gal 5:17) It happens for the sake of our perfect sanctification, therefore, that every fleshly appetite is subjected to our enlightened and enlivened spirit— that is, to our good will. And just as we see now that we lack many childish pleasures, which tormented us very violently if they were denied us when we were children, it must be believed that this will be the case with every fleshly pleasure once perfect holiness has restored the whole person. But now, as long as there is anything in us that may resist a good will, we stand in need of God's help through good men and good angels, so that until our wound is healed it will not trouble us to such a degree as even to destroy our good will.

Because of our sin we deserved death. This sin was previously completely in our free will, when in paradise no resentment about having denied himself pleasure stood in the way of the human being's free will, as it does now. For example, if there is anyone who has never enjoyed hunting, he is completely free whether he wishes to hunt or not, and anyone who prohibits it does not torment him. But if he makes bad use of his freedom and hunts when he is not allowed to, pleasure gradually creeps in and kills the soul, so that even if he wished to abstain he could not do so without difficulty and anguish, although he might not have done this with complete ease. Therefore *the sting of death is sin* (1 Cor 15:56), because on account of sin there arose a pleasure that could now resist free will and be restrained with difficulty. Inasmuch as this pleasure exists in the weakness of a soul that has grown wicked, we rightly call it death. *But the strength of sin is the law* (1 Cor 15:56), because what a law prohibits is contravened with much greater wickedness and disgrace than if it were not prohibited by a law. And so death will be swallowed up in victory[385] when through sanctification fleshly pleasure will be overthrown in every part of the human person by a perfect pleasure in spiritual things.

---

385. See 1 Cor 15:54.

LXXI. On what is written: *Bear one another's burdens, and thus you will fulfill the law of Christ* **(Gal 6:2)**

1. Because the observance of the old covenant was marked by fear, it could not be pointed out more clearly that the gift of the new covenant was charity than in this place, where the Apostle says, *Bear one another's burdens and thus you will fulfill the law of Christ* (Gal 6:2). For he is understood to be speaking of the law of Christ in which the Lord himself commanded that we love one another, putting so much force in the wording of the precept that he said, *By this it will be recognized that you are my disciples, if you love one another* (Jn 13:35). It is the duty of this love to bear one another's burdens. But this duty, which does not last forever, should certainly lead to everlasting beatitude, in which there will be none of those burdens of ours that we are ordered to bear for each other. But now, while we are in this life, which is to say on this journey, let us bear one another's burdens, so that we may be able to attain to that life in which there are no burdens at all. Some learned persons who possess knowledge of this sort have written this about stags: When they cross over a body of water to an island in order to feed, they arrange themselves so as to put the burden of their heads, which are heavy with antlers, upon each other in such a way that the one behind stretches his neck and places his head on the one before him. And since there has to be one who leads the rest and has no one in front of him to lay his head on, they are said to take turns, so that the one who is in the lead and is worn out by the burden of his head goes to the end of the line, and the one whose head he bore, when he himself was first, takes his place. Bearing one another's burdens in this fashion they cross over the water until they come to solid ground.[386] Perhaps it was this characteristic of stags that Solomon was alluding to when he said, *May the stag of friendship and the chick of your graces converse with you* (Prv 5:19). For nothing so proves a friend as bearing a friend's burden.

2. Yet we would not bear one another's burdens if both persons who were to carry each other's burdens were weak at the same time, or if they had a single kind of weakness. But different times and different kinds of weakness make it possible for us to bear one another's burdens. For

---

386. See Pliny, *Natural History* VIII,114. Augustine liked this charming image well enough to use it in at least two other places. See *Exposition of Psalms* 41[42],4; 129 [130],4. Stags are, in general, beneficent creatures in early Christian symbolism. See *Physiologus* 45.

example, you will bear your brother's anger when you are not angry with him so that, in turn, when anger has overcome you he will put up with you with mildness and calm. This example touches upon the different times for bearing burdens, although the weakness itself is not different, for the anger of each of them is borne by the other in both cases. Another example, however, is useful relative to the different kinds of weakness. If someone has conquered talkativeness in himself and has not yet conquered obstinacy, while someone else is still talkative but no longer obstinate, the former must in charity bear the latter's talkativeness and the latter the former's obstinacy until the one is healed in the former and the other in the latter. Of course, if the same weakness occurs in two people at the same time, they are unable to put up with one another, since it puts them at odds with each other. Now two angry people agree with each other and tolerate each other in the face of a third person, although they should not be said to tolerate each other reciprocally but rather to offer comfort to each other. Likewise, persons who are sad about a particular thing bear with each other and, so to speak, lean on each other more than if one were sad and the other happy. But if they are sad about each other, then they are utterly unable to tolerate each other. And consequently, in feelings of this sort, the very weakness from which you wish the other person to be freed by you must to some extent be taken on, and it must be taken on in such a way as to help the other, not so that you both end up equally miserable. It is thus, for example, that a person leans over to stretch out his hand to someone who has fallen down; for he does not put himself in such a position that both fall down but only bends to the extent that he may raise up the one who has fallen.

3. Nothing makes this gracious task of giving oneself to bearing others' burdens easier than reflecting upon how much the Lord has suffered for us. And so the Apostle makes us aware of this when he says, *Have this sense in you that was also in Christ Jesus, who, although he was in the form of God, did not think it robbery to be equal to God, but emptied himself, taking on the form of a slave, having been made in the likeness of men and found in appearance as a man. He humbled himself, having become obedient unto death, even the death of a cross.* (Phil 2:5-8) For he had said just before, *No one favoring what is his but what is another's* (Phil 2:4). To this phrase he joined what was said, as follows: *Have this sense in you that was also in Christ Jesus* (Phil 2:5), which is to be understood in this way: just as he,

being the Word, was made flesh and dwelled among us[387] and, although he was without sin, took up our sins and looked out not for his own interests but for ours, so likewise, in imitation of him, we should gladly bear one another's burdens.

4. That consideration leads to another—that *he took up* humanity,[388] whereas *we are* human beings and must realize that we could or can have the weakness of soul or body that we see in someone else. Let us, then, show the person whose weakness we wish to bear what we would wish to be shown us by him if perchance it were ours and not his. What the Apostle himself says is apropos here: *I have become all things to all people in order to gain all* (1 Cor 9:22)—namely, by realizing that he himself was capable of possessing the vice from which he wished to free someone else. For it was a matter of being compassionate and not of lying, as some people suppose, and especially those who, in order to defend their own lying, which they cannot deny, need the protection of some imposing example.[389]

5. Finally, this too must be considered—that there is no one who could not possess a good quality that you do not yet possess, even if it is concealed, which could make him unquestionably superior to you. This consideration is useful for breaking down and vanquishing pride, so that you do not think that, because in fact your good qualities stand out and are apparent, another person does not have any good qualities; they may be concealed and perhaps more impressive, causing him to rise above you, even though you do not know it. For the Apostle commands us not to be led astray by adulation, or rather not to take advantage of it, when he says, *Not by strife or by empty boasting but in humility of mind, each one thinking that the other is superior to him* (Phil 2:3). For we must not think this in such a way that we feign our thoughts, but we should genuinely think that there can be something concealed in a person that would make him superior to us, even if our good quality, which seems to make us superior to him, is not concealed. These considerations, which suppress pride and arouse charity, cause one another's brotherly burdens to be endured not only with equanimity but even with great gladness. In no way, however,

---

387. See Jn 1:14.
388. "He took up humanity": *ille suscepit hominem.* See note 11.
389. That 1 Cor 9:22 was used by some persons both to assert that Paul was lying and to justify their own lying was troublesome enough to Augustine for him to mention it in at least three other places—*The Lord's Sermon on the Mount* II,19,65; *Lying* 42; *Against Lying* 26.

should a judgment be made about an unknown person, and no one is known except through friendship.[390] Consequently, we should endure the bad qualities of our friends more steadfastly because we enjoy and understand their good ones.

6. And so the friendship of no one who seeks to become our friend should be rejected—not that he should be received at once [into our friendship] but that we should be open to receiving him and to treating him in such a way that he can be received. For we can say that a person has been received into our friendship when we dare to disclose all our thoughts to him. And if there is anyone who does not dare to make friends with us because he is embarrassed on account of some temporal honor or dignity of ours, we should approach him on his own level and offer him with a certain courtesy and humility of soul what he dares not ask for of himself.

It sometimes happens, to be sure, although it is rather rare, that the bad qualities of a person whom we wish to receive into our friendship become known to us before his good ones do, that we are offended and to a certain extent repelled by them, and that we leave him and never find out his good qualities, which are perhaps somewhat concealed. And so the Lord Jesus Christ, who wishes us to become his imitators, admonishes us to tolerate the person's weakness, so that we may be led by way of a charitable tolerance to those healthy qualities whose enjoyment would give us pleasure. For he says, *A physician is needed not for the healthy but for the* sick (Mt 9:12). Hence, if for the love of Christ we should not cast out from our soul even someone who perhaps is ailing in every respect, because he can be healed by the word of God, how much less should we cast out someone who can seem to us to be completely sick because we were unable to endure certain frailties of his at the outset of our friendship and—what is worse—dared, with an offended spirit, to make a rash judgment about that person in his whole being, not fearing what is said: *Do not judge, lest you be judged* (Mt 7:1), and, *By the measure that you have measured it shall be measured out to you* (Mt 7:2).

But often good qualities are the first to appear. A rash but kindly judgment in their regard should be cautioned against as well, lest, having thought of someone as totally good, the bad qualities that appear later

---

390. Augustine devotes most of the rest of this question to the topic of friendship, to which he gave much thought during the course of his life. For a summary of his views on this matter see Joseph T. Lienhard, "Friendship, Friends," in Fitzgerald 372-373.

come upon you when you are settled and unprepared and they offend you all the more, so that you hate more passionately the person whom you had so rashly loved, which is wicked. For even if no good qualities were evident to begin with, and those that first stood out were those that would later prove to be bad, they should still be tolerated until you had done everything in his regard that usually contributes to healing in such cases. How much more should this be the case when those good qualities have come first that serve as pledges and that ought to constrain us to tolerate the later ones.

7. This, then, is the law of Christ—that we should bear one another's burdens. But by loving Christ we easily endure another's weakness, even when it is someone whom we do not yet love on account of his own good qualities. For we realize that the Lord whom we love died on his behalf. This charity the apostle Paul brought to our attention when he said, *Because of your knowledge, the weak brother for whom Christ died will perish* (1 Cor 8:11). Thus, if we love a weak person less because of the vice that made him weak, we should consider him in light of the one who died on his behalf. Not to love Christ, however, is not weakness but death. Hence we should be very careful and implore God's mercy lest we neglect Christ because of a weak person, when we should love the weak person because of Christ.

LXXII. On the eternal times[391]

It can be asked how the apostle Paul could say, *Before the eternal times* (Ti 1:2). For if it is a matter of times, how could they be eternal? Or if it is a matter of things eternal, how could they be times? But perhaps he wanted "before all times" to be understood because, if he had said "before the times" and not added *eternal*, it could be taken to mean "before certain times," which would have other times before them. But perhaps he preferred to say *eternal* rather than "all" because time did not begin from time. Or maybe *eternal times* signified eternity, between which and time

---

391. An expression that Paul himself probably did not linger over, in Ti 1:2, has become for Augustine an agonizing conundrum. The Greek, πρὸ χρόνων αἰωνίων, rendered "so long ago" (New Jerusalem Bible) and "ages ago" (Revised Standard Version) in English, was an oxymoron in the Latin text that Augustine had before him: *ante tempora aeterna*. It provides, in any event, fuel for his speculation on time, which is one of his great philosophical themes. The two certitudes that emerge from this very brief question are 1) that time did not begin in time and 2) that time is mutable while eternity is stable. See John M. Quinn, "Time," in Fitzgerald 832-838 for a helpful discussion.

there is this difference—that the former is stable whereas time is mutable.

LXXIII. On what is written: *And found in* habitus *as a man* (Phil 2:7)[392]

1. We use *habitus* in many ways—in reference to the soul, when it is the taking in of some learning that is then strengthened and consolidated by use; or in reference to the body, when we say that one thing is more vigorous or healthy than another, which customarily is more appropriately called a habitude (*habitudo*); or in reference to the things that are fitted externally to our members, which we call clothing or shoes or weaponry and so forth. In all of these kinds of things, inasmuch as this word is taken from the verb "to have" (*habere*), it is clear that *habitus* is used in the context of something affecting someone, such that an effect can either be had or not. For teaching affects a soul, and vigor and strength a body, and there is no doubt that clothing and weaponry affect our members, such that the soul can also be uninstructed if no teaching affects it, and the body feeble and sluggish if our organs are without vigor and strength, and a person can be naked without clothing and defenseless without weapons and barefoot without shoes. *Habitus,* therefore, is used in the context of something affecting us such that an effect is had.

But there is this difference—that some of the things that affect us so as to constitute a *habitus* are not changed by us, but they themselves change us into them, while they remain whole and inviolate. For example, when wisdom affects a person, it itself is not changed, but it changes the person, whom it transforms from foolish to wise. But some things affect others in such a way that they both change and are changed. For example, food loses its own form and is turned into our body, and when we have eaten food we are changed from being feeble and sluggish into being strong and vigorous. There is a third possibility, when the things that affect others are changed so as to constitute a *habitus* and in a certain way they are shaped by the things for which they constitute the *habitus*. Clothing is an example

---

392. After defining the term *habitus* and listing its four usages, Augustine claims that the third usage applies to Christ's assumption of humanity. As Augustine explains it, this usage implies a change wrought in one thing, such as clothing, that affects (he employs forms of the verb *accidere* here) another thing, such as a body, which, although affected, is not changed by it. Christ's human nature, then, is analogous to clothing. See also Sermon 264,4. The second part of this question is rich in references to *assumptus homo* Christology, especially in the form of *induere hominem* ("clothing himself in humanity"). See note 11.

of this, for when it is taken off or set aside it does not have the form that it assumes when it is worn and placed over one's members. When it is worn, therefore, it takes on a form that it did not have when unworn, although the body's members themselves stay as they are both when clothed and unclothed. There can also be a fourth possibility, when the things that affect others so as to constitute a *habitus* neither change the things they affect nor are changed by them. The relationship of a ring to a finger is an example of this, if it is not looked at too closely. But this alternative is either nonexistent, if you investigate it carefully, or exceedingly rare.

2. When the Apostle was speaking of the only-begotten Son of God, then, as far as his divinity is concerned, according to which he is most true God, he said that he was equal to the Father and that it was not like robbery to him—that is, something else to desire, so to speak—if he were to abide always in that equality and did not wish to be clothed in humanity and to appear as a man to men. *But he emptied himself,* not changing his form but *taking the form of a slave* (Phil 2:7), and, having been changed and transformed into a man, his unchangeable stability did not depart from him but, taking up true humanity, he who took it up *was made in the likeness of men* (Phil 2:7), not for himself but for those to whom he appeared, and he *was found in* habitus *as a man* (Phil 2:7)—that is, by having (*habendo*) humanity he was found as a man. For he could not be found by those who had an unclean heart and who were unable to see the Word with the Father[393] unless he took up what they were able to see, and thus they could be brought interiorly to that light. But this *habitus* is not of the first kind, for the nature of the man, remaining as it was, did not change the nature of God; nor of the second, for it did not come about that the man both changed God and was changed by him; nor of the fourth, for the man was not taken up in such a way that he would neither change God nor be changed by him. Rather it is of the third kind, for he was taken up in such a way that he would be changed for the better and in an ineffable fashion be formed more excellently and harmoniously than clothing when it is taken off by a person. By this word *habitus*, therefore, the Apostle showed quite well what he meant by saying *having been made in the likeness of man* (Phil 2:7), because he became such not by transformation into a man but by a *habitus,* when he was clothed in the humanity that he somehow united and conformed to himself and joined to his own immortality and eternity.

---

393. See Jn 1:1.

The Greeks refer to the *habitus* which has to do with the taking in of wisdom and learning as ἕξις while what we speak of as clothing or weaponry they call σχῆμα. From this it is clear what kind of *habitus* the Apostle meant when in Greek texts the word, σχῆμα is in fact written, which we have as *habitus* in our Latin ones. The use of this word indicates that the Word was not changed by the taking up of humanity, just as a body's members are not changed when clothing is worn, although that taking up joined in an ineffable way the humanity that was taken up with the one who took it up. But to the extent that human words can be accommodated to ineffable things, lest the God who assumed human frailty be thought to have changed, it was foreseen that that taking up would be referred to in Greek as σχῆμα and in Latin as *habitus*.

LXXIV. On what is written in Paul's letter to the Colossians: *In whom we have redemption, the remission of sins, who is the image of the invisible God* (Col 1:14-15)[394]

Image and equality and likeness must be differentiated, because where there is an image there is necessarily a likeness but not necessarily equality; where there is equality there is necessarily a likeness but not necessarily an image; where there is a likeness there is not necessarily an image and not necessarily equality. Where there is an image there is necessarily a likeness but not necessarily equality, as in a person's image in a mirror: because it is a reflection of him it must also be a likeness, but there is no equality because many things are lacking to the image that are in the thing whose reflection it is. Where there is equality there is necessarily a likeness but not necessarily an image, as in the case of two of the same eggs: because there is equality there is also a likeness, for whatever properties one of them has the other has as well, but there is no image because neither of them is a reflection of the other. Where there is a likeness there is not necessarily an image and not necessarily equality; to be sure, every egg is like every other egg inasmuch as it is an egg, but a partridge egg, although it is like a chicken egg inasmuch as it is an egg, is nonetheless not its image because it is not a reflection of it, nor is it its equal because it is smaller and contains another kind of animal.

But when "not necessarily" is said, it means that it can sometimes exist. An image can exist, therefore, in which there is also equality. For example, in parents and their children there is an image as well as equality and likeness, even though there is a difference in age, for the image of the child is a reflection

---

394. Although this question is introduced with a text from Paul, its tone is entirely philosophical, with an emphasis on logic.

of the parent, so that it is correctly called an image, and it can be so close that it is correctly called equality as well, except that the parent is older. From this it is clear, too, that equality sometimes possesses not only a likeness but also an image, as is evident from the previous example. There can also sometimes be likeness and equality, although there is no image, as we said in the case of the same eggs. There can be both a likeness and an image, although there is no equality, as we showed with respect to a mirror. There can also be a likeness where there are both equality and an image, as we mentioned regarding children, except that the parents are older, for we say that one syllable is equal to another, although one precedes and the other follows.

But because God is not conditioned by time, for God cannot correctly be understood to have begotten in time the Son through whom he created time, the consequence is that he is not only his image because he is from him and his likeness because he is his image, but there is also such an equality that there is no difference in time to serve as a delay.

LXXV. On God's inheritance

1. As the Apostle says to the Hebrews, *The testament of a testator becomes valid at death* (Heb 9:17). Hence Christ's death on our behalf declares that a new testament has become valid[395] whose likeness was an old testament in which the death of the testator was prefigured by a victim.[396] If, then, the question is asked as to how we are, in the words of the same Apostle, coheirs of Christ and children and heirs of God,[397] since an inheritance is acquired upon the proven death of the deceased and there is no other way that an inheritance can be understood, the response should be that by that very death we have become heirs, because we have also been called his children: *The bridegroom's children,* it says, *do not fast as long as the bridegroom is with them* (Mt 9:15). We are called his heirs, then, because he has left us the possession of the Church's peace through the faith of the temporal dispensation, which we possess in this life because he attested and said, *I give you my peace, peace I leave you* (Jn 14:27). But we shall become his coheirs when, at the end of the world, death is swallowed up in victory.[398] For then *we shall be like him, because we shall see him as he is* (1 Jn 3:2). We do not acquire this inheritance upon

---

395. See Heb 9:15.
396. See Heb 9:18-20.
397. See Rom 8:17.
398. See 1 Cor 15:54.

the death of his Father, who cannot die, but when he himself becomes our inheritance, according to what is written: *The Lord is the portion of my inheritance* (Ps 16:5). But, inasmuch as when we were called we were still little children and unable to contemplate spiritual things, the divine mercy extended itself to our lowly thoughts so that, as much as we strained to see what we did not see in a clear and evident way, the very thing that we saw obscurely dies when we have begun to see face to face.[399] For it is appropriately said that what will be removed will die: *When what is perfect has come, what is partial will be removed* (1 Cor 13:10). Thus the Father somehow dies to us in obscurity, and he himself becomes our inheritance when he is seen face to face—not that he himself dies, but our imperfect vision of him is destroyed by a perfect vision. And yet, unless that former one had sustained us, we would not be prepared for the other in all its fullness and clarity.

2. Even if the devout mind admits this of the Lord Jesus Christ not in regard to the Word, who was God with God in the beginning,[400] but in regard to the boy who grew in age and wisdom,[401] while maintaining that assumption [of humanity] that is his alone[402] and not common to other human beings, it is clear whose inheritance he possesses as though by death. For we cannot be his coheirs unless he himself is the heir. But if devotion does not admit that the Lordly Man[403] saw partially at first and then completely, although he was said to grow in wisdom, his heir may be understood as his body, which is the Church, whose coheirs we are, just as we are called the children of this mother although she is composed of ourselves.

3. But, once more, it can be asked by whose death we became God's inheritance, in keeping with the words, *I will give you the nations as your inheritance* (Ps 2:8), if not perhaps by that of this world, under whose domination, so to speak, we used to be held. But later, when we say, *The world has been crucified to me, and I to the world* (Gal 6:14), Christ possesses us once that which used to possess us has died. When we renounce it, we die to it and it to us.

---

399. See 1 Cor 13:12.
400. See Jn 1:1.
401. See Lk 2:52. On Augustine's view of Christ's boyhood ignorance, which the Lukan verse seems to attest to, see note 167.
402. "While maintaining that assumption [of humanity] that is his alone": *propria illa susceptione servata.* See note 11.
403. "The Lordly Man": *homo dominicus.* See note 44.

LXXVI. On what the apostle James says: *Do you wish to know,*
O foolish person, that faith without works is useless? **(Jas 2:20)**[404]

1. Since the apostle Paul, declaring that *a person is made righteous by*
faith apart from works (Rom 3:28), has not been properly understood by
those who have accepted what he said in such a way as to think that, once
they have believed in Christ, they can be saved by faith even if they have
acted badly and lived in a vicious and shameful manner, the passage from
this letter [of James] sets out the same meaning as the apostle Paul's and how
he should be understood.[405] And so [James] dwells on the example of
Abraham in order to show that faith is empty if one does not act well,[406] since
the apostle Paul also used the example of Abraham to prove that a person
was made righteous by faith apart from the works of the law.[407] For when
[James] recalls Abraham's good works, which followed upon his faith,[408] he
clearly shows that the apostle Paul does not use Abraham to teach that a
person is made righteous by faith apart from works, as if it were a matter of
indifference whether someone who believed acted well, but rather so that no
one would think that he had attained to the gift of righteousness, which is in
faith, by the merits of his previous good works. For the Jews desired to give
themselves preference over the gentiles who believed in Christ, because
they said that they had attained to gospel grace by the merits of the good
works that are in the law, and therefore many were scandalized who had
believed because of them, because the grace of Christ was being given over
to uncircumcised gentiles.[409] Hence the apostle Paul says that a person can
be made righteous by faith apart from antecedent works.[410] For how can a
person who has been made righteous by faith act other than righteously from
that point on, even though previously he had done nothing righteously and
had attained to the righteousness of faith not by the merits of good works but
by the grace of God, which cannot be lacking in him[411] since now, by love, he
is acting well? If soon after having believed he departs from this life, the
righteousness of faith remains with him—neither on account of antecedent

---

404. Augustine confronts two classic apparently contradictory statements in Paul and James here,
    as he does later at greater length in *Exposition of Psalm* 31 [32],2,3-8, and comes to the
    conclusion that in fact they are complementary. Paul, he says in section 2, "is speaking of
    works that are antecedent to faith and [James] of those that follow upon faith."
405. See Jas 2:14-26.
406. See Jas 2:21-24.
407. See Rom 3:21-4:25.
408. See Jas 2:21-22.
409. See Acts 11:1-3.
410. See Rom 3:28.
411. See 1 Cor 15:10.

good works, because he attained to it not by merit but by grace, nor on account of subsequent ones, because none were permitted him in this life. Hence what the apostle Paul says is clear: *For we consider that a person is made righteous by faith apart from works.* Yet this must not be understood to mean that, once a person has accepted faith and if he lives, we may call him righteous, even if he lives badly. So the apostle Paul uses the example of Abraham[412] because he was made righteous by faith apart from the works of the law, which he had not received, and so does James, because he shows that good works resulted from the faith of Abraham,[413] and he indicates how what the apostle Paul preached should be understood.

2. For those who consider that the words of the apostle James contradict the words of the apostle Paul can also think that Paul contradicts himself, because he says in another place, *For those who listen to the law are not made righteous before God, but those who do the law shall be made righteous* (Rom 2:13), and in still another place, *But the faith that works by love* (Gal 5:6), and again, *For if you live according to the flesh you shall die, but if by the spirit you put to death the deeds of the flesh you shall live* (Rom 8:13). He indicates what the deeds of the flesh are that must be put to death by spiritual works when he says in another place, *But the works of the flesh are clear. They are fornications, impurities, worship of idols, sorcery, enmities, disputes, jealousies, animosities, dissensions, heresies, envies, drunkenness, gluttony and things like that. I declare to you, as I have declared, that those who do such things shall not possess the kingdom of God* (Gal 5:19-21), and to the Corinthians, *Make no mistake: neither fornicators nor idolators nor adulterers nor the effeminate nor those who sleep with men nor thieves nor the avaricious nor drunkards nor slanderers nor the greedy shall possess the kingdom of God. And that is in fact what you were. But you have been washed clean, but you have been sanctified, you have been made righteous in the name of our Lord Jesus Christ and in the Spirit of our God.* (1 Cor 6:9-11) With these words he teaches very clearly that they did not attain to the righteousness of faith on account of past good works, nor that grace was given by reason of their merits, when he says, *And that is in fact what you were* (1 Cor 6:11). But when he says, *Those who do such things shall not possess the kingdom of God* (Gal 5:21), he makes it quite obvious that those who have come to

---

412. See Rom 3:21-4:25.
413. See Jas 2:22.

faith from such circumstances must act well. James also says this, and in many places throughout his writings the same Paul declares clearly and openly that all who have believed in Christ must live rightly lest they be punished. The Lord himself refers to this also when he says, *Not everyone who says to me, Lord, Lord, shall enter into the kingdom of heaven. But he who does the will of my Father who is in heaven shall enter into the kingdom of heaven* (Mt 7:21), and elsewhere, *Why do you say to me, Lord, Lord, and not do what I tell you?* (Lk 6:46) and, *Everyone who hears these words of mine and does them, him I shall liken to a wise person who built his house upon rock* (Mt 7:24), and so forth, *And he who hears these words of mine and does not do them, him I shall liken to a foolish person who built his house upon sand* (Mt 7:26), and so forth. Accordingly, the words of the two apostles Paul and James are not mutually contradictory, when one says that *a person is made righteous by faith apart from works* and the other says that faith apart from works is empty,[414] because the former is speaking of works that are antecedent to faith and the latter of those that follow upon faith, just as Paul himself also shows in many passages.

LXXVII. On whether fear is a sin[415]

Every perturbation is a passion and every desire is a perturbation; therefore every desire is a passion. But when any passion is in us, we suffer from that passion, and we suffer insofar as it is a passion. When any desire is in us, therefore, we suffer from that desire, and we suffer insofar as it is a desire. But not every passion, insofar as we suffer from that passion, is a sin. And thus, if we suffer fear, it is not a sin. It is as if it were to be said, "If that is two-footed it is not an animal." If, then, this does not follow, inasmuch as there are many two-footed animals, neither does the former follow, inasmuch as there are many sins that we suffer. For it is a contradiction to say that it does not follow that, if we suffer fear, it is not a sin, yet you concede[416] that there are some sins that we suffer.

---

414. See James 2:20.
415. For a better understanding of this exercise in logic it is useful to know that "passion" and "suffer" are related words in Latin; the perfect participle of "suffer" in Latin is *passus*. Both *passio* ("passion") and *passus* connote an element of passivity. Although some sins are passive, fear, which is also passive, is not among them.
416. The abrupt intrusion of the second person singular (*concedas*) here suggests that this question was once part of a dialogue between Augustine and someone else.

LXXVIII. On the beauty of images[417]

That most lofty art of almighty God, by which he made everything from nothing and which is also called his wisdom,[418] is also operative in craftsmen, so that they make things that are beautiful and harmonious, although they do not make them from nothing but from some material such as wood or marble or ivory or another kind of material that is at the craftsman's disposal. Yet these persons cannot fashion something out of nothing, because they work by way of their bodies, although in their minds they receive those numbers and geometrical patterns that they imprint upon other bodies by way of their own bodies thanks to that loftiest wisdom which has imprinted those numbers and patterns upon the whole world in a far more skillful manner,[419] because it has been fashioned[420] out of nothing. In it are also the bodies of animals, which are fashioned[421] from something—namely, the elements of the world—but with much greater efficacy and excellence than when skillful persons imitate those same bodily figures and shapes in their own works. For not every harmonious element (*numerositas*) of the human body is found in a statue, yet whatever is found there comes by way of the craftsman's soul from that wisdom which fashions the human body itself in conformity with nature. But those who fashion or love such works must not on that account be considered great because, with their souls intent upon the less important things that they make with their bodies according to a bodily pattern, they cling that much less to that most lofty wisdom from which they acquire their skills. They use them badly as long as they exercise them externally, for when they love those things upon which they exercise [their skills] they pay no heed to their unchangeable inner form, and they become foolish and weak. But from this it can be understood that those who even go so far as to worship such works deviate greatly from the truth because, if they worshiped the actual bodies of animals that have been

---

417. Augustine mainly envisages three-dimensional art in this question, and the conclusion of the question suggests that this art is pagan in its subject matter. (Christian three-dimensional art, especially statuary, was in any event only in its infancy in his day.) Indeed, in the translation of the Bibliothèque Augustinienne (1,10,341) the title reads: "De la beauté des statues païennes." Much of the artistic theory of this question is repeated in *Confessions* X,34,53. In his judgment of what is beautiful Augustine seems to be guided here as elsewhere by mental preconceptions rather than by sensual refinement. See H.-I. Marrou, *Saint Augustin et la fin de la culture antique* (Paris: Boccard,1938) 184, n. 1. It is noteworthy that at the very beginning of the question he compares—of course with qualifications—artists to the divine wisdom, which is the Son of God.

418. See 1 Cor 1:24.

419. On the role of numbers—which represent an order or harmony that ultimately comes from God, to which the artist, or artisan, must conform if he wishes to make something beautiful—see also *Free Will* II,16,42; *Music* VI,17,57.

420. Reading *fabricatum* instead of *fabricata*.

421. Reading *fabricantur* instead of *fabricator*.

much more excellently fashioned and of which those [works] are imitations, what could we say was more wretched than they?

LXXIX. Why did Pharaoh's magicians perform certain miracles like Moses, the servant of God?[422]

1. Every soul partly exercises powers of its own that have a certain private quality and partly is controlled and ruled by the laws of the universe, which can be called public. Since, therefore, every visible thing whatsoever in this world has an angelic power placed over it, as sacred scripture testifies in a few passages,[423] the thing over which it has been placed acts in one way as though by a private law and is in another way compelled to act as it were publicly. For the universe is more powerful than any part of it, because even that which acts privately there is allowed to act only as much as the law of the universe allows. But a given soul is that much more cleansed by piety to the extent that it takes less pleasure in its private affairs and is attentive to and devoutly and willingly observant of the law of the universe. For the law of the universe is divine wisdom. But to the extent that [a soul] finds greater joy in its private concerns and, neglecting God who watches over all souls to their profit and benefit, wishes to take the place of God in relation to itself and, when it can, to others, loving its own power over itself and others rather than God's power over all, the more contemptible it is and the more it is compelled, as punishment, to submit to the divine, or public, laws. To the extent, then, that the human soul abandons God and takes pleasure in its own honors or power, the more enslaved it is to the powers that find joy in their own private gain and desire to be honored by human beings as if they were gods. It is often permitted them by the divine law even to perform something miraculous for those whom, in conformity with their merits, they have brought under their sway; this they do by their private power in matters where they may vaunt themselves and over which they have been placed by the lowest yet most well-arranged ordering of powers. But when the divine or public law commands, it overcomes private license, although private license itself would be naught without the permission of the universal divine law.

---

422. See Ex 7-8. The present question seeks to explain how not only wicked human beings but also wicked spirits can perform miracles—an issue that is addressed again in the *Miscellany of Questions in Response to Simplician* II,1 (which deals with the related matter of an evil man possessing a prophetic spirit) and II,3 (= *Eight Questions of Dulcitius* 6); *The Trinity* III,7,12-10,21; IV,1,14. That spiritual powers do whatever they do, including evil deeds, with God's permission is the insight that appears already in Jb 1-2.
423. See, e.g., Mt 18:10; Rv 1:20.

And so it happens that when it is appropriate for the holy servants of God to have this gift, in accordance with the public and (so to say) commanding law, which is the power of the most high God, they may command the lowest powers to perform certain visible miracles. For in them it is God himself, whose temples they are[424] and whom they most ardently love while disdaining their own private power, who issues the commands. But in magical conjurations, for the pleasure of deception and in order to bring under their sway those to whom they allow such things, they produce an effect as a result of their entreaties and rituals, bestowing by their private law what it is permitted them to bestow upon those who honor and serve them and enter into a kind of covenant with them in their sacraments.[425] And when magicians seem to issue commands, they terrify lower beings by using the names of higher ones so that they may display to those who marvel at them a few visible things that seem great to persons who, on account of the weakness of their flesh, are unable to perceive the eternal things that the true God manifests to those who love him. But God, who regulates everything justly, allows these things in order to apportion slavery or freedom in keeping with their desires and choices, and if ever they obtain something in keeping with their evil desires after invoking the most high God, it is a punishment and not a favor. For not without reason does the Apostle say, *God handed them over to the desires of their hearts* (Rom 1:24). For an ease in committing certain sins is the punishment for those [sins] that have gone before.

2. A person who uses the names of some of the lowest powers and has cast out a minor demon may think that these words of the Lord—*Satan cannot cast out Satan* (Mk 3:23)—are false. But he should understand that they were said because Satan, even if he spares the body or the body's senses, spares them so that, by a still greater triumph, he may master a person's will through the error of his impiety. In this way Satan does not leave but rather enters into a person's innermost parts so as to work in him just as the Apostle says, *According to the prince of the power of this air, who works now in the children of disobedience* (Eph 2:2). For he did not disturb and torment the senses of their bodies or beat their bodies, but he ruled in their wills or, rather, in their desires.

3. But when he says that false prophets will perform many signs and prodigies so as to deceive even the elect, if that were possible,[426] he warns us that we should understand that even wicked persons perform miracles such as the

---

424. See 1 Cor 3:16.
425. These are of course not sacraments in the same sense as explained in note 43 but rather perversions of them. An implicit contrast is made with the Christian sacraments that are mentioned in section 4.
426. See Mt 24:24.

saints cannot perform. Nor must they be thought to occupy a preferential position in God's presence. For the magicians of the Egyptians were not more acceptable to God than the people of Israel because that people could not do what the others did (although Moses was capable of still greater things by the power of God).[427] But these things are not bestowed upon all the saints lest the weak be deceived by a most pernicious error, thinking that there are greater gifts in such deeds than in the works of righteousness by which eternal life is obtained. Therefore the Lord forbids his disciples to rejoice on this account when he says, *Do not rejoice because the spirits are subjected to you, but rejoice because your names are written in heaven* (Lk 10:20).

4. When, therefore, magicians do what the saints sometimes do, they indeed appear to be the same on the surface, but they happen for a different purpose and by a different law. For the ones do these things to seek their own glory, while the others seek the glory of God;[428] the former engage, so to speak, in private trade and cull private advantage in their own ranks through what is allowed them by the powers, while the latter do so for the public weal at the command of him to whom the whole creation is subject. For it is one thing when a horse's owner is forced to give it to a soldier and another when he hands it over to a buyer or donates it or lends it to someone. And just as most bad soldiers, whom imperial discipline condemns, terrify some property owners by the ensigns of their emperor and extort from them something that is not publicly commanded, so bad Christians and schismatics and heretics, in the name of Christ or through Christian words or sacraments, claim something from the powers that have been enjoined to yield to Christ's honor. But when they yield in their will to those that issue wicked commands, they yield in order to seduce people in whose error they rejoice. And so magicians perform miracles in one way, good Christians in another and bad Christians in yet another: magicians through private pacts, good Christians through public righteousness and bad Christians through the signs of public righteousness. It is not surprising that these signs have validity when they are used by them since, thanks to the honor of the most excellent emperor, they continue to have validity even when they are usurped by strangers who have not so much as enrolled in the army. One of these was the man of whom the disciples told the Lord that he cast out devils in his name, although he was not of their following.[429] But when the powers of this sort do not yield to these signs, God himself restrains them in secret ways when he judges that to be just and advan-

---

427. See Ex 7-10.
428. For an expansion of the same thought see *The City of God* XIV,28.
429. See Lk 9:49.

tageous. For in no way do any spirits dare to disdain these signs, for they tremble at them whenever they see them. But, without people's realizing it, another command is divinely given—either to confound the wicked when they deserve to be confounded, as we read in the Acts of the Apostles about the sons of Sceva, to whom an unclean spirit said, *I know Jesus and I know Paul, but who are you?* (Acts 19:15) or to admonish the good so that they may make progress in faith and be able to do this not boastfully but profitably, or to discern the gifts of the Church's members, as the Apostle says, *Do all have strengths? Do all have the gifts of healing?* (1 Cor 12:30) Very often for these reasons, then, as has been said, without people's realizing it, commands are divinely given—that is, so that when signs of this sort are used the powers may not submit to the will of men.

5. But frequently, so that the wicked may harm the good for a time, they receive power over them for the greater advantage of the good, that their patience may be exercised. Hence the Christian soul is always attentive, in the course of its tribulations, to follow the will of its Lord, lest by resisting God's plan it obtain for itself a more severe judgment. For that is what the Lord himself, acting in his humanity,[430] said to Pontius Pilate, which Job could also have said to the devil: *You would have no power over me unless it had been given you from above* (Jn 19:11). It is not therefore the will of him to whose malice power is given over the good but rather the will of him *by* whom this power is given that must be most dear to us, *because tribulation works patience, but patience brings proving, and proving brings hope; but hope does not deceive, because the charity of God has been poured into our hearts through the Holy Spirit who has been given to us* (Rom 5:3-5).

LXXX. Against the Apollinarians[431]

1. Certain heretics, who are said to have been named after Apollinarius, their founder, assert that our Lord Jesus Christ, insofar as he deigned to become a man, did not have a human mind, and some of their adherents have also delighted their eager listeners with the perversity whereby he diminished the man in God, when he said that he did not have the mind, or rational soul, by

---

430. "The Lord himself, acting in his humanity": *ipse dominus agens hominem*. See note 11.
431. The position of the Apollinarians is clear from this question: they claimed that Christ had the external accoutrements of humanity with none of its internal properties—i.e., a mind or a soul. Apollinarius (c. 310-c. 390) was the bishop of Laodicea and both a clever opponent of the paganizing policy of Julian the Apostate and a strong defender of Nicean Christianity against Arianism. His christological system was an attempt to account for the unity of Christ's humanity and divinity while emphasizing the latter in opposition to the Arians. As seems particularly appropriate, Augustine uses *homo assumptus* terminology several times in the question. See note 11.

which a human being is interiorly distinguished from the beasts.[432] But there were those with them who thought that it had to be acknowledged that, if this were the case, the only-begotten Son of God, the wisdom[433] and Word of the Father, through whom all things were made,[434] might be believed to have taken on some kind of animal with the shape of a human body, and they displeased them—yet not so much that they corrected them with a view to their returning to the way of truth and confessing that a human being in his entirety was taken up by the wisdom of God[435] with no detriment to his [divine] nature. Instead, using still greater audacity, they removed from him even his very soul and all the means of life, saying that he had taken up human flesh alone, and they even cited testimony from the gospel; and in their perverse misunderstanding of that text they dare to contend against Catholic truth, saying that it is written: *The Word was made flesh and dwelled among us* (Jn 1:14). For by these words they wish to understand that the Word was so joined to and compounded with flesh that not only no human mind but not even a human soul could come between them.

2. To these persons it must first be responded that the gospel expresses itself in this way because that assumption of human nature by the Lord was accomplished by including even the visible flesh, and in the unity—in its totality—of that assumption the Word is the original factor, whereas the flesh is least and last. And so the evangelist, wishing for our sake to refer to the love of humility of a God who humbled himself, and showing how far he humbled himself, mentioned the Word and the flesh but omitted the nature of the soul, which is inferior to the Word but nobler than the flesh. For he makes more of this humility by saying, *The Word was made flesh*, than if he said that the Word was made man. For if people look too closely at these words, someone else no less perverse could use these words so to misrepresent our faith in such a way as to say that the Word himself was changed into flesh and ceased to be the Word, because it is written: *The Word was made flesh*. That would be like saying that human flesh, since it becomes ashes, is not flesh and ashes but is ashes made from flesh and, according to a well-known expression, whatever comes into being that did not use to be ceases to be what it was. Yet that is not how we understand these words. But even [these heretics] themselves understand along with us that, while the Word remained what he was, he took the

---

432. "Mind": *mentem*; "rational soul": *rationalem animam*; "interiorly": *secundum animum*. The distinction between *mens* and *animus* is occasionally lost in Augustine. See Bibliothèque Augustinienne 1,10,705-706.
433. See 1 Cor 1:24.
434. See Jn 1:3.
435. See 1 Cor 1:24.

form of a slave,[436] not that he was changed by some sort of mutation into that form, so that it might be said, *The Word was made flesh.*

Finally, if, whenever the flesh is spoken of and the soul goes unmentioned, this is to be understood in such a way that the soul should be believed not to exist, then they do not have a soul of whom it is said, *And all flesh shall see the salvation of God* (Lk 3:6), and in a psalm, *Hear my prayers; to you all flesh will come* (Ps 65:2), and in the gospel, As *you gave him power over all flesh, so that everything that you gave him would not perish but would have eternal life* (Jn 17:2). From this it is clear that human beings are often signified by mentioning the flesh alone, so that what was said—*The Word was made flesh*—can be understood in light of this manner of speaking as well and as meaning nothing else than that the Word was made man. For just as the part implies the whole and a man is understood when the soul alone is mentioned, as in the words, *So many souls went down to Egypt* (Gn 46:27), so also the part implies the whole and a man is understood when the flesh alone is mentioned, as in the cases that we cited.[437]

3. Accordingly, just as we respond to this objection of theirs, which they put forward as gospel-based, in such a way that no one would be so foolish as to think that we are compelled by these words to believe and profess that the mediator of God and humankind, the man Jesus Christ,[438] did not have a human soul, so I ask how they can respond to these very clear objections of ours, by which we have shown from innumerable gospel passages what was said of him by the evangelists—that he possessed feelings that cannot exist without a soul. For I submit statements that do not come from me but from the many that the Lord himself utters: *My soul is sad even unto death* (Mt 26:3 8), and, *I have power to lay down my soul and power to take it up again* (Jn 10:18), and, *Greater love has no one than that he would lay down his soul for his friends* (Jn 15:13). An obstinate opponent can tell me that these things were spoken figuratively by the Lord, just as it is obvious that he said many things in parable form. But even if this is not so [as I have described it] there is still no need to be contentious, when we have the narratives of the evangelists, thanks to which we know him and his having been born of the virgin Mary,[439] and his having been seized by the Jews and scourged and crucified and killed

---

436. See Phil 2:7.
437. The same broader definition of "flesh" is offered in *Exposition of Psalm* 56 [57],5; *The Trinity* II,6,11; *Continence* 4,11; *The City of God* XIV,2.
438. See Tm 2:5.
439. See Mt 1:18-23.

and buried in a tomb[440]—all of which no one can understand to have happened without a body. Even someone very foolish would not say that these things should be taken figuratively, since they were recounted by those who narrated these events as they remembered them. Just as they testify, then, that he had a body, so those feelings that cannot exist except in the soul, which we read about in the very same narratives of the evangelists, indicate that he had a soul. Jesus was astonished[441] and angry and sad[442] and gladdened[443] and countless other things that also demonstrate the combined functions of soul and body, such as the fact that he hungered,[444] that he slept,[445] that he was wearied from traveling and sat down,[446] and other things of this sort. For they cannot say that in the ancient books[447] as well God's anger[448] and joy[449] and several emotions of this sort were spoken of and that it does not follow therefore that God should be believed to have had a soul. For those things were said with prophetic imagination and not with the veracity characteristic of historical narrative. For God's members were also spoken of—his hands[450] and feet[451] and eyes[452] and face[453] and so forth. Just as the latter do not mean that he has a body, neither do the former mean that he has a soul. But just as what is narrated, when Christ's hands and head and so forth are mentioned, points to his body, so also what is mentioned regarding the emotions of his soul in the course of the same narration points to his soul. It is foolish to believe the evangelist when in his narrative he says that [the Lord] ate and not to believe that he was hungry. For even if it does not follow that everyone who eats is hungry—for we also read that an angel ate, but we do not read that he was hungry[454]—nor that everyone who is hungry eats, when a person restrains himself for some reason or when the

---

440. See Mt 26:47-27:60.
441. See Mt 8:10.
442. See Mk 3:5.
443. See Jn 11:15.
444. See Mt 4:2.
445. See Mt. 8:24.
446. See Jn 4:6.
447. "The ancient books" are the Old Testament.
448. See, e.g., Ex 32:12.
449. See, e.g., Dt 28:63.
450. See, e.g., Ez 1:3.
451. See, e.g., Ps 99:5.
452. See, e.g., Ps 33:18.
453. See, e.g., Ex 33:23.
454. See Gn 18:2-8.

food and the wherewithal for eating are lacking to him, nonetheless, when an evangelist puts both in his narrative, both must be believed, because he wrote both fact and deed as an indicator of things that were done. But since the fact that he ate cannot be understood without a body, neither could his hunger have occurred without a soul.

4. Nor does that foolish and absurd fallacy frighten us when they say with malicious hostility that he was subject to necessity if he truly possessed these inclinations of the soul. Our response is easy indeed: he was subject to necessity because he was seized, scourged, crucified and died. Thus they may at last understand, if they wish and if they renounce their stubbornness, that he took up true passions—that is, movements—of the soul, in accord with the divine plan and yet as it pleased him, just as in the same accord with that plan he took up the passions of the body apart from any necessity. Just as we do not die in accord with our will, neither are we born in accord with our will. He, however, did both in accord with his will, as was fitting, and yet he did them most truly. Therefore, just as no one tears away either us or them, in the name of necessity, from believing in that truest passion by which his corporeality is proven, so neither does anyone deter us, in the name of necessity, from believing in that truest affectivity (*affectionis*) by which we recognize his soul, and it should not deter them from assenting to Catholic belief if a fatal embarrassment at changing an opinion that is false but that has been obstinately defended over a long period does not deter them.

LXXXI. On quadragesima and quinquagesima[455]

1. The whole discipline of wisdom, which is for the purpose of instructing human beings, consists in distinguishing the creator and creation and in worshiping the one as master and acknowledging the other as subject. Now the creator is God, from whom are all things and through whom are all things and in whom are all things,[456] who is therefore a Trinity, Father, Son and Holy Spirit. Creation, however, is partly invisible (like the soul) and partly visible (like the body). The number three is associated with the invisible, because we

---

455. The Latin word *quadragesima* means "forty" and is associated here with the forty days of Lent. *Quinquagesima* means "fifty" and refers here to the fifty-day period from Easter to Pentecost. Augustine works out the numerological significance of forty and fifty—the former symbolizing this-worldly toil and sorrow, the latter heavenly peace—and concludes with an interpretation of the 153 fish of Jn 21:11, recalling a somewhat different treatment of the same theme in question LVII. For other discussions of the relationship of quadragesima, quinquagesima and the number 153 see Letter 55,28-32; Sermon 252; *Teaching Christianity* II,16,25. See also note 99.

456. See Rom 11:36.

are commanded to love God in a threefold way, with all our heart and all our soul and all our mind,[457] while the number four is associated with the body on account of its most obvious characteristics—that is, warmth and cold, moisture and dryness. The number seven, therefore, is associated with creation in its entirety. Hence all the discipline which consists in distinguishing and separating the creator and creation is suggested by the number ten.

This discipline, to the extent that it deals in the temporal activities of bodies, is based upon believing, and as with milk it nourishes small children[458] by events that have taken place which occur and then pass away, so that it may make them fit to contemplate what does not occur and then pass away but abides forever. Once there have been divinely narrated to a person those events that have transpired in time for the salvation of men, or which are announced as being still in the future and must yet transpire, if he clings to them in faith and hopes in what has been promised and strives to fulfill with unwavering charity what the divine authority enjoins, he shall live uprightly this life of necessity and time. This [life] is called to mind by the number forty (*quadragenario*) because the number ten, which suggests the whole of discipline, multiplied four times (multiplied, that is, by the number associated with the body, because service, which it has been said is based upon belief, takes place through bodily activities), produces the number forty. Thus he attains to a wisdom that is unchanging and not bound by time, which is called to mind by the number ten, so that ten may be added to forty, because the unvarying parts of the number forty, once added together, come to fifty (*quinquaginta*). For the number forty possesses unvarying parts —first forty ones, then twenty twos, ten fours, eight fives, five eights, four tens, two twenties. Therefore one and two and four and five and eight and ten and twenty, added together, produce fifty. Hence, just as the number forty, added up in its unvarying parts, begets ten more and produces fifty, so also the time of faith concerning events that have transpired for our salvation and that must yet transpire, along with an upright life, attains to an understanding marked by abiding wisdom, so that discipline may be based not only upon belief but also upon understanding.

2. And so that which is now the Church—although we are the children of God, yet before it appears what we shall be[459]—carries on in toil and affliction, and in it the upright person lives by faith.[460] For, it says, *unless you believe, you shall not understand* (Is 7:9). And this is the age when we groan

---

457. See Mt 22:37.
458. See 1 Cor 3:1-2.
459. See 1 Jn 3:2.
460. See Rom 1:17.

and are in pain[461] as we await the redemption of our body, which is celebrated at quadragesima. *But we know that when he appears, we shall be like
him, because we shall see him as he is* (1 Jn 3:2). Then the number ten will be
added to the number forty (*quadragenario*), so that we may merit not only to
believe what pertains to faith but also to understand the truth in its clarity.
This Church, in which there shall be no sadness, no mingling with bad men,
no wickedness, but joy and peace and gladness, is foreshadowed by the celebration of quinquagesima. Consequently, after our Lord rose from the dead
and had completed forty days with his disciples,[462] having by this very same
number alluded to the temporal dispensation that pertains to faith, he
ascended into heaven.[463] And when ten more days had gone by he sent the
Holy Spirit[464] for this purpose—that, for the sake of contemplating not
human and temporal but divine and eternal things, by a certain breathing and
burning of love and charity ten might be added to forty. And so this
total—that is, the number fifty in terms of days—must be marked by a celebration of joy.

3. But our Lord also symbolizes these two ages, one of toil and worry and
the other of gladness and security, by the nets cast into the sea. For an
account is given, before [Christ's] passion, of a net cast into the sea and of so
many fish being caught that they could hardly be drawn to shore, and the
nets were torn.[465] For they were not cast on the right side, since the Church of
this age possesses many bad persons, nor on the left side, since it also
possesses good persons,[466] but indiscriminately, in order to symbolize the
mingling of the good and the bad. The fact that the nets were torn, however,
symbolizes the springing up of many heresies once charity has been
violated. But after the resurrection, when [Christ] wished to foreshadow the
Church of the future age, when all will be perfect and holy, he commanded
that the nets be cast on the right side,[467] and one hundred and fifty-three huge
fish were caught, while his disciples were amazed at the fact that, although
they were so big, the nets were not ripped.[468] Their great size symbolizes the
greatness of wisdom and righteousness, and their number symbolizes that
discipline which has been perfected by both the temporal dispensation and

---

461. See Rom 8:22-23.
462. See Acts 1:3.
463. See Acts 1:9.
464. See Acts 2:1-4.
465. See Lk 5:5-6.
466. On the symbolism of right=good and left=bad see Mt 25:33.
467. See Jn 21:6.
468. See Jn 21:11.

eternal regeneration, which we said was called to mind by the number fifty. For inasmuch as there will be no need then of bodily sustenance, and faith and wisdom will be held fast by the soul, and inasmuch as we have said that the number three was associated with the soul, we multiply fifty times three, and one hundred and fifty results. The Trinity is added to this number because all of this perfection has been consecrated in the name of the Father and of the Son and of the Holy Spirit. Thus one hundred and fifty-three results, which is the number of the fish caught on the right side.

LXXXII. On what is written: *Whom the Lord loves he corrects; he scourges every son whom he receives* (Heb 12:6)

1. Many of those who murmur under God's discipline are provoked to questioning when they see the righteous often undergoing grave trials in this life, as though the fact that they serve God is of no value to them, because they endure bodily hardships and those of loss and insult indiscriminately and in common with everyone else, which mortals consider to be evils, or even to a greater extent than others on account of [their love of] the Word of God and righteousness, which are burdensome to sinners and arouse tumultuous uprisings and plots and hatred against those who preach this. To these the response will be that, if this life were the only one that people had, it would not seem absurd that a righteous life would be valueless or even harmful in all cases. Even so there would not be lacking those who would make the sweetness of righteousness and its inner joy equal to all the bodily hardships and trials that the human race endures on account of its mortal condition, and equal also to all those things that, because of their very righteousness, are stirred up most wrongfully against those who live righteously. Quite apart from any hope for a future life, they would submit to torture out of a love for the truth with more joy and gladness than voluptuaries would banquet out of a desire to get drunk.

2. But there are those who think that God is unjust when they see the righteous oppressed by sorrows and hardships (even if they do not dare to *say* that God is unjust), who feel that he either takes no interest in human affairs or that he at one time established the Fates, against whom even he himself can do nothing, lest he be believed to disturb through fickleness the order of things that he arranged, or who hold another opinion—that God, having been weakened to some degree, is unable to keep bad things from happening to the righteous. To these it must be said that there would have been no righteousness in human beings if God had taken no interest

in human affairs, because all this righteousness of human beings, which the human mind can either lay hold of by acting uprightly or lose by sinning, would not have been imprinted upon the soul did some immutable righteousness not exist, to be discovered in its integrity by the righteous when they are converted to it and to be abandoned in its integrity by sinners when they turn away from its light. This immutable righteousness is of course God's, and he would not offer it for the enlightenment of those who converted to him if he took no interest in human affairs. But if he allowed the righteous to endure heavy burdens because he did not want to go against the order of things that he arranged, he would not be righteous then either, not because he wishes to maintain his own arrangement but because he has arranged the very order of things in such a way that the righteous are afflicted with undeserved sufferings. But whoever holds the opinion that God is too weak to ward off the bad things that the righteous undergo is foolish, because he does not understand that it is just as wicked to deny God's omnipotence as it is to call him unjust.

3. To respond briefly to the question that was raised: to those who agree that it is unspeakably wicked to doubt that God exists and that he is just and omnipotent, no reason seems more likely as to why righteous persons suffer frequently in this life than that this is advantageous to them. For the righteousness of human beings that now exists and that is aimed at obtaining eternal life is one thing, while that which a person living in paradise needs then in order to maintain and not lose that same eternal salvation is another. For just as it is characteristic of God's justice to command what is beneficial and to apportion punishments to the disobedient and rewards to the obedient, so it is characteristic of man's righteousness to obey beneficial commands. But since beatitude is to the soul what health is to the body, and just as in regard to the body one medicine is prescribed so that good health may not be lost whereas another is prescribed so that what has been lost may be restored, so in regard to humankind's total condition some commands have been given so that humankind may not lose immortality then whereas others are enjoined so that it may obtain it now. Now, in regard to the body's health, if a person does not heed his physician's prescriptions, which are given for the purpose of maintaining his good health, and falls into some illness, he is given other prescriptions so that he can get better; these are frequently of no avail if the illness is advanced, unless certain supplementary treatments are administered by the physicians that often cause pain and discomfort while nonetheless contributing to the restoration of health; and so it happens that, even when a person pays heed to his physician, he still suffers pain not only from the illness itself, when it is not

yet cured, but even from supplementary medical treatment. Similarly, when through sin humankind fell into the sickly and ruinous mortality of this life because he chose not to heed what was first enjoined, which would have enabled him to grasp and keep hold of eternal salvation, in his illness he received a second injunction, and when he heeds this he is in fact correctly said to be living righteously; but still he endures the hardships that he suffers either from his as yet uncured illness or from the supplementary medical treatment. It is this supplementary medication that is referred to in the text, *Whom the Lord loves he corrects; he scourges every son whom he receives* (Heb 12:6). But those who pay no heed to health-giving injunctions live wickedly and constantly increase their illnesses, and either from them or from added punishments they endure the misery of innumerable hardships and pains, so that what is not healthy is affected and feels pain and those who are in these straits are mercifully warned that, once they have taken their medication, they can be cured through the grace of God. If they disdain all of this—namely, what has been enjoined in the form of words and pains—they will merit just and eternal condemnation after this life. And so he can say that these things happen unjustly who thinks that this mortal life alone exists, which we now lead, and does not believe in what is to come, which has been divinely announced. He will be meted out very heavy punishments for his persistence in sin and his lack of faith.

LXXXIII. On marriage[469]

If the Lord allows the renunciation of a spouse because of fornication alone[470] and does not forbid the renunciation of a pagan marriage,[471] it follows that paganism is equated with fornication. But it is clear that the Lord is making fornication the sole cause by way of exception when he speaks in the gospel of renouncing a spouse. It is not forbidden here for a pagan marriage to be renounced, however, because, although the Apostle advised in this matter that a believer should not renounce an unbelieving spouse who was willing to stay with him, he said, *I say* [*this*], *not the Lord* (1 Cor 7:12). Thus it should be understood that the Lord does not in fact order that [the unbelieving spouse] be renounced, lest the Apostle appear to give advice contrary to his [i.e., the Lord's] command, but he nonethe-

---

469. The issue discussed here briefly is treated at greater length in *The Lord's Sermon on the Mount* I,14,39-16,50; *Adulterous Marriages*, passim. Note also *Faith and Works* 16,28 = *Eight Questions of Dulcitius* 1,7.
470. See Mt 5:32.
471. See 1 Cor 7:15.

less allows it, so that a person is not under the obligation of law in this matter but may act freely of his own accord. But if anyone claims that the Lord admits fornication as the sole cause for renouncing a spouse—fornication being the word used in popular speech for engaging in unlawful copulation—he can say that the Lord, when he was speaking about this matter, said with respect to each of the two believers, husband and wife, that, if both are believers, it is permitted to neither to leave the other except because of fornication; paganism cannot be understood here since each of the two is a believer. For the Apostle seems to make this distinction when he says, *But to those who are married I command—not I but the Lord—the wife not to leave her husband; but if she departs she must remain unmarried or be reconciled to her husband* (1 Cor 7:10-11). Here it is understood that, even if there is only one cause whereby the abandonment of a marriage is permitted, the wife who has parted from her husband must stay married or, if she does not restrain herself, must be reconciled to her husband, who has either improved or should at least be tolerated, rather than marry someone else. But the next words say, *And a husband must not renounce his wife* (1 Cor 7:11), briefly applying the same formula to the husband that [the Apostle] enjoined with regard to the wife. After he has brought in these things from the Lord's command he continues as follows: *To the others I say, not the Lord, If any brother has an unbelieving wife, and she consents to live with him, he must not renounce her; and if a wife has an unbelieving husband, and he consents to live with her, she must not renounce her husband* (1 Cor 7:12-13). Here he gives it to be understood that the Lord was speaking of persons neither of whom would renounce the other if both were believers.

Miscellany of Questions in Response to Simplician

Introduction

In *Revisions* II,1,1 Augustine identifies the Simplician of this work's title as the bishop of Milan who succeeded Ambrose in 397. Paulinus of Milan, the author of Ambrose's biography, indicates that he was to all intents hand-picked by Ambrose himself for the position, despite his advanced age.[1] Simplician had been instrumental in the conversion to Catholic Christianity of the famous Roman rhetor Marius Victorinus in the 350s and in that of Ambrose as well in 374.[2] Years after his death, which occurred about 400, Augustine spoke of him in *The City of God*[3] as a "saintly old man" and used him as a reference regarding the doctrine of the Incarnation. It is clear that Simplician was a man capable of making an enduring impression. But, as one author observes, he is "better known by what we hear of his influence over others more famous than himself, than by any writings of his own," and this influence, "which was very great, was shewn more in drawing forth their thoughts than in recording his own."[4] Certainly Simplician's letter to Augustine, now lost, which he wrote sometime in the mid-390s in order to request answers to eight questions on scripture, succeeded in drawing forth from his addressee some thoughts of considerable consequence.

We know from *Revisions* II,1,1 that the *Miscellany of Questions in Response to Simplician* was the first work that Augustine wrote as a bishop. Since he was ordained to the episcopacy in Hippo in 395, the treatise is dated to the period 396-398. Not possessing Simplician's letter of request to Augustine, we know nothing other than what the *Miscellany* tells us of his questions. Their order, which Augustine probably did not alter, is slightly unusual in that the first book is devoted to two questions on the Epistle to the Romans while the second goes back to the Old Testament and covers six questions from the Books of Kings (specifically 1 and 2 Samuel and 1 Kings).

From Augustine's own treatment of the *Miscellany* in his *Revisions* it is obvious that the first book overshadows the second in importance: in particular he dwells at some length on the meaning of the first book's second ques-

---

1. See *Life of Saint Ambrose* 46.
2. See Augustine, *Confessions* VIII,2,3-5.
3. X,29.
4. William Smith and Henry Wace, eds., *A Dictionary of Christian Biography* IV (London: John Murray, 1887) 688, 689.

tion and calls attention to its significance, while he deals quite conventionally with the six questions contained in the second book. And the excerpts from *The Predestination of the Saints* and *The Gift of Perseverance* that are included in this volume make it even more evident how much of a turning point in his theological development the second question in the first book represents.

Augustine had already written two works on Paul's Epistle to the Romans —the *Commentary on Some Statements in the Epistle to the Romans* and the *Unfinished Commentary on the Epistle to the Romans*—and had interpreted three passages from it in his *Miscellany of Eighty-three Questions* 66-68 when, in response to Simplician's request, he once more addressed himself to this crucial New Testament text, which would in fact continue to preoccupy him for the rest of his life.

The topic of the first question is a lengthy passage from the seventh chapter of this epistle, in which Paul, while insisting that the Old Testament law is good, points to the interior struggle that its very existence inspires or at least throws into relief. Augustine follows Paul closely and, like him, emphasizes the law's goodness. Although Simplician had asked for an explanation of Rom 7:7-24, Augustine begins and ends his exegesis with the preceding verse, which distinguishes between the spirit and the letter of the law. This verse is the key to the lines that follow, for the spirit of the law is the love that frees from the letter that kills.

In the course of this first question, however, as in his *Commentary on Some Statements in the Epistle to the Romans,* Augustine takes two positions that he will later disavow.[5] The first position, which he states at the outset of the question,[6] is that Paul is speaking in this passage not in his own person but in that of someone under the law other than himself. Twenty years later, in his writings against the Pelagians, Augustine repudiates this view as characteristically Pelagian and asserts that Paul himself was no more removed from the struggle with sin than was any other human being.[7] The second of these two positions is that the very beginnings of the life of grace are within the scope of human ability. As Augustine says in I,1,11, "willing itself is in our power," even

---

5. See *Revisions* I,23,1.3, where he blames himself for having held in the *Commentary* the two views that will be discussed. The first, regarding the person of Paul, is in section 41 but is not glaring. The second, concerning grace, comes across very clearly in section 61: "It is ours to believe and to will, but [God's] to give to those who believe and will the faculty of doing good through the Holy Spirit."

6. See I,1,1. See also I,1,9.

7. See, e.g., *The Grace of Christ and Original Sin* I,39,43; *Answer to the Two Letters of the Pelagians* I,8,13-11,24.

though accomplishing the good that one has willed is impossible. And in I,1,14 he states: "What in fact is left to free choice (*libero arbitrio*) in this mortal life is not that a person may fulfill righteousness when he wants to but that by suppliant piety he may turn to him by whose gift he may be enabled to fulfill it." In other words a person may turn to God by his own initiative, although it is only God himself who gives the power to act rightly once the turn has been made. The notion that the human will could at least on occasion anticipate the action of divine grace was later espoused by John Cassian in the famous thirteenth of his twenty-four *Conferences* and came to be referred to as semi-Pelagianism or, more recently and perhaps more correctly, as semi-Augustinianism. Having initially entertained this notion in responding to Simplician's first question, Augustine goes on to reject it in his answer to the second.

In this question, at Simplician's request, Augustine interprets the text of Rom 9:10-29, in which Paul works out a theology of human merit and divine grace based upon the Genesis narrative of Jacob and Esau. Augustine tells us in *Revisions* II,1,2 that "in answering this question I in fact strove on behalf of the free choice of the human will, but God's grace conquered. . . . " He had not expected, he seems to be saying, that his response to Simplician would turn out as it did. Perhaps at the time, despite his account thirty years later in the *Revisions* and elsewhere, he did not even appreciate how greatly the second question was at variance with the first. For why, after having said what he did in the second, did he not immediately return to the first and revise it from the perspective of his new insight? In any event, only the conclusion that he came to in his second question could make sense of the words that Paul wrote else-where, which cast light on the text from Romans: *What do you possess that you have not received? But if you have received, why do you boast as if you had not received?* (1 Cor 4:7)

If the passage from Romans that Augustine had interpreted in the first part of the first book of his *Miscellany* left an opening for the human will to make a salvific decision without the assistance of grace, Paul's meditation on the story of Jacob and Esau allowed for no such opening. For Paul made it clear—at least to Augustine—that nothing good whatsoever, whether will or merit, whether faith or work, precedes the influence of grace. Neither Jacob nor Esau, who were conceived at the same moment and born only moments apart and who seemed to be morally identical, had done anything to merit that one should serve the other or that one should be loved by God and the other, in the hyperbolic language of scripture, be hated by him. The reason why one was chosen and the other rejected lies in God's mysterious purpose (*propositum*), which cannot be explained away by suggesting that he made his choice (*electio*) based on his foreknowledge of Jacob's future faith and good works and of Esau's future evil will and misdeeds: this would only make God's foreknowledge and grace dependent upon human activity.[8]

Once he has settled the issue of the absolute primacy of grace, Augustine turns to the distinction that is made in Mt 20:16: *Many are called, but few are chosen.* It is one thing for a person to be the object of God's call (*vocatio*) and quite another for him to be chosen. As Augustine would explain it, to have been called is to have been visited by grace, but not all who have been visited by grace are moved by it; only those who have been moved constitute "the few" who have been chosen. This is the basis for what theologians would later refer to as the distinction between "operating" or "sufficient" grace on the one hand and "cooperating" or "efficacious" grace on the other.

Why are some called and others not? And why, even among those who are called, are some chosen and others not? The response can only be that, since Adam's transgression, the whole human race is "a kind of single mass of sin (*una quaedam massa peccati*)," as Augustine describes it in I,2,16, and as such is deserving of punishment in its entirety. If God allows some of the "mass of sin" to pay the debt of punishment that is owed him but forgives the same debt of others, so that they may experience being made righteous (*justificatio*), no one may reasonably object. "It should be maintained with unflinching faith," he says in I,2,17, "that there is no injustice with God, who either forgives or exacts what is owed him, and neither can the one from whom he rightly exacts it complain of his injustice nor ought the other to whom it is forgiven boast of his own merits. For the one only repays what is owed while the other has only what he has received."

Augustine must find a place for free will here, and toward the end of the question he emphasizes it—only to cast its ultimate value into doubt by adding a qualification inspired by Rom 7:14: "The free choice of the will (*liberum voluntatis arbitrium*) counts for a great deal, to be sure. But what does it count for in those who have been sold under sin?" (I,2,21)

As he approaches his conclusion Augustine wonders rhetorically what sort of person might be chosen by God. Would it be someone whose sins were few and who had, in addition, useful learning, intelligence, mental refinement? Yet people with unlikely backgrounds, prostitutes and actors among others, are converted and enjoy a sudden inrush of virtue that could not have been anticipated. What preparation did Paul himself have for the conversion that conquered his "rabid, raging, blind will" (I,2,22)? And so Augustine's final

---

8. This was the solution to the problem of the interaction of grace and free will offered by Augustine's greatest predecessor, Origen. See his *On Prayer* 6,2-5.

words on the subject are an appeal to recognize the inscrutability of God's judgments and to join in the canticle of praise that should ever greet those judgments—an appeal to which, it may be noted, only the chosen would respond.

Having completed his discussion of these two passages from Romans, Augustine begins a second book in which he deals with Simplician's remaining six questions. In his brief preface he remarks that the matters that he will cover originate in books shrouded in mystery, and he thanks Simplician for not having asked him to provide a prophetic (i.e., allegorical) interpretation of the various texts, since that would have been much more difficult and taken much more time. Thus, although he does not refer to it as such here, he uses an approach that he would elsewhere call literal or historical in answering Simplician's questions about problems that arose from his reading of the Books of Kings.[9]

Each of the initial three questions of this second book concerns some aspect of the history of Saul. In the first and longest question Augustine makes use of two verses (1 S 10:10 and 16:14) that Simplician adduces, which describe Saul's experience of spirits, to discuss how prophecy occurs; how this gift may be possessed even by bad persons like Saul in his later years, in accordance with God's hidden plan; how God employs spirits both good and bad for his own purposes; and how it may be known whether a spirit to which scripture refers is either good or bad or is perhaps the Holy Spirit himself. The conclusion of the question alludes to the Donatists, whose ecclesiology was of grave concern to Augustine at the time.

The second question confronts the words attributed to God in 1 S 15:11: *I regret having made Saul king.* The Old Testament practice of describing God in human terms, and particularly as experiencing regret, had been discussed by Christians since at least the time of Marcion (died c. 154).[10] Here Augustine takes up this ancient issue, which he had already addressed—although with much greater brevity and much less detail—in the *Miscellany of Eighty-three Questions* 52, where he had commented on words also attributed to God in Gn 6:7: *I regret having made man.* The notion of regret in God immediately calls to mind the concept of God's foreknowledge, which seems to preclude regret. Yet, in light of God's knowledge, to which all things are present, his foreknowledge, which implies future things, also seems to be precluded. These observations lead Augustine to reflect in turn on the nature of human—including scriptural—language as it is applied to God. In order to

---

9. See *The Literal Meaning of Genesis* I,17,34 for a distinction between the allegorical (or prophetical) on the one hand and the historical (or literal) on the other.
10. See Tertullian, *Against Marcion* II,23-24.

be used in the context of the divine, words that describe human qualities such as anger, mercy, jealousy and even knowledge must be purged especially of their mutable elements. There are some praiseworthy human qualities, finally, such as modesty, which are not fittingly ascribed to God, whereas on the other hand certain blameworthy human qualities may actually be attributed to him. Taking all of this into consideration, then, Augustine says that regret, as well as knowledge and foreknowledge, may be spoken of in God.

Augustine next answers Simplician's question about the unclean spirit in the necromancer which, at the plea of Saul, caused a vision of Samuel to be seen, as narrated in 1 S 28:7-19. Here Augustine follows a tack similar to the one that he took in the first question of the second book, in which he allowed a certain place for the activity of evil spirits, or demons, subject to the constraints of the divine plan. Thus there is nothing untoward in the fact that an unclean spirit would have been able, with divine permission, to contact Samuel or even rouse his spirit from the regions of the dead. Perhaps, indeed, it was not his spirit itself that was seen but rather a phantasm which, as Augustine explains, could quite fittingly be referred to by Samuel's name. As for an unclean spirit speaking words of truth, scripture offers several examples of demons or evil spirits saying something truthful, although they often distort the truth with lies. Samuel's telling Saul that he would soon be with him might well be—although it need not be—an instance of demonic deception of this sort. Augustine's commentary on this strange episode was one of a long series of attempts by early Christian writers to make sense of the text, beginning with a brief mention in Justin's *Dialogue with Trypho* 105, in the middle of the second century, and including a controversial sermon by Origen in the early third century. Augustine himself discusses the matter again in *The Care to be Taken of the Dead* 18, and he repeats in its entirety what he wrote for Simplician in his *Eight Questions of Dulcitius* 6.

Simplician's fourth question, about the meaning of the words in 2 S 7:18, *King David went in and sat before the Lord,* offers Augustine the opportunity to say something about both where David may have prayed (either before the ark of the covenant or in a quiet, remote place or in the depths of his heart) and, more importantly, the physical disposition for prayer. Augustine's indifference here to the body's position during prayer (but see *The Care to Be Taken of the Dead* 5.7, where he acknowledges the value of bodily gesture while not insisting on its necessity) represents a break with tradition, since standing, usually with arms outstretched and facing towards the east, was the classic posture. Kneeling was a penitential practice, and sitting or lying down were generally frowned upon except in illness.[11]

The answer to Simplician's fifth question, which is about the intent of Elijah's words in 1 K 17:20, *O Lord, witness of this widow, since I am living with her you have acted badly by killing her son,* turns on how the phrase is spoken. If it is transformed into a question—"Have you acted badly by killing her son?"—to which a negative answer can be given, then it will take on a meaning that is more in conformity with Elijah's real understanding of how God would act and with how he would speak to God. For, in Augustine's view, which is implicit in his solution to the problem that Simplician poses, Elijah would neither believe that God would allow the widow's son to die (or worse, that God would kill him) nor permit himself to speak complainingly to God. The same sort of concern, which is about the correct pronunciation of scriptural questions so that they might yield orthodox responses, is taken up in *Teaching Christianity* III,3,6.

The *Revisions* does not mention a sixth question in the second book, but in some manuscripts a sixth was joined to the fifth. Having to do with 1 K 22:19-23, which tells of the lying spirit by which King Ahab was deceived, this question is a very brief representation for the most part of material already found in questions 1 and 3 of this second book.

---

11. See Tertullian, *On Prayer* 16-17.23; Origen, *On Prayer* 31,2-3; Cyprian, *On the Lord's Prayer* 20; Basil, *On the Spirit* 27,66.

Revisions II,1

1. The first two books that I worked on as a bishop are addressed to Simplician, bishop of the church of Milan, who succeeded the most blessed Ambrose, on a miscellany of questions. Two of them I took from the epistle of the apostle Paul to the Romans and put in the first book.

2. The first of these is on that which is written: *What, then, shall we say? That the law is sin?* (Rom 7:7) up to the point where it says: *Who will liberate me from the body of this death? The grace of God through Jesus Christ our Lord.* (Rom 7:24-25) In it I explained those words of the Apostle—*The law is spiritual, but I am fleshly* (Rom 7:14), and so forth, by which the flesh is shown to struggle with the spirit—in such a way as to see humankind described as being *still under the law* and *not yet under grace* (Rom 6:14). For it was not until long afterwards that I realized that those words can as well—and this is more likely—pertain to the spiritual person.

3. The second question in this book is from the place where it says: *As well as that* [i.e., Sarah's story], *there is also Rebecca, who from a single act of intercourse conceived from our father Isaac* (Rom 9:10) up to the point where it says: *Unless the Lord of hosts had left us offspring, we would have become like Sodom, and we would have been like Gomorrah* (Rom 9:29). In answering this question I in fact strove on behalf of the free choice of the human will, but God's grace conquered, and otherwise I would have been unable to arrive at understanding what the Apostle said with the most evident truthfulness, *For who sets you apart? What do you possess that you have not received? But if you have received, why do you boast as though you had not received?* (1 Cor 4:7) The martyr Cyprian also, wishing to demonstrate this, summed it all up with this very title when he said, "No one must boast of anything since nothing is ours."[1]

4. Other questions are treated in the second book and answered in accordance with whatever ability we had. They all concern the so-called Books of Kings.[2]

---

1. *Testimonies* 3,4, also referred to by Augustine in *The Predestination of the Saints* 3,7. Cyprian of Carthage (200?-258) is often cited by Augustine as an authority of high standing.
2. What Augustine knew as the four books of Kings are now divided into two books of Samuel and two books of Kings.

5. The first of these is on that which is written: *And the spirit of the Lord came over* Saul (1 S 10:10), inasmuch as it is said elsewhere: *And there was an evil spirit of the Lord in Saul* (1 S 16:14). In explaining this I said, "Although it is in a person's power to will something, nonetheless it is not in his power to be able to do it." I said this because we do not say that something is in our power unless what we will happens. The first and most important thing is the willing itself. Without any hiatus whatsoever the will itself is present when we will. But we also receive the power from on high for living a good life when our will is prepared by the Lord.[3]

6. The second question asks how it was said: *I regret having made Saul king* (1 S 15:11).

7. The third is on whether the unclean spirit that was in the necromancer was able to bring it about that Samuel was seen by Saul and spoke with him.[4]

8. The fourth is on that which is written: *King David went up and sat before the Lord* (2 S 7:18).

9. The fifth is on what Elijah said: *O Lord, witness of this widow, since I am living with her you have acted badly by killing her son* (1 K 17:20).

10. This work begins thus: "[In sending me your questions, Father Simplician, you have shown me] the clearly most welcome and delightful [honor]."

3. See Prv 8:35 LXX.
4. See 1 S 28:7-19.

The Predestination of the Saints 4,8[1]

You certainly see what I believed then about faith and works, even though I tried to emphasize the grace of God. I see now that such is the view that those brothers of ours hold because, as they did not make an effort to read my books, they did not advance along with me in them.[2] For, if they had made an effort, they would have found that question answered in accordance with the truth of the divine scriptures in the first of the two books that I wrote at the very beginning of my episcopate to Simplician of blessed memory, the bishop of the church of Milan and the successor of Saint Ambrose. Perhaps, on the other hand, they were unaware of them. In that case, see to it that they are aware of them. I spoke first of the first of those two books in the second book of the *Revisions*. My words there are as follows:

"The first two books that I worked on as bishop are addressed to Simplician, bishop of the church of Milan, who succeeded the most blessed Ambrose, on a miscellany of questions. Two of them I took from the epistle of the apostle Paul to the Romans and put in the first book.

"The first of these is on that which is written: *What, then, shall we say? That the law is sin?* (Rom 7:7) up to the point where it says: *Who will liberate me from the body of this death? The grace of God through Jesus Christ our Lord.* (Rom 7:24-25) In it I explained those words of the Apostle—*The law is spiritual, but I am fleshly* (Rom 7:14), and so forth, by which the flesh is shown to struggle with the spirit—in such a way as to see humankind described as being *still under the law* and *not yet under grace* (Rom 6:14). For it was not until long afterwards that I realized that those words can as well—and this is more likely—pertain to the spiritual person.

"The second question in this book is from the place where it says: *As well as that* [i.e., Sarah's story], *there is also Rebecca, who from a single act of intercourse conceived from our father Isaac* (Rom 9:10) up to the point where

---

1. Written in 428-429 and addressed to Prosper of Aquitaine and a certain Hilary.
2. The brothers to whom Augustine refers are monks of southern Gaul, centered in Marseilles, whose understanding of grace was the same as that of Augustine himself in the *Miscellany of Questions in Response to Simplician* I,1. Whereas he had revised his thinking, however, in the second half of the first book of the *Miscellany*, they still clung to a view of grace that on occasion allowed human initiative to precede divine action.

it says: *Unless the Lord of hosts had left us offspring, we would have become like Sodom, and we would have been like Gomorrah* (Rom 9:29). In answering this question I in fact strove on behalf of the free choice of the human will, but God's grace conquered, and otherwise I would have been unable to arrive at understanding what the Apostle said with the most evident truthfulness, *For who sets you apart? What do you possess that you have not received? But if you have received, why do you boast as though you had not received?* (1 Cor 4:7) The martyr Cyprian also, wishing to demonstrate this, summed it all with this very title when he said, 'No one must boast of anything since nothing is ours.' "[3]

This is why I previously said that, when I thought otherwise about this matter, I myself had also been convinced in particular by this testimony of the Apostle.[4] God revealed this to me in the answer to the question that, as I said, I was writing to Simplician. This testimony of the Apostle, then, when he said, in order to check human boastfulness, *For what do you possess that you have not received?* does not permit any of the faithful to say, "I have faith that I have not received." This utterly prideful response is completely checked by these words of the Apostle. Not even this much can be said: "Although I do not have a perfect faith, still I have the beginning of it, thanks to which I first believed in Christ." For the response here as well is: *But what do you possess that you have not received? But if you have received, why do you boast as though you had not received?*

---

3. *Testimonies* 3,4.
4. See 1 Cor 4:7.

The Gift of Perseverance 20,52; 21,55[1]

But they say, "It was not necessary that the hearts of so many persons of little intelligence be disturbed by the uncertainty of this kind of discussion, since the Catholic faith has been upheld no less advantageously over the course of so many years without this definition of predestination, occasionally against others but especially against the Pelagians, thanks to the books that we already have, both by Catholics and by others."[2] I am quite surprised that they say this and do not consider that those books of ours (to say nothing here of others) were written and published before the Pelagians came upon the scene, and that they do not notice in how many places in them, without our even having been aware of it, we cut to pieces the future Pelagian heresy by extolling the grace by which God frees us from our wicked errors and behavior, which he does in accordance with his own gratuitous mercy and apart from any antecedent merits of ours. I began to understand this more fully in the treatise that I wrote at the beginning of my episcopate to Simplician of blessed memory, the bishop of Milan, when I realized and affirmed that the beginning of faith is God's gift....

Let them see, I say, whether in the final sections of the first book of the two that I wrote at the beginning of my episcopate, before the Pelagian heresy came upon the scene, to Simplician, the bishop of Milan, anything remains that might call into doubt the fact that God's grace is not given in accordance with our merits; whether I did not make it clear that even the beginning of faith is God's gift; and whether, from what was said there, it does not plainly follow—even if it is not openly expressed—that final perseverance is not given except by him who has predestined us for his kingdom and glory.

---

1. Written in 428-429 as a sequel to *The Predestination of the Saints* and likewise addressed to Prosper and Hilary.
2. Augustine is quoting a letter from Hilary to him, which is included in Augustine's own correspondence. See Letter 226,8. Hilary is in turn citing the position of those who say that Augustine's definition of predestination is confusing and inopportune. Augustine's response in both excerpts from *The Gift of Perseverance* that are reproduced here is that his theology of grace was ultimately not reactive to Pelagius (whose understanding of grace was diametrically opposed to Augustine's) but had already existed in all its principal elements, implicitly including final perseverance and predestination, by the time of the composition of the *Miscellany of Questions in Response to Simplician* I,2, well before Pelagius came to Augustine's attention. In her *Rethinking Augustine's Early Theology: An Argument for Continuity* (Oxford 2006) 142-154, esp. 150-154, Carol Harrison argues that Augustine's characteristic theology of grace predated even the *Miscellany* and that in I,1 he was merely experimenting with the notion of grace that he presents there, to see whether he could maintain some small role for human freedom. See Chad Tyler Gerber's sympathetic but critical review of Harrison's thesis in *Journal of Early Christian Studies* 15 (2007) 120-122.

Letter 37, to Simplician

To Simplician, his most blessed lord and father, who deserves to be reverently embraced with most sincere love, Augustine sends greetings in the Lord.

1. I have received the letter that was sent at the behest of Your Holiness. It is full of pleasant joys because I hold a place in your memory and you love me as you always have, and because whatever gifts of his the Lord has deigned to confer upon me—not by my own merits but by his mercy—are a source of gladness for you. In it, my most blessed Lord, who deserves to be reverently embraced, I drank from your most kindly heart a not unexpected and new fatherly feeling towards me, but I claimed it as something evidently proven and known.

2. But how is it that our literary exertions, which have engaged our efforts in the writing of some books, have had such good fortune as to be read by Your Honor? It must be that the Lord, to whom I have submitted my soul, wished my troubles to be assuaged and to release me from the concern, which is my ineluctable preoccupation in such labors, that, being perhaps somewhat ignorant and rash, I might cause offense anywhere even while on the most level plain of truth. For if my writing pleases you, I know whom [else] it pleases, since I know who dwells within you. Indeed, the same one who distributes and bestows every spiritual gift has confirmed my obedience through your judgment. For whatever those writings possess that is worthy of your admiration, it was God who, in my ministry, said, "Let it be done," and it was done, but it was in your approval that God saw that it was good.[1]

3. Even if I were hindered by my own obtuseness and did not understand the questions that you deigned to command me to elucidate, I would approach them with the assistance of your merits. This alone I seek—that you beseech God on behalf of my weakness and, whether in these matters in which you have desired to occupy me in kindly and fatherly fashion or in others when something of ours may perhaps fall into your holy hands, that, inasmuch as I recognize my own errors as well as I do God's gifts, you not only exercise a reader's care but also provide a critic's judgment.

---

1. See Gn 1:3-4.

First Book

In sending me your questions, Father Simplician, you have shown me the clearly most welcome and delightful honor, and I would consider myself not only insolent but also ungrateful if I did not attempt to reply to them. And in fact the things that you proposed should be answered with regard to the apostle Paul had already been discussed by us to some degree or other and had been committed to writing.[1] But still I am not satisfied with my previous research and explanation, since I may have negligently overlooked something pertinent, and I have gone through the Apostle's words and the sense of his statements more carefully and attentively. For, if it were a quick and easy matter to understand them, you would not consider that they should be investigated.

First Question

1,1. You have wished us to elucidate the first question—from the place where it is written: *What, then, shall we say? That the law is sin? Of course not!* (Rom 7:7) up to the place where it says: *The law, then, is good for me when I am willing* (Rom 7:21), and I believe what remains as far as: *Wretched man that I am! Who will liberate me from the body of this death? The grace of God through Jesus Christ our Lord.* (Rom 7:24-25) In this text it seems to me that the Apostle has put himself in the place of someone who is under the law, whose words he speaks in his own person. He had said a little before, *We are rid of the law, in which imprisonment we were dead, so that thus we may serve in the new way of the spirit and not in the old way of the letter* (Rom 7:6). But because he could thus seem as it were to have rebuked the law by these words, he immediately added, *What, then, shall we say? That the law is sin? Of course not! But I did not know sin except through the law, for I did not know about covetousness* (concupiscentiam) *except that the law said, You shall not covet* (concupisces). (Rom 7:7)

1,2. Here again there is something striking: If the law is not sin but implants sin, it is nonetheless censured in these words. This is why it must be understood that the law was given not that sin might be instilled nor that it might be extirpated but only that it might be made manifest. In this way it would make the human soul, seemingly secure in its innocence, guilty by the very manifestation of sin so that, inasmuch as sin could not be conquered apart from the

---

1. Augustine is undoubtedly referring to his *Commentary on Some Statements in the Letter to the Romans* 37-46, 60-65 and to the *Miscellany of Eighty-three Questions* 66, 68.

grace of God, [the soul] would be turned by its uneasy awareness of guilt to a receptivity to grace. And so he does not say, "I did not commit sin except through the law," but, *I did not know sin except through the law.* Nor, again, does he say, "For I did not have covetousness except that the law said, You shall not covet," but, *I did not know about covetousness except that the law said, You shall not covet.* From this it is clear that covetousness was not instilled by the law but made manifest by it.

1,3. But the consequence was that, since grace had not yet been received and the human person could not resist covetousness, it was even increased, because this covetousness grew even more, since, when by acting even against the law it is joined to the offense of transgression (*crimine praevaricationis*), it takes on greater strength than it would have done had there been no law forbidding it. And so [Paul] adds what follows: *But, having seized the occasion, sin brought about every kind of covetousness in me through the commandment* (Rom 7:8). For it also existed before the law, but it was not all-encompassing when the offense of transgression was still lacking. Hence he says in another place, *For where there is no law there is no transgression* (Rom 4:15).

1,4. To this he adds, *For without the law sin was dead* (Rom 7:8). It was as though he said that it was hidden—that is, it was thought to be dead. Shortly thereafter he says more clearly, *But once I lived without the law* (Rom 7:9)—that is, I was unafraid of death from sin because it had not appeared when there was no law. *But with the coming of the commandment sin came back to life* (Rom 7:9)—that is, it made its appearance. *But I died* (Rom 7:10)—that is, I knew that I was dead for the reason that the guilt of transgression threatens me with the certain punishment of death. Clearly, when he said, *Sin came back to life with the coming of the commandment*, he indicated in this way that sin once lived—that is, that it was known, in my opinion, at the transgression of the first man, because he himself had also received a commandment.[2] For in another place he says, *But the woman, once seduced, fell into transgression* (1 Tm 2:14); and again, *In the likeness of the transgression of Adam, who is the form of the one who is to come* (Rom 5:14). For unless [sin] was once alive it cannot come back to life. But it was dead—that is, hidden—when mortal men who were born without the law's commandment lived in pursuit of the covetous desires of the flesh without any knowledge, because there was no prohibition. Therefore he says, *Once I lived without the law*, and in this way he demonstrates that he is speaking not just for himself but for human beings in general. *But with the coming of the commandment sin came back to life. But I died, and the commandment, which was for*

---

2. See Gn 2:16-17.

life, turned out to be death for me. (Rom 7:9-10) For if one is obedient to the commandment, life is certainly there. But it turns out to be death as long as the commandment is contravened, so that it not only becomes sin, which was committed even before the commandment, but becomes it in a more widespread and pernicious fashion, such that sin is now committed by a knowing transgressor.

1,5. *For,* he says, *having seized the occasion, sin deceived me through the commandment, and in this way it killed me* (Rom 7:11). Sin, using the law unlawfully, grew more desirable because of its prohibition and became sweeter, and so it deceived. For deception is a sweetness that is followed by more and greater bitter punishments. Since, then, it is quite reasonably admitted by those who are not yet in possession of spiritual grace that there is a prohibition, sin deceives by a false sweetness; but because the guilt of transgression is also present, it kills.

1,6. *And so, to be sure, the law is holy, and the commandment is holy and righteous and good* (Rom 7:12), for it enjoins what should be enjoined and prohibits what should be prohibited. *Has, then, what is good become death for me? Of course not!* (Rom 7:13) There is vice in using a thing badly, not in the commandment itself, which is good, *because the law is good if a person uses it lawfully* (1 Tm 1:8). But a person uses the law badly if he does not submit to God with devout humility so that the law may be fulfilled through grace. And so he who does not use it lawfully receives it for no other purpose than that his sin, which before its prohibition lay hidden, may begin to appear through transgression, and to appear without limit, because now it is not only a matter of committing sin but also of contravening the commandment. He continues, therefore, and adds, *But sin, in order to appear as sin, worked death in me through what was good, so that the sinner and the sin might, thanks to the commandment, be without limit* (Rom 7:13). From this it is evident what he meant when he said previously, *For without the law sin was dead,* not because it did not exist but because it was not manifest, and how it was said, *Sin came back to life,* not that it might be just what it was before the law but that it might be made manifest inasmuch as it contravened the law, since he says in this place, *But sin, in order to appear as sin, worked death in me through what was good*; for he does not say "in order to be sin" but *in order to appear as sin.*

1,7. Then he gives the reason why this is so: *For we know that the law is spiritual, but I am fleshly* (Rom 7:14). In saying this he clearly indicates that the law cannot be fulfilled except by spiritual persons, who do not become such apart from grace. For a person becomes that much more conformed to the spiritual law—that is, he rises all the more to a spiritual disposition—the more he fulfills it, because he takes that much more delight in it when he is no longer worn down by its burdensomeness but energized by its light. For the precept of the Lord is lucid and enlightens the eyes,[3] and the law of the Lord is unsullied, transforming souls.[4] By grace he forgives sins and pours out the spirit of love, which is why practicing righteousness is no longer burdensome but indeed joyful.

Although he plainly said, *But I am fleshly*, what he meant by *fleshly* must be clarified. For even those who are already living in grace, who have already been redeemed by the blood of the Lord[5] and renewed by faith, are referred to as fleshly to a certain degree. To them the same Apostle says, *And I, brothers, have not been able to speak to you as to spiritual persons but as to fleshly ones. Since you are little children in Christ, I have given you milk to drink, not solid food.* (1 Cor 3:2) By saying this he shows that those who were little children in Christ and had to be given milk to drink have in fact already been reborn through grace, and yet he still refers to them as fleshly. The person who is not yet under grace but under the law is fleshly in that he has not yet been reborn from sin but is *sold under sin* (Rom 7:14), because he willingly accepts the sweet price of the deathly pleasure by which he is being deceived and also delights in contravening the law, since the less it is allowed the more attractive it is.[6] This sweetness he cannot enjoy as the price of his condition unless he serves his appetites like a bought slave. For he who is prohibited and knows that he is justly prohibited and nonetheless does the deed is aware that he is the slave of the desire that masters him.

1,8. *For,* he says, *I know not what I do* (Rom 7:15). He does not say *I know not* here as though he did not know that he was sinning. For that contradicts what he said [previously], *But sin, in order to appear as sin, worked death in me through what was good*, and what came before that, *I did not know sin except through the law.* For how is it made manifest or how did he know what he did not know? But he said this in the same way that the Lord will say to the wicked, *I do not know you* (Mt 25:12). For there is nothing that is hidden from God, since *the face of the Lord is over those who do wickedness, to destroy their memory from the earth* (Ps 34:16). But we are sometimes said not to know what we do not approve of. It is in that sense, then, that he says, *I know not what I do*—that is, "I do not approve of it." This he shows in what follows, when he says, *For I do not do what I want, but I do what I hate* (Rom 7:15). When he says, *I hate,* it means "I do not know," because, regarding those to

---

3. See Ps 19:8.
4. See Ps 19:7.
5. See 1 Pt 1:18-19.
6. "Since the less it is allowed the more attractive it is": *cum tanto magis libet, quanto minus licet.*

whom the Lord will say, *I do not know you*, it is also said to him, *Lord, you hate all who do evil* (Ps 5:5).

1,9. *But if I do what I do not want, I consent to the law because it is good* (Rom 7:16), for neither does the law want it, since the law forbids it. He consents to the law, then, not insofar as he does what it prohibits but insofar as he does not want to do what he does. He is overcome, not yet having been liberated by grace, although through the law he already both knows that he is doing wrong and does not want to do it. But the next thing that he says is: *It is no longer I that do it but the sin that dwells in me* (Rom 7:17). He does not say this because he does not consent to committing sin, although he consents to the law that disapproves of it (for he is still speaking in the person of someone who is living under the law and not yet under grace,[7] who is actually drawn to do wrong under the mastery of covetousness and by the deceptive sweetness of forbidden sin, although he disapproves of this by reason of his knowledge of the law), but he says, *It is not I that do it*, because he has been overcome. It is in fact desire (*cupiditas*) that does it, to whose victory he surrenders. But it is grace that sees to it that there is no surrender and that a person's mind is fortified against desire. Of this he will speak later.

1,10. *For I know*, he says, *that good does not dwell in me—that is, in my flesh* (Rom 7:18). As regards what he knows, he consents to the law; but as regards what he does, he surrenders to sin. Perhaps someone would ask, "Whence comes it that he says that good does not dwell in him, meaning that sin does?" What would the answer be except that it comes from the passing on of mortality and the constant repetition of sensual pleasure? The former derives from the punishment for the original sin,[8] the latter from the punishment for repeated sin; with the former we are born into this life, while the latter we augment over the course of our lives. These two things, which we may call nature and habit, create a very strong and unconquerable covetousness once they have been joined together, which [Paul] refers to as sin and says dwells in his flesh—that is, possesses a certain sovereignty and rule, as it were. This is why the psalm says, *I have preferred to be cast down in the house of the Lord than to dwell in the tents of sinners* (Ps 84:10)—as though he who has been cast down, wherever that may be, is not dwelling, although he is there. And so he suggests that "dwelling" is to be understood with a note of mastery. But if

---

7. In the *Revisions* Augustine qualifies his position here by saying: "It was not until long afterwards that I realized that those words can as well—and this is more likely—pertain to the spiritual person."
8. "The original sin": *originalis peccati*. This is Augustine's first use of a term that would probably be more closely associated with him than any other. It is translated here with the article "the" in order both to emphasize that it is in fact Adam's sin in its origin and to suggest that it is not yet a popular expression, which not using the article might connote.

what he says in another place should happen to us through grace—that sin should not rule in our mortal body to make us obey its desires[9]—it is no longer properly said to dwell there.

1,11. *For to will the good is close at hand, but the doing of it is not* (Rom 7:18). To those who do not correctly understand he seems with these words to be abolishing free choice. But how can he be abolishing it when he says, *To will is close at hand*? For willing itself is in our power since it is close at hand, but the fact that doing the good is not in our power is part of the deserts of the original sin. For nothing remains of this first nature of humankind but the punishment of sin, through which mortality itself has become a kind of second nature, and it is from this that the grace of the creator frees those who have submitted to him through faith. But those are the words of a person who lives now under the law and not under grace. For he who is not yet under grace does not do the good that he wants but he does the evil that he does not want,[10] thanks to the domination of covetousness, which is strengthened not only by the bond of mortality but also by the millstone of habit. But if he does what he does not want, it is no longer he that does it but the sin that dwells in him, as was stated and explained previously.

1,12. *I find it, therefore, to be a law,* he says, *that, when I want to do good, evil is close at hand* (Rom 7:21)—that is, I find the law to be a good thing for me when I want to do what the law maintains, because evil is close at hand and hence easy to do, since what he said previously, *To will is close at hand*, he said with reference to its being easy. For what is easier for a person living under the law than to will good and to do evil? For the one he wills without difficulty, although he does not do with such ease what he easily wills, and the other, which he hates, he easily possesses, although he would not will it. It is like someone who, once having been pushed, easily continues to fall, even though he does not want to and hates what is happening. I have said this in light of the expression that he uses—*is close at hand.* A person who is living under [the law] and who has not yet been freed by grace bears witness that the law is good. It certainly bears witness to him, inasmuch as he restrains himself from contravening the law and finds that it is a good thing for him even when he wills to do what it enjoins and is unable to do so because covetousness has overwhelmed him. And thus he sees that he is caught up in the guilt of transgression, so that he must beg for the grace of the liberator.

1,13. *For I am delighted,* he says, *with the law of God according to the inner person* (Rom 7:22), and certainly with the law that says, *You shall not*

---

9. See Rom 6:14, 12.
10. See Rom 7:19.

covet. But, he says, *I see another law in my members, opposing the law of my mind and making me captive under the law of sin that is in my members* (Rom 7:23). He refers to the law in his members as the very burden of mortality, under which we groan who are burdened by it.[11] *For the body that is corruptible weighs down the soul* (Wis 9:15). Because of this it often happens that what is impermissible is ineluctably delightful. Therefore he refers to the law as an oppressive and burdensome weight, because it was assigned as punishment by divine judgment and imposed by him who warned the man when he said, *On the day you eat you shall die* (Gn 2:17). This law opposes the law of the mind, which says, *You shall not covet*, and in which one delights according to the inner person. And, before someone is under grace, [this law] opposes [the law of the mind] in such a way that it also holds [its subject] captive under the law of sin—that is, under itself. For, when he says *that is in my members* (Rom 7:23), he indicates that this is the same as that of which he had spoken earlier: *I see another law in my members.*

1,14. But all of this is said in order to make it clear to humankind, which is held captive, that it must not presume on its own strength. This is why [Paul] reproved the Jews who boasted proudly of what they thought were their works of the law, although they were drawn by covetousness to whatever is unlawful, since the law about which they boasted says, *You shall not covet.* Humankind vanquished, condemned and held captive, which even after having received the law is not victorious but rather a transgressor, must humbly say, must humbly cry out, *Wretched man that I am, who will liberate me from the body of this death? The grace of God through Jesus Christ our Lord.* (Rom 7:24-25) What in fact is left to free choice in this mortal life is not that a person may fulfill righteousness when he wants to but that by suppliant piety he may turn to him by whose gift he may be enabled to fulfill it.

1,15. In respect to this whole ensemble of the apostolic text that we have been treating, whoever holds that the Apostle thought that the law was bad—because he says, *The law entered in so that wrongdoing might abound* (Rom 5:20); and, *The administering of death written in letters of stone* (2 Cor 3:7); and, *The power of sin is the law* (1 Cor 15:56); and, *You have died to the law through the body of Christ, so that you might belong to another, who has risen from the dead* (Rom 7:4); and, *The passions of sin, which are through the law, were at work in our members, so that they bore fruit for death, but now we are rid of the law, in which imprisonment we were dead, so that thus we may serve in the new way of the spirit and not in the old way of the letter* (Rom 7:5-6); and other things along these lines which we have found

---

11. See 2 Cor 5:4.

that the Apostle said—should consider that these things were said in view of the fact that the law increases covetousness because of its prohibitions and, because of transgression, binds the guilty person, since it enjoins what human beings in their weakness cannot fulfill unless in piety they turn to God's grace. And for that reason those over whom it rules are said to be under it; it rules over those whom it punishes, and it punishes all transgressors. But those who have received the law transgress it unless through grace they arrive at the possibility of doing what it enjoins. Thus it comes about that it no longer rules over those who were at one time condemned under the fear of it but who now, under grace, are fulfilling it through love.

1,16. For if what was said causes anyone to think that the Apostle found fault with the law, what are we to make of his saying, *For I am delighted with the law of God according to the inner person?* In saying this he certainly praises the law. When those persons hear this, they reply that in this passage the Apostle is referring to another law—that is, the law of Christ, not that which was given to the Jews. If we ask them, then, what law he is speaking about when he says, *The law entered in so that wrongdoing might abound,* they will doubtlessly reply, "That which the Jews received." See, then, whether that is the one of which it is said, *Having seized the occasion, sin brought about every kind of covetousness in me through the commandment.* What does *brought about every kind of covetousness in me* mean if not *so that wrongdoing might abound?* See also whether these words are consistent: *So that the sinner and the sin might, thanks to the commandment, be without limit.* For what this means is that sin might become limitless—that is, that sin might abound. If we have shown, then, that the commandment is good from which, *having seized the occasion, sin has brought about every kind of covetousness* so that it might be without limit, let us also show that the law is good which *entered in so that wrongdoing might abound*—that is, so that sin might bring about every kind of covetousness and become limitless. Let them listen to the same Apostle, then, when he says, *What, then, shall we say? That the law is sin? Of course not!* This, they say, was said of the law of Christ; this refers to the law of grace. Let them respond, therefore, as to how they understand what follows: *But I did not know sin except through the law, for I did not know about covetousness except that the law said, You shall not covet. But, having seized the occasion, sin brought about every kind of covetousness in me through the commandment.* The very phrasing makes it clear enough about what law he said, *That the law is sin? Of course not!* He was speaking, namely, about that [law] through whose commandment an occasion was given to sin, so that it might bring about every kind of covetousness—about that [law], therefore, which entered in so that wrongdoing might abound, and which they think is evil. But what is plainer than what he says a little later: *And so, to be sure, the law is holy, and the commandment is holy and righteous and good*? This, they say again, was said not of the law that was given to the Jews but of the gospel. For so unspeakably blind is this perversity of the Manicheans![12] For they pay no heed to what follows, which is very plain and clear: *Has, then, what is good become death for me? Of course not! But sin, in order to appear as sin, worked death in me through what was good, so that the sinner and the sin might, thanks to the commandment, be without limit*—that is, through the holy and righteous and good commandment, which nonetheless entered in so that sin might abound, that is, so that it might be without limit.

1,17. Why, then, if the law is good, is it referred to *as the administering of death*? Because *sin, in order to appear as sin, worked death in me through what was good*. You should not be surprised when it is said of the very preaching of the gospel: *We are the good odor of Christ in those who are to be saved and in those who are perishing—for some, indeed, the odor of life unto life, while for others the odor of death unto death* (2 Cor 2:15-16). For in regard to the Jews, for whom it was even written in stone because of their hardness, the law is called *the administering of death*, but not in regard to us, who fulfill the law through love. *For love is the fulfillment of the law* (Rom 13:10). For the law itself, which is written in letters of stone, says, *You shall not commit adultery, you shall not kill, you shall not steal, you shall not covet* (Ex 20:14.13.15.17), and so forth. The Apostle states that this law is fulfilled through love when he says, *The one who loves his fellow human being has fulfilled the law. For you shall not commit adultery, you shall not kill, you shall not steal, you shall not covet, and any other commandment that there is, is summed up in this phrase: You shall love your neighbor as yourself* (Rom 13:8-9), because this too is written in the same law.

Why is the law the power of sin if the law is good? Because sin worked death through what was good, so that it might be without limit—that is, so that it might acquire still greater strength from transgression.

Why have we died to the law through the body of Christ if the law is good? Because we have died to a law that was dominating us and were liberated from that disposition which the law punishes and condemns. For

---

12. Here it becomes clear that the Manicheans are the ones who are denying that the Old Testament law is good and who, when Paul refers to the law's goodness, claim that he means the law of Christ. The Manicheans, whose name comes from the Persian religious figure Mani (216-277), rejected the Old Testament in its entirety. Much of Augustine's earliest polemical work is directed against them. On the point that he makes here see also the *Answer to Faustus, a Manichean* XV,8; XIX,7. (The Manichean Faustus' view of the law is given in his own words *ibid.* XIX,1-6.)

the law is very commonly referred to in the context of warning and instilling fear and punishing. And so the same precept is law for the fearful and grace for those who love. Hence it says in the gospel, *The law was given through Moses, but grace and truth were brought about through Jesus Christ* (Jn 1:17). This very same law, which was given through Moses in order to inspire fear, became grace and truth through Jesus Christ in order to be fulfilled. Therefore it was said, *You died to the law* (Rom 7:4) as though to say that you died to the law's punishment, *through the body of Christ* (Rom 7:4), through which the sins have been forgiven that were under the constraint deserving of lawful punishment.

Why do the passions of sin stem from the law if the law is good? Because he [i.e., the Apostle] wanted them to be understood here as the passions of sin that have already been frequently spoken of, an increase of covetousness resulting from prohibition and the guilt of punishment resulting from transgression —that is, because *it worked death through what was good, so that the sinner and the sin might, thanks to the commandment, be without limit.*

Why *are we freed from the law, in which imprisonment we were dead, so that thus we may serve in the new way of the spirit and not in the old way of the letter,* if the law is good? Because the law *is* the letter for those who do not fulfill it through the spirit of love, which is the domain of the New Testament. And so those who have died to sin are freed from the letter in which are imprisoned the wrongdoers who do not fulfill what is written. For what is the law other than a letter, pure and simple, for those who know how to read it but are unable to fulfill it? For it is not unknown to those for whom it was written, but, inasmuch as it is known only to the extent that it is read as a piece of writing and not to the extent that it is fulfilled as an object of love, it is nothing but a letter for such persons. This letter is not a help to its readers but rather a witness against sinners. Those who are renewed through the spirit, then, are freed from its condemnation so that they are no longer bound to the punishment of the letter but are united to its understanding through righteousness. This is why it says, *The letter kills, but the spirit gives life* (2 Cor 3:6). For the law, if it is only read but not understood and not fulfilled, does indeed kill; it is then that it is called "the letter." But the spirit gives life, because the fullness of the law is the love which *has been poured into our hearts through the Holy Spirit who has been given to us* (Rom 5:5).

Second Question

2,1. But now, in my opinion, it is time to pass on to the second question that you posed. It is a matter of discussing the entire text from where it is written: *As well as that* [i.e., Sarah's story], *there is also Rebecca, who from a single act of intercourse conceived from our father Isaac. For when they were not yet born and had not done anything good or evil* (Rom 9:10-11) up to the point where it is written: *Unless the Lord of hosts had left us offspring, we would have become like Sodom, and we would have been like Gomorrah* (Rom 9:29). This is exceedingly obscure. But I know for a certainty that, because of your feelings in my regard, you could not request me to interpret these words unless you had interceded with the Lord that I could do so. Having been reassured by this help, I proceed.

2,2. And in the first place I shall seize upon the Apostle's main thought, which is evident throughout the epistle that I am going to consider. Now this is that no one should boast of the merits of his works. The Israelites dared to boast of them on the grounds that they had observed the law that had been given to them[13] and so had received the grace of the gospel as though it were due them for their merits, because they observed the law. Hence they did not want that same grace to be given to the gentiles, whom they saw as unworthy, unless they took up the Jewish sacraments[14] (which is an issue that, when it arose, was dealt with in the Acts of the Apostles[15]). For they did not understand that the grace of the gospel is not dependent on works; otherwise grace is no longer grace.[16]

And in many places [the Apostle] frequently testifies that grace comes before works not in order to do away with works but in order to show that works do not precede but follow upon faith—in other words, so that a person may not think that he has obtained grace because he has done good works but that he cannot do good works unless he has obtained grace through faith.[17] But a person begins to obtain grace when he begins to believe in God, having been moved to faith by either an internal or an external urging.[18]

Now it is important to know if grace is poured out more fully and more manifestly at certain moments of time or at the celebration of the sacraments. For catechumens do not lack belief; if they do, then Cornelius, to whom an

---

13. See Rom 2:17-23.
14. On the broad understanding of the term "sacrament" in Christian antiquity see p. 50, note 43. Here of course the word refers to Old Testament rituals and observances.
15. See Acts 15.
16. See Rom 11:6.
17. See Rom 5:2.
18. See Rom 10:14.

angel was sent, did not believe in God when he was making himself worthy through his almsgiving and prayers.[19] But in no way would he have done these things unless he had believed beforehand; in no way would he have believed, however, unless he had been called by secret urgings that his mind or spirit could perceive or by more evident ones coming to him through his bodily senses.[20] But in certain persons, like catechumens and like Cornelius himself, before he was incorporated into the Church by participating in the sacraments, the grace of faith, as great as it is, is insufficient to attain to the kingdom of heaven;[21] but in others it so great that they are already counted as belonging to the body of Christ and to the holy temple of God. *For the temple of God is holy,* [the Apostle] says, *which you are* (1 Cor 3:17). And the Lord himself says, *Unless a person has been born of water and the Holy Spirit he shall not enter the kingdom of heaven* (Jn 3:5). Certain beginnings of faith, therefore, are like conceptions. Yet, in order to arrive at eternal life, one must not only be conceived but also be born. But none of this is without the grace of God's mercy, because even if works that are good follow that grace, as they say, they do not precede it.

2,3. The Apostle wishes to emphasize this, because as he says in another passage, *It is not because of us but is a gift of God; it is not because of works, lest perhaps anyone be inflated* (Eph 2:8-9). Therefore he provided proof by referring to those who had not yet been born. For no one could say that Jacob, who was not yet born, had been meritorious before God on account of his works, so that it might be said as divinely inspired: *The older shall serve the younger* (Gn 25:23). Therefore he says, *It was not only Isaac who was promised* (Rom 9:10) when it was said, *At this time I will come and Sarah shall have a son* (Rom 9:9). [Isaac] had certainly not been meritorious before God on account of any works so that a promise would be made that he was to be born, so that the seed of Abraham would be named in Isaac[22]—that is, that they would share in the lot of the saints, which is in Christ, understanding that they were children of the promise[23] and not boasting of their own merits but attributing the fact that they were co-heirs in Christ[24] to the grace of their calling.[25] For, when it was promised that they would exist, they who did not yet exist had been deserving of nothing. [And he continues:] *But also Rebecca, who from a single act of intercourse conceived from our father Isaac*

---

19. See Acts 10:1-4.
20. See Rom 10:14.
21. See Acts 10:44-48.
22. See Rom 9:7.
23. See Rom 9:8.
24. See Rom 8:17.
25. See Rom 9:12.

(Rom 9:10). He says with great precision, *from a single act of intercourse.* For it was twins who were conceived. Otherwise it might be attributed to the father's merits, and someone could say that such and such a son was born because his father was influenced in a particular way at the time when he sowed him in his mother's womb, or his mother was influenced in a particular way when she conceived him. For he sowed both at the same time and she conceived both at the same time. [Paul] says *from a single act of intercourse* in order to emphasize that there is no room for astrologers here or rather for those whom they call *genethliaci,* who make conjectures about behaviors and destinies on the basis of people's birthdays.[26] For they have no idea what to say when the one conception occurs at one precise moment, when the heavens and the stars are arranged in a particular way so that no differences whatsoever in this respect can be discerned with regard to either of the twins, and [yet] there is a great difference between them. And, if they wish, they can easily see that the oracles which they sell to wretched people come not from a familiarity with any scientific theory but from fortuitous inklings.[27]

But (to speak rather of the matter at hand) these things are recalled for the purpose of smashing and overturning the pride of persons who are unthankful for the grace of God and who dare to boast of their own merits. *For when they were not yet born and had not done anything good or evil, not because of their works but because of him who called them it was said to her that the older would serve the younger* (Rom 9:11-12). Grace, then, comes from him who calls, but good works come as a consequence from him who receives grace; they do not beget grace but are begotten by grace. For a fire does not heat *in order* to burn but *because* it burns, nor does a wheel run well *in order* to be round but *because* it is round. Thus no one does good works *in order* to receive grace but *because* he has received it. For how can a person live righteously who has not been made righteous? In the same way that a person cannot live holily who has not been made holy or live at all if he has not been given life. It is grace that makes righteous,[28] so that one who has been made righteous can live righteously. Grace, therefore, comes first, and good works are second. As [the Apostle] says in another passage, *To a person who works, wages are owed not as a grace but as a debt* (Rom 4:4). A case in point would be if immortality following upon good works were demanded as a debt. In the words of the same

---

26. *Genethliaci:* the Latin form of a Greek word meaning "pertaining to the day of one's birth."

27. The case of twins with different life histories was a classic objection to the claims of astrologers that the arrangement of the heavens at the time of conception or birth was determinative of a person's life course. Augustine, who emphasizes the single moment of Jacob and Esau's conception, often avails himself of this objection. See *Confessions* VII,6,8-10; *Teaching Christianity* II,22,33-34; *The City of God* V,1-6.

28. See Rom 3:24.

[Apostle]: *I have fought the good fight, I have finished the race, I have kept the faith. For the rest there remains for me a crown of righteousness which the Lord, the just judge, will render me on that day.* (2 Tm 4:7-8) For, perhaps because he said *will render* (*reddet*), it is a matter of debt. But when he ascended on high and led captivity captive, he did not render but *gave* (*dedit*) gifts to men.[29] For how would the Apostle himself presume that a debt, as it were, was being rendered to him if he had not first received a grace that was not owed him, by which, as one who had been made righteous,[30] he could fight the good fight? For he had been a blasphemer and a persecutor and a reviler, but he obtained mercy, as he himself testifies,[31] believing in him who makes righteous not the one who is upright but the one who is wicked, so that he may make him upright by making him righteous.[32]

2,4. *Not because of their works,* he says, *but because of him who called them it was said, to her that the older would serve the younger* (Rom 9:12). To this pertains what was said, *For when they were not yet born and had not done anything good or evil* (Rom 9:11), so that it could be said, *Not because of their works but because of him who called them.* This is why a person may ask why he said, *That God's purpose would abide in accordance with his choice* (Rom 9:11). For how is a choice righteous or of any quality at all when there is no distinction [between persons]? For if Jacob, who was not yet born and had not yet done any works, was not chosen on account of any merit, he could not have been chosen in any sense of the word when there was no difference [between him and his brother] on the basis of which he might be chosen. Likewise, if Esau, who also was not yet born and had not yet done any works, was not rejected on account of any merit when it was said, *And the older shall serve the younger,* how can his rejection be called righteous? Based on what act of discernment and on what equitable judgment are we to understand what follows: *I loved Jacob but I hated Esau* (Rom 9:13)? This was, to be sure, written in a prophet, who long afterwards prophesied how they were born and died.[33] Yet that phrase, *And the older shall serve the younger,* seems to have been used both before they were born and before they did any works. How could this or any other choice be made if, since they were not yet born and had not yet done any works, they had no opportunities for merit? Were they perhaps somehow of different natures? Who could claim this, inasmuch as they had the same father and the same mother, came from a single act of inter-

---

29. See Eph 4:8.
30. See Rom 3:24.
31. See 1 Tm 1:13.
32. See Rom 4:5.
33. See Mal 1:2-3.

course and had the same creator? As the same creator brought forth from the same earth different living and self-reproducing beings,[34] did he from the same union and embrace of [two] human beings bring forth different offspring in twins, one whom he loved and another whom he hated? There would be no choice, therefore, until there was something to be chosen. For if Jacob was made good so that he would be pleasing, how was he pleasing before he was made, so that he would be made good? And so he was not chosen in order to be made good but, once made good, he was able to be chosen.

2,5. Is it *in accordance with his choice* that God, knowing all things in advance, would see future faith in Jacob, who was not yet born? Thus, although a person does not merit to be made righteous because of his works, since in fact he cannot do good works unless he is made righteous, yet, inasmuch as God makes the pagans righteous by faith[35] and no one believes except by free will, did God foresee this very future will to believe and in his foreknowledge choose someone who was not yet even born in order to make him righteous? If a choice is made through foreknowledge, then, and God foreknew Jacob's faith, how do you prove that he did not also choose him because of his works? If it was the case, then, that they had not yet been born and had not yet done anything either good or evil, it was also the case that neither of them had yet believed. But foreknowledge sees who will believe. Thus foreknowledge could see who would do works, so that, as one person may be said to have been chosen because of a future faith that God foreknew, another could say that he, for his part, was chosen because of future works that God likewise foreknew. How, then, does the Apostle show that these words, *The older shall serve the younger*, were not said on account of works? Because if they were not yet born, it applied not only to works but also to faith, since those who were not yet born lacked both. He did not want it to be understood, therefore, that it was the result of foreknowledge that the younger was chosen with a view to his being served by the older. For he wanted to show that this did not happen because of works, and so he added the words, *For when they were not yet born and had not done anything good or evil*; otherwise it could have been said to him, "But God already knew who was going to do what." The question, therefore, is just how that choice was made. Because if it was not based on works, which did not exist in those who were not yet born, nor based on faith, because that itself did not exist, how then did it happen?

2,6. Must it be said that there would have been no choice had there not been some difference in their mother's womb, whether of faith or of works or of

---

34. See Gn 1:24.
35. See Gal 3:8.

some kind of merits, whatever they might have been? But it is said that *God's purpose would abide in accordance with his choice*, and so we try to discover why it was said. Perhaps this sentence should be construed in a different way—so that we would not understand the words, *so that God's purpose would abide in accordance with his choice,* as following on from *not because of their works but because of him who called them was it said that the older would serve the younger* but rather as referring to the example given of persons yet unborn, who have not yet accomplished any works, so that no choice [based on works] could be understood here. *For when they were not yet born and had not done anything good or evil, so that God's purpose would abide in accordance with his choice*—that is, *they had not done anything good or evil* which would allow for some choice to be made of a person who had something good, based on that very action. Since, therefore, no choice was made of someone who had done something good, on account of which God's purpose would abide, it was *not because of their works but because of him who called them* that *it was said to her that the older would serve the younger.* In other words, it was because of him who, by calling the wicked to faith, makes him righteous by grace.[36]

God's purpose, therefore, does not abide on account of a choice, but the choice results from the purpose—that is, it is not because God discovers in human beings good works that he chooses, and that therefore his plan of making righteous abides, but because it abides in order to make righteous those who believe, and that therefore he discovers works that he may now choose for the kingdom of heaven. For unless a choice were made there would be no chosen ones, nor would it correctly be said, *Who will accuse God's chosen ones?* (Rom 8:33) Yet it is not making a choice that precedes making righteous but making righteous that precedes making a choice. For no one is chosen unless he is already entirely different than a person who is rejected. Hence I do not see how these words, *God chose us before the foundation of the world* (Eph 1:4), could have been said if not with foreknowledge. But what he says here, *Not because of their works but because of him who called them it was said to her that the older would serve the younger,* he wanted to be understood not of a choice based upon merits, which occur after a person has been made righteous by grace, but of the generosity of God's gifts, lest anyone be inflated because of his works. *For by God's grace we have been saved. And this is not because of us but is a gift of God; it is not because of works, lest perhaps anyone be inflated.* (Eph 2:8-9)

---

36. See Rom 4:5.

2,7. Now the question is whether faith merits humankind's being made righteous. Do faith's merits precede God's mercy, or should even faith itself not be numbered among the gifts of grace? For in the passage where he said, *Not because of their works*, he did *not* say, "Because of their faith it was said to her that the older would serve the younger," but he *did* say, *But because of him who called them*. For no one believes who is not called. But it is a merciful God who calls, bestowing this [gift] when there are no merits of faith, because the merits of faith follow the call rather than precede it. For *how will they believe him whom they have not heard? And how will they hear without a preacher?* (Rom 10:14) If God's mercy does not precede by way of a call, therefore, a person cannot believe, so that from this he may begin to be made righteous and to receive the capacity to do good works. Before every merit, then, there is grace, since Christ died for the wicked.[37] Hence it was not because of any merits of his own, but because of him who called, that the younger received [the grace] to be served by the older. This also explains the phrase, *I loved Jacob*, which was because of God who called and not because of Jacob's works.

2,8. What then of Esau? On account of what evil deeds of his did he merit to serve his younger [brother] and to have it written [of him]: *I hated Esau*? For neither had *he* been born yet or done anything good or evil when it was said, *And the older shall serve the younger*. Is it perhaps that, just as that was said of Jacob, who had no merits for any good deed, so Esau was hated, who had no merits for any evil deed? For, if God predestined him to serve his younger [brother] because he foreknew his future evil works and predestined Jacob as well, so that his older [brother] would serve him, because he foreknew his future good works, what he says now is false: *Not because of their works*. But if it is true that this did not occur because of their works and that [God] approves of this, inasmuch as it is said of persons who were not yet born and had not yet done any works, and that it was not done because of faith either, which similarly did not exist in persons not yet born, on the basis of what merit was Esau hated before he was born? For there is no doubt that God loves what he has made. But if we say that he hated what he made, it contradicts another text of scripture that says, *You did not create anything in hatred, but you hate nothing that you have made* (Wis 11:24). For by what merit was the sun made the sun? Or how did the moon offend, that it is so inferior to it? Or how did it merit to be created so much brighter than the other stars? But all of these were

---

37. See Rom 5:6.

created good, each in its own kind.[38] For God would not say, "I loved the sun but I hated the moon," or, "I loved the moon but I hated the stars," as he *did* say, *I loved Jacob but I hated Esau*. But he loved all those things, even though they were placed in different ranks of excellence, because God saw that they were good when he created them by his word.[39] But it is unjust that he would have hated Esau when there was no unrighteousness to merit it. If we grant this, then Jacob begins to be loved because of the merit of righteousness. If this is true, then it is false that it is not because of works. Was it perhaps because of the righteousness of faith? How do these words, *For when they were not yet born*, support your position, then, when in fact there could not have been any righteousness of faith in someone who was not yet born?

2,9. And so the Apostle saw what effect his words could have on the mind of his hearer or reader, and he immediately added, *What, then, shall we say? Is there injustice with God? Of course not!* (Rom 9:14) And as if teaching how absurd this is, he says, *For Moses says, I will have mercy on whom I will have mercy, and I will show compassion to whom I will be compassionate* (Rom 9:15). With these words he solves the problem—or, rather, complicates it further. For this is the very thing that is so disturbing: if he will have mercy on whom he will have mercy and show compassion to whom he will be compassionate, why was this compassion lacking in regard to Esau, so that by it he might have been good, just as by it Jacob became good? Or was this said, *I will have mercy on whom I will have mercy, and I will show compassion to whom I will be compassionate*, because God will have mercy on a person in order to call him, will be merciful to him so that he may believe, and will show compassion to him to whom he is compassionate—that is, will make him compassionate, so that he may also do good works? From this we are warned that it is not right for anyone to boast or to be inflated even because of his works of mercy, [saying] that he is deserving of God [by claiming God's works] as if they were his own, when in fact he who will show compassion to whom he will be compassionate showed him the very compassion that he was to have. If a person boasts that he has merited this by believing, he should know that [God], who by inspiring faith has mercy on whom he is merciful, has shown it to him in order to communicate his call to one who was without faith up until that moment. For the one with faith is already differentiated from the wicked. *For what do you have*, he says, *that you have not received? But if you have received, why do you boast as if you had not received?* (1 Cor 4:7)

---

38. See Gn 1:16-18.
39. See Gn 1:16-18.

2,10. Well said! But why was this compassion withdrawn from Esau? Why was he not called in such a way that, once called, he would be inspired with faith and, as a believer, become compassionate, so that he might do good works? Was it perhaps because he did not will to? If, then, Jacob believed because he willed to, God did not bestow faith on him, but he conferred it upon himself by an act of will, and he had something that he did not receive. Is it the case that, because no one can believe unless he wills to and no one can will to unless he is called, but no one can confer it upon himself to be called, God, by calling, also confers faith, because no one can believe without being called, although no one believes unwillingly? *For how will they believe him whom they have not heard? And how will they hear without a preacher?* And so no one believes who has not been called, but not everyone who has been called believes, *for many are called, but few are chosen* (Mt 20:16); these are the ones who have not disdained him who calls but, by believing, have followed him. Without doubt, however, they have believed willingly. What is this, then, that follows: *It is not a matter of willing or of running, therefore, but of a merciful God* (Rom 9:16)? Can we not will unless we are called, and does our willing count for naught unless God helps to bring it to completion? It is necessary, then, to will and to run, for it was not without purpose that it was said, *Peace on earth to men of good will* (Lk 2:14), and, *Run in such a way that you may seize the prize* (1 Cor 9:24). Yet *it is not a matter of willing or of running but of a merciful God* that we obtain what we will and arrive where we will. Esau did not will, therefore, and did not run. But, if he had both willed and run, he would have arrived with the help of God, who would also have bestowed willing and running upon him by calling him if he had not, by disdaining the call, made himself disapproved. For in one way God bestows so that we may will, and in another he bestows what we have willed. For he has willed that our willing be both his and ours—his by calling and ours by following. He alone bestows, however, what we have willed—that is, the ability to act well and to live blessedly forever. But Esau, who was not yet born, could neither will nor not will anything. Why, then, was he disapproved when he was in the womb? This brings us back to those difficulties which are all the more complex by reason of both their obscurity and also our frequent repetition.

2,11. For why was Esau, who was not yet born, disapproved, when he was unable to have faith in him who called him or to disdain his call or to do anything either good or evil? If God foreknew his [i.e., Esau's] future evil will, why was Jacob not also approved through God's foreknowledge of his future good will? If you but once concede that a person could have been either approved or disapproved on the basis of what was not yet in him but because God foreknew what was going to be in him, it follows that he could also have been approved on the basis of the works that God foreknew were going to be in him, although he had not yet done any works, and the fact that they were not yet born when it was said, *The older shall serve the younger,* will not support your position at all, since you must then show that this was not said because of works, inasmuch as he had not yet done any works.

2,12. If you also pay close attention to these words, *It is not a matter of willing or of running, therefore, but of a merciful God,* the Apostle will be seen to have said this because it is not only by God's help that we attain to what we will but also in the context of that effort to which he refers in another text: *Work out your salvation with fear and trembling. For it is God who, for the sake of a good will, works in you both the willing and the working.* (Phil 2:12-13) Here he shows clearly that even a good will itself comes about in us through God's working. For if it is only said that it is not a matter of willing but of a merciful God, because the human will does not suffice for us to live in rectitude and righteousness unless we are aided by God's mercy, it can therefore also be said that it is not a matter of a merciful God but of human willing, because God's mercy alone does not suffice unless our will's consent is joined to it. But it is evident that we will to no avail unless God is merciful. I do not know how it may be said, on the other hand, that God is merciful to no avail unless we will. For if God is merciful, we also will. It pertains to the same mercy, in fact, that we will, *for it is God who, for the sake of a good will, works in us both the willing and the working.* For if we asked whether a good will was God's gift, it would be strange if someone dared to deny it. For, since it is not a good will that precedes a call but a call that precedes a good will, it is rightly ascribed to God who calls that we will what is good, but it cannot be ascribed to us that we are called. It must not be thought, then, that these words, *It is not a matter of willing or of running but of a merciful* God, were said because without his aid we cannot attain to what we will but rather because without his call we do not will.

2,13. But if this call brings about a good will in such a way that everyone who has been called follows it [i.e., the call], how is it correct that *many are called, but few are chosen* (Mt 20:16)? If this is correct and the one who has been called does not follow and submit to the call, because it is built into his will not to submit, it can also rightly be said that it is not a matter of God's being merciful but of man's willing and running, because the mercy of him who calls is insufficient unless there follows the obedience of the one who has been called. What if those who have been called in this way do not consent? Could they, if called in another way, accommodate their will to faith? Thus this would be correct: *Many are called, but few are chosen,* so that, although many have been called in one way, yet, because not all have been touched in one way, only they would follow the call who are found fit to grasp it. And this would be no less correct: *It is not a matter of willing or of running, therefore, but of a merciful God*, who called in a way that was appropriate for those who followed the call. The call has indeed reached others, but because it was such that they could not be moved by it and were not suited to grasp it, they could indeed be said to have been called but not chosen, and it is no longer similarly correct that it is not a matter of God's being merciful but of man's willing and running. For the effectiveness of God's mercy cannot be in man's power, so that he would be merciful to no avail if man were unwilling, because, if he should will to have mercy even on those persons [who were mentioned shortly before], he could call them in such a way as would be appropriate for them, so that they would be moved and would understand and would follow. This, then, is correct: *Many are called, but few are chosen*. For the chosen are those who have been called in an appropriate way, whereas those who did not consent and were not obedient to the call are not chosen, because they did not follow even though they were called. Likewise this is correct: *It is not a matter of willing or of running but of a merciful God*, because, even if he calls many, he still has mercy on those whom he calls in such a way as is appropriate for them to be called so that they may follow. It is incorrect, however, if anyone says that it is not a matter of God's being merciful but of man's willing and running, because God has mercy on no one in vain. But the person on whom he has mercy he calls in such a way as he knows is appropriate for him, so that he may not reject him who calls.

2,14. At this point someone will say, "Why, then, was Esau not called in such a way that he would will to obey?" For we see that others have been moved to faith when these same things have been shown or signified. For example, Simeon, when the Spirit revealed it to him, recognized our Lord Jesus Christ when he was still a tiny infant and believed in him.[40] Nathanael, when he had heard one sentence of his, *Before Philip called you, when you were under the fig tree, I saw you* (Jn 1:48), responded, *Rabbi, you are the Son of God, you are the king of Israel* (Jn 1:49). When Peter confessed this much later, he merited to hear that he was blessed and that the keys of the kingdom of heaven would be given to him.[41] When the miracle was performed at Cana in Galilee that the evangelist John mentions as the first of his signs, when water was turned into wine, his disciples believed in him.[42] When he spoke he invited many to faith,

40. See Lk 2:25-35.
41. See Mt 16:16-19.
42. See Jn 2:1-11.

but there were many who did not believe when he raised the dead.[43] Even the disciples were terrified by his cross and death and wavered,[44] yet the thief believed when he saw him not as one more excellent in his deeds but as his equal in the fellowship of the cross.[45] After his resurrection one of the band of disciples believed not so much because of his living members as because of his fresh wounds.[46] There were many from the number of those by whom he was crucified who saw him performing miracles and disdained him, but they believed his disciples when they preached him and did similar things in his name.[47]

Since, therefore, one person is moved to faith in one way while another is moved in another way, and frequently the same thing said to one person at one time moves him but said to another at another time does not move him, and it moves one and does not move another, who would dare to say that God lacked that way of calling by which Esau as well could have applied his mind and joined his will to that faith in which Jacob was made righteous?

If the resistance of a person's will can be so great that a mental revulsion hardens him against any manner of calling, it may be asked whether this very hardening comes from a divine punishment, when God has abandoned a person by not calling him in such a way that he will be moved to faith. For who would say that the manner in which he might be persuaded to have faith was lacking to the Almighty?

2,15. But why do we ask this? For the Apostle himself adds, *For in scripture* [God] *says to Pharaoh, It was for this that I raised you up, so that I might display my power in you and so that my name might be made known throughout the earth* (Rom 9:17). The Apostle appended this statement, however, in order to prove what he had said before: *It is not a matter of willing or of running, therefore, but of a merciful God.* For as though he were being asked what the source of his teaching was, he declares, *For in scripture* [God] *says to Pharaoh, It was for this that I raised you up, so that I might display my power in you and so that my name might be made known throughout the earth.* In this way he shows that *it is not a matter of willing or of running but of a merciful God,* and he concludes as follows, *Therefore he has mercy on whom he wills, and whom he wills he hardens* (Rom 9:18), since neither had been mentioned previously. For these words, *It is not a matter of willing or of running but of a merciful God,* are not said in the same way that these others are: "It is not a matter of being unwilling or of disdaining but of a God who

---

43. See Lk 16:13.
44. See Mt 26:56.
45. See Lk 23:40-42.
46. See Jn 20:27-29.
47. See Acts 2:37-41; 5:12-16.

hardens." From this it becomes clear that what [the Apostle] previously said, *Therefore he has mercy on whom he wills, and whom he wills he hardens*, can fit in with the previous phrase [i.e., *It is not a matter of willing or of running but of a merciful God*] so that [it is understood that] God's hardening is an unwillingness to be merciful. Thus he imposes nothing whereby a person may become worse, but nothing is given to the person whereby he may become better. If this occurs when there is no difference in merits, who would not burst out into those words that the very Apostle uses against himself: *And so you say to me, Why is there still complaint? For who resists his will?* (Rom 9:19) For God often complains of human beings, as is clear from countless passages of scripture, because they are unwilling to believe and to live uprightly. Hence those who are faithful and carry out God's will are said to live *without giving rise to complaint* (Lk 1:6), because scripture does not complain of them. But why is there complaint, he asks, *for one who resists his will* (Rom 9:18), when *he has mercy on whom he wills, and whom he wills he hardens?* Yet let us consider what was said previously, and on that basis let us, to the degree that the Lord himself assists, shape our own perspective.

2,16. For he said shortly before, *What, then, shall we say? Is there injustice with God? Of course not!* Let this, then, be something fixed and settled in minds that are devoutly serious and steadfast in faith—that there is no injustice with God. And thus this very thing—that God *has mercy on whom he wills, and whom he wills he hardens*, which means that he has mercy on whom he wills and does not have mercy on whom he does not will—may be believed with utter tenacity and firmness as pertaining to a kind of justice that is hidden from that which is sought and must be observed in our human affairs and earthly agreements. Unless we held fast there to certain clearly marked vestiges of eternal justice, our frail efforts would never aim at and long for the holiest and purest resting place and sanctuary of spiritual precepts. *Blessed are those who hunger and thirst for justice, for they shall be satisfied* (Mt 5:6). In the aridity of our life and of this mortal condition, therefore, unless there were a sprinkling from on high of, so to speak, the slightest mist of justice, we would wither away more quickly than we thirst. Hence, since it is by giving and receiving that human society is bound together, while it is things either owed or not owed that are given and received, who would not see that no one—and certainly not he who would willingly forgive what is owed him—can be accused of injustice who exacts what is owed him, and that this [i.e., whether a debt should be exacted or not] falls under the judgment not of those who owe the debt but of the one to whom the debt is owed? This thought or vestige (as I said above) has been clearly marked upon the affairs of men from the highest summit of justice.

Therefore, all human beings—since, as the Apostle says, *all die in Adam* (1 Cor 15:22), from whom the origin of the offense against God spread throughout the whole human race—are a kind of single mass of sin owing a debt of punishment to the divine and loftiest justice, and whether [the punishment that is owed] be exacted or forgiven, there is no injustice. They are debtors, however, who proudly judge from whom it should be exacted and by whom it should be forgiven, like those who, having been brought to that vineyard, were unjustly angered when precisely as much was gifted to the others as was paid to them.[48] And so the Apostle beats back this impudent question in this way: *O man, who are you that you talk back to God?* (Rom 9:20) For he talks back to God when it displeases him that God complains of sinners, as if God would compel someone to sin, although he himself compels no one to sin but only does not bestow on certain sinners the mercy of being made righteous by him, and for that reason it is said that he hardens certain sinners because he does not have mercy on them, not because he forces them to sin. But to those to whom he is not merciful he judges, with a most secret justice that is far removed from human understanding, that mercy must not be shown. For *inscrutable are his judgments and unfathomable his ways* (Rom 11:33). Justly, however, does he complain of sinners as one who does not force them to sin. And likewise [he complains] so that those to whom he shows mercy may possess a call [to grace] as well. Thus, as God complains of sinners, their hearts may be pricked and they may turn to his grace. Justly and mercifully, then, does he complain.

2,17. But if it is disturbing that no one resists his will, because whom he wills he sustains and whom he wills he abandons, since both the one whom he sustains and the one whom he abandons come from the same mass of sinners and, although both owe a debt of punishment, yet it is exacted from one and forgiven another—if it is disturbing, *O man, who are you that you talk back to God?* For I think that the meaning of *man* is the same here as in the passage, *Are you not men and do you not walk as men do?* (1 Cor 3:3) For by this term they are designated as fleshly and animal persons, as when it is said to them, *I have not been able to speak to you as to spiritual persons but as to fleshly ones* (1 Cor 3:1); and, *You were not able, and you are still not able, for you are still fleshly* (1 Cor 3:2); and, *The animal man, however, does not grasp the things that are of God's Spirit* (1 Cor 2:14). To these, therefore, it is said, *O man, who are you that you talk back to God? Does what has been fashioned say to the one who fashioned it, Why did you make me thus? Or does the potter not indeed have the power to make from the same lump of clay one vessel for*

---

48. See Mt 20:1-12.

honor and another for reproach? (Rom 9:20-21) With those very words he seems to show with sufficient clarity that he is speaking to fleshly man, because the mire itself alludes to that from which the first man was formed.[49] And since, as I have already noted, according to the same Apostle, *all die in Adam,* he says that there is a single lump for all. And although one vessel is made for honor and another for reproach, nonetheless even the one that is made for honor has to begin in fleshly fashion and from there rise up to spiritual maturity, since they had already been made for honor and already been reborn in Christ. Yet, because he is addressing little children, he also refers to them as fleshly when he says, *I have not been able to speak to you as to spiritual persons but as to fleshly ones. Since you are little children in Christ, I have given you milk to drink, not solid food. For you were not able, and you are in fact still not able, for you are still fleshly.* (1 Cor 3:1-2) Although he says that they are fleshly, then, still they have already been born in Christ and are little children in him and must drink milk. And what he adds—*you are in fact still not able*—indicates that it will be possible for them to make progress because grace had already begun in them when they were spiritually reborn. These, therefore, were vessels made for honor, to whom it may still rightly be said, *O man, who are you that you talk back to God?* And if this is rightly said to such as them, it is much more rightly said to those who either have not yet been regenerated in this way or have even been made for reproach. Only it should be maintained with unflinching faith that there is no injustice with God, who either forgives or exacts what is owed him, and neither can the one from whom he rightfully exacts it complain of his injustice nor ought the other to whom it is forgiven boast of his own merits. For the one only repays what is owed while the other has only what he has received.

2,18. But at this point we must strive to see, with the Lord's assistance, how both these statements are true: *You hate nothing that you have made* and *I loved Jacob but I hated Esau.* For if he hated Esau because he was a vessel made for reproach, and it was the same potter who made one vessel for honor and another for reproach, how is it that *you hate nothing that you have made?* For obviously he hates Esau, because he made him a vessel for reproach. This problem is solved if we understand that God is the maker of all creatures. But every creature of God is good,[50] and every human being, insofar as he is a human being and not insofar as he is a sinner, is a creature. God, therefore, is the creator of the human body and soul. Neither of these is evil and neither is hated by God, for he hates nothing that he has made. The soul, however, is

---

49. See Gn 2:7.
50. See 1 Tm 4:4.

more excellent than the body, but God, the author and creator of each, is more excellent than both soul and body, and he hates nothing in the human being other than sin. Sin, however, is a disorder and a perversion in the human being—that is, a turning away from the creator, who is more excellent, and a turning to created things, which are inferior.[51] God, therefore, does not hate Esau the human being, but God does hate Esau the sinner, as is said of the Lord: *He came unto his own, and his own did not accept him* (Jn 1:11). To these he himself says, *You do not hear me because you are not of God* (Jn 8:47). How are they his own and how are they not of God if not because the one thing is said of human beings whom the Lord himself made while the other is said of sinners whom the Lord himself was rebuking? Yet the same persons are themselves both human beings and sinners—but human beings by God's doing and sinners by their own will.

As far as his loving Jacob is concerned: was he not a sinner? But he loved in him not the guilt that he did away with but the grace that he bestowed. For Christ also died for the wicked[52]—yet not that they might remain wicked but that, having been made righteous, they might be changed from their wickedness and believe in him who makes the wicked righteous. For God hates wickedness. And so in some he punishes it by condemning them, while in others he removes it by making them righteous, just as he himself judges by his inscrutable judgments[53] must be done in their regard. And, because he makes vessels for reproach from the number of the wicked whom he does not make righteous, he does not hate in them the fact that he makes them, for they are accursed insofar as they are wicked, but insofar as they are made vessels they are made for a certain use, so that, by way of the punishments that have been decreed for them, the vessels that are made for honor may advance [in holiness]. And so God does not hate them insofar as they are human beings, nor insofar as they are vessels—that is, [he does not hate] what he does in them in creation nor what he does in them by his decree. For he hates nothing that he has made. Yet, in that he makes them vessels of perdition to use in correcting others, he hates the wickedness in them that he himself did not make. For as a judge hates theft in a person but does not hate the fact that he is sent to the mines[54]— for a thief does the former and a judge the latter—neither does God hate what he makes because out of a lump of the wicked he makes vessels of perdition—that is, a work decreed by him for the punishment owed to those who are perishing, in

---

51. "A turning away . . . a turning to": *aversio . . . conversio*. This definition of sin is notable for its brevity and its breadth.
52. See Rom 5:6.
53. See Rom 11:33.
54. Laboring in the state-controlled mines was a standard form of criminal punishment.

which those on whom he has mercy discover their opportunity for salvation. Thus it was said to Pharaoh: *It was for this that I raised you up, so that I might display my power in you and so that my name might be made known throughout the earth.* This manifestation of God's power and the making known of his name throughout the earth are of benefit to those for whom such a calling is fitting so that they may be fearful and correct their ways. Accordingly he says as follows, *But if God, who is willing to display his wrath and to manifest his power, has borne with great patience the vessels of wrath that have been produced for perdition* (Rom 9:22). The implication is: *Who are you that you talk back to God?* When we join this text to the previous words, this is the meaning: If God, who is willing to display his wrath, has borne with the vessels of wrath, who are you that you talk back to God? He is willing, however, not only to display his wrath and to manifest his power, having borne with great patience the vessels of wrath that have been produced for perdition, but also, as in the words that follow, *to reveal the riches of his glory for the vessels of mercy* (Rom 9:23). For what profit is there to the vessels produced for perdition in God's patiently enduring them when, in accordance with his decree, he destroys and uses them as a means of salvation for those others on whom he has mercy? But it does indeed profit those for whose salvation he thus uses them, so that, as it is written, the righteous hand may wash in the blood of the sinner[55]—that is, that it may be cleansed of evil works through the fear of God, when it sees the punishments of sinners. That he is willing to display his wrath and has borne with the vessels of wrath, therefore, contributes to a beneficial fear to which others must be exposed and to the making known of the riches of his glory to the vessels of mercy, *which he has prepared for glory* (Rom 9:23). And indeed that hardening of the wicked demonstrates two things —both what should be feared, so that through goodness a person may be converted to God, and what great thanks are owed to the mercy of God, who shows in the punishment of the ones what he forgives in the others. But if what he exacts of the ones is not a just punishment, then nothing is forgiven the others, from whom he does not exact it. But because it is just and there is no injustice with God when he punishes, who can give adequate thanks to him who remits what, if he willed to exact it, no one would rightly say he did not owe?

2,19. *Us whom he also called, not only from the Jews but also from the gentiles* (Rom 9:24)—that is, *the vessels of mercy which he has prepared for glory.* For those [who are called] are not all Jews, but they are *from* the Jews; nor are they absolutely all the peoples of the gentiles, but they are *from* the gentiles. For from Adam has come a single mass of sinners and wicked

---

55. See Ps 58:10.

persons; it is far from God's grace, and both Jews and gentiles belong to the one lump of it. For if from the same lump the potter makes one vessel for honor and another for reproach, and if it is obvious that from the Jews, as from the gentiles, some vessels are for honor and some are for reproach, it follows that they should all be understood to belong to one lump.

Then he begins to offer prophetic testimonies to individual cases in reverse chronological order. For he had spoken first of the Jews and afterwards of the gentiles, but [now] he submits testimony on behalf of the gentiles first and then on behalf of the Jews. Thus: *As Hosea says, I will call a people that was not mine, my people, and that was not loved, loved, and in the place where it was said, You are not my people, there they shall be called the children of the living God* (Rom 9:25-26). This is understood to have been said of the gentiles, because they did not have a single place designated for sacrifices as did the Jews in Jerusalem. But apostles were sent to the gentiles so that those *to whom he gave the power to become children of God* (Jn 1:12) would believe, each of them in their own place, and so that wherever they had come to faith they would also offer there a sacrifice of praise.[56]

But Isaiah, he says, *cries out for Israel* (Rom 9:27). Lest, on the other hand, all the Israelites be believed to have fallen into perdition, he also teaches there that some vessels have been made for honor and others for reproach. *If,* he says, *the number of the children of Israel were like the sands of the sea, a remnant will be saved* (Rom 9:27). The remaining vessels, then, are the throng that has been produced for perdition. *For the Lord,* he says, *will carry out his brief and swift word upon the earth* (Rom 9:28)—that is, in order to save those who believe[57] through grace by the simplicity of their faith, not through the innumerable observances by which that multitude was burdened and oppressed as though they were slaves. Through grace he carried out his brief and swift word upon the earth for us when he said, *My yoke is easy, and my burden is light* (Mt 11:30). And shortly thereafter this is said: *The word is near you, in your mouth and in your heart—that is, the word of faith that we preach. Because if you confess in your mouth that Jesus is Lord and believe in your heart that God has raised him from the dead, you shall be saved. For with the heart there is belief unto righteousness, while with the mouth confession is made unto salvation.* (Rom 10:8-10) This is the brief and swift word that the Lord has carried out upon the earth. By its brevity and swiftness the thief was made righteous who, with all his members fastened to the cross but with these two [members] unhindered, believed with his heart unto righteousness and

---

56. See Ps 50:14.
57. See 1 Cor 1:21.

confessed with his mouth unto salvation, and immediately he deserved to hear:[58] *Today you shall be with me in paradise* (Lk 23:43). For his good works would have followed had he, upon receiving grace, lived for a long time among men. Yet they had not come in advance so as to merit the same grace by which he who was fastened to the cross as a thief was borne away from the cross to paradise.

And, he says, *as Isaiah predicted, Unless the Lord of hosts had left us offspring, we would have become like Sodom, and we would have been like Gomorrah* (Rom 9:29). What he says here, *had left us offspring,* appears elsewhere as *a remnant will be saved.* But others who owed the debt of punishment perished as vessels of perdition. And the fact that not all would perish as at Sodom and Gomorrah was not due to anything that they had merited; it was rather the grace of God leaving a seed from which another harvest would spring throughout the whole earth. A little later he also says this: *And so, therefore, at this time as well a remnant exists that was chosen by grace. But if by grace, then not by works; otherwise grace is no longer grace. What then? What Israel was seeking it did not find. The chosen found it, however, while the rest were blinded.* (Rom 11:5-7) The vessels of mercy found it but the vessels of wrath were blinded; yet, like all the gentiles, they are from the same lump.

2,20. There is a certain passage of scripture that is very pertinent to the matter at hand, which provides marvelous proof of what has been explained. It is in the book that is called Jesus Sirach by some and Ecclesiasticus by others, and in it there is written as follows: *All human beings come from the ground, and from the earth Adam was created. In the abundance of discipline the Lord separated them and changed their ways. Some he blessed and exalted, and these he sanctified and brought to himself. Some he cursed and humbled and turned to dissension. Like clay in a potter's hand, for shaping and forming, all its ways according to his plan, so is man in the hands of the one who made him, the one who deals with him according to his judgment. In contrast to evil there is good, and opposed to death there is life, in the same way the sinner is opposed to the righteous man. Look thus upon the work of the Most High, in twos, one opposed to the other.* (Sir 33:10-15)

The first thing that is mentioned here is God's discipline. *In the abundance of discipline,* it says, *the Lord separated them*—from what if not from the blessedness of paradise?—*and changed their ways* (Sir 33:11), so that they would now live as mortals. Then a single mass was made of all of them, which came from the transmission of sin and the punishment of mortality, although, thanks to God's forming and creating them, they are good. For in all people

---

58. See Lk 23:32-43.

there is a beauty and cohesion of body with such harmony among its members that the Apostle used this to illustrate how charity should be maintained;[59] in all people there is also a vital spirit that gives life to their earthly members; and the whole nature of the human person is regulated in marvelous fashion by the mastery of the soul and the servitude of the body. But the fleshly desire that results from the punishment for sin has, because of the original guilt, cast abiding confusion into everything, and now it presides over the whole human race as one complete lump. But there also follows: *Some he blessed and exalted, and them he sanctified and brought to himself. Some he cursed and humbled and turned to dissension.* (Sir 33:12)

As the Apostle says, *Or does the potter not have the power to make from the same lump of clay one vessel for honor and another for reproach?* (Rom 9:2 1) And so the passage that has been cited uses the same imagery: *Like clay in a potter's hand,* it says, *for shaping and forming, all its ways according to his plan, so is man in the hands of the one who made him* (Sir 33:13-14). But the Apostle says, *Is there injustice with God?* Notice, therefore, what is added here: *He deals with him according to his judgment* (Sir 33:14). But although just punishments are assigned to those who have been condemned, yet, because this very thing is turned to the advantage of those to whom mercy is shown so that they may advance [in holiness], pay attention to what remains: *In contrast to evil there is good, and opposed to death there is life; in the same way the sinner is opposed to the righteous man. Look thus upon all the work of the Most High, in twos, one opposed to the other.* (Sir 33:15) Thus, from the conjunction of two bad things, better things emerge and advance [in holiness]. Yet, because they are better through grace, it is as though [the writer] were saying, *A remnant will be saved.* Speaking in the person of that remnant, he goes on to say, *And I have been the last to keep watch, like someone who gleans after the vintagers* (Sir 33:16). And where is the proof that this is not the result of merits but of God's mercy? *In the blessing of the Lord,* he says, *I myself have hoped, and like one who gathers the vintage I have filled the winepress* (Sir 33:17). For although he was the last to keep watch, nevertheless, because, as is said, the last shall be first,[60] the people of Israel, which has been gleaned from the rest[61] and which hopes in the Lord, has filled its winepress from out of the abundance of the vintage, which has flourished throughout the world.

2,21. The main thought of the Apostle, then, as well as of those who have been made righteous, through whom an understanding of grace has been given to us, is none other than that whoever boasts should boast in the

---

59. See 1 Cor 12:12-27.
60. See Mt 20:16.
61. See Jer 6:9.

Lord.[62] For would anyone question the works of the Lord, who from the same lump condemns one person and makes another righteous? The free choice of the will counts for a great deal, to be sure. But what does it count for in those who have been sold under sin?[63] *The flesh,* [the Apostle] says, *lusts against the spirit, the spirit against the flesh, so that you do not do the things that you want* (Gal 5:17). It is commanded that we live uprightly, and in fact this reward has been offered—that we merit to live blessedly forever. But who can live uprightly and do good works without having been made righteous by faith?[64] It is commanded that we believe so that, having received the gift of the Holy Spirit through love, we may be able to do good works. But who can believe without being touched by some call—that is, by the evidence of things? Who has it in his power for his mind to be touched by such a manifestation as would move his will to faith? Who embraces in his heart something that does not attract him? Who has it in his power either to come into contact with what can attract him or to be attracted once he has come into contact? When, therefore, things attract us whereby we may advance towards God, this is inspired and furnished by the grace of God; it is not obtained by our own assent and effort or by the merits of our works because, whether it be the assent of our will or our intense effort or our works aglow with charity, it is he who gives, he who bestows it. We are ordered to ask so that we may receive, and to seek so that we may find, and to knock so that it may be opened to us.[65] Is not this particular prayer of ours sometimes so lukewarm, or rather cold and practically non-existent, indeed, sometimes so utterly non-existent, that we do not notice this in ourselves without sorrow? Because if this actually makes us sorry, we are already praying. What else, then, is being shown to us than that it is he who orders us to ask and seek and knock who enables us to do these things? *It is not a matter of willing or of running, therefore, but of a merciful God,* since in fact we could neither will nor run if he did not move and rouse us.

2,22. If there is some choice that is made here, such as we understand from the words, *A remnant that was chosen by grace* (Rom 11:5), the choice is not of those who, for the sake of eternal life, have been made righteous. It is, rather, that those are chosen who are to be made righteous,

---

62. See 2 Cor 10:17.
63. See Rom 7:14.
64. See Rom 5:1.
65. See Mt 7:7.

and this choice is so very hidden that it can by no means be discerned by us who are in the same lump. Or, if it is discernible to some, I for my part acknowledge my incompetence in the matter. For, if in my thoughts I am allowed some insight into this choice, I cannot see how persons are chosen for the grace of salvation apart from either greater endowments or lesser sins or both. We may also add, if you wish, learning that is good and useful. Whoever, then, has been ensnared in and sullied by only the very least sins—for who could be without *any*?—and is endowed with intelligence and has been refined by the liberal arts seems as if he must have been chosen for grace. But when I arrive at this conclusion, he who has chosen the weak things of the world to confound the strong, and the foolish things of the world to confound the wise,[66] laughs at me in such a way that, as I gaze upon him and am checked by shame, I myself begin to make fun of many who are more chaste than certain sinners and better speech-makers than certain fishermen.[67] Do we not notice that many of us who are faithful and who walk in God's way by no means possess endowments comparable not only, I would say, to those of some heretics but even to those of actors? On the other hand, do we not see some persons of both sexes living peacefully in married chastity, who are nonetheless heretics or pagans or even members of the true faith and the true Church and who are so lukewarm that we marvel at how they are surpassed not only by the patience and temperance but even by the faith, hope and charity of prostitutes and actors who have experienced sudden conversions?

The upshot, then, is that wills are chosen. But the will itself, unless it comes into contact with something that attracts and beckons the soul, can by no means be moved. But that it may come into contact with this is not in a person's power. What did Saul want to do but attack, seize, enchain and kill Christians? What a rabid, raging, blind will![68] Yet at a single voice from heaven he fell prostrate and, having had such an experience that his mind and will, broken by savagery, were turned about and directed toward

---

66. See 1 Cor 1:27.
67. These lines bear a remarkable resemblance to a scene recounted in *Confessions* VIII,11,27, in which Continence, appearing to Augustine in a kind of vision and bringing before his mind's eye a throng of the chaste of every condition (analogous to the many who are weak and foolish in the view of the world), mocks him because he fears that he cannot be chaste himself, whereupon he blushes. The present work and the *Confessions* were written at most within a year or two of each other.
68. See Acts 8:3; 9:1-2.

faith, he was at once transformed from a famous persecutor of the gospel to its still more famous preacher.[69]

And yet *what shall we say? Is there injustice with God*, who exacts from whom he pleases and gives to whom he pleases but who never exacts what is not owed him and never gives what is not his? *Is there injustice with God? Of course not!* Yet why is one person treated one way and another person another way? *O man, who are you?* If you do not repay what is owed, you have reason to be grateful; if you do repay it, you have no reason to complain. Let us only believe, even if we cannot understand, that he who made and established the whole of creation, spiritual and corporeal, arranges everything according to number and weight and measure.[70] But *inscrutable are his judgments and unfathomable his ways* (Rom 11:33). Let us say "Alleluia" and join in the canticle, and let us not say "Why this?" or "Why that?" For all things have been created in their own time.[71]

---

69. See Acts 9:3-22.

70. See Wis 11:20.

71. See Sir 39:21. This and the preceding allusion to Wis 11:20, which is one of Augustine's favorite verses, is intended to hint at the order that governs creation, even though it may not always be immediately apparent.

Second Book

I think that I have responded adequately now to what was asked of me in reference to the Apostle. Now I shall begin another volume about what you requested of me concerning the Books of Kings which, like many and nearly all of the books of the Old Testament, tend to be figurative and wrapped in the veils of mysteries. But, although the veil may be removed inasmuch as we have passed to Christ,[1] nonetheless now we see obscurely, but then face to face.[2] A veil in fact completely cuts off our view, but the obscurity is as it were through a mirror, as the same Apostle says, *We see now through a mirror in obscurity* (1 Cor 13:12), and it neither exposes the clearest traces nor utterly conceals the truth. Let us begin this too, then, with the Lord as our guide and lifted up by your prayers rather than weighed down by your commands, especially since I understood from your letter that you were not looking for what these things might signify prophetically. In that regard it would truly be very difficult for me to obey because the intention would have to be deduced from the entire ensemble of those same books, and, as eager as my mind may be, the vastness of the enterprise would still be daunting; if it has to be undertaken, much more effort and time are necessary. But now you have deigned to give consideration to how I understand the meanings of the deeds that are expressed in the words that you have called to my attention and to be open to my explanation.

First Question

1,1. And the first thing, which is from the First Book of Kings, that you have commanded me to explain is why it was said: *And the spirit of the Lord came over Saul* (1 S 10:10), inasmuch as it is said elsewhere: *And there was an evil spirit of the Lord in Saul* (1 S 16:14).[3]

This is what is written: *And it came about that, when he turned his back to go away from Samuel, God changed Saul's heart, and all the signs came about on that day. And he went from there to a high place, and behold, a band of prophets met him, and the spirit of God came over him, and he prophesied in*

---

1. See 2 Cor 3:16.
2. See 1 Cor 13:12.
3. The Latin word *spiritus* has sometimes been capitalized in the pages that follow and sometimes not, depending on its context; but the fluid meaning of the term demands a fluid use of capitalization. Augustine himself addresses the ambiguity of the word in II,1,5 without arriving at a certain conclusion.

their midst. (1 S 10:9-10) In fact Samuel had foretold these things to him when, having been commanded, he anointed him.[4] And indeed I do not think that there is anything questionable here, since the Spirit blows where it wills,[5] and no contact with any soul can sully the spirit of prophecy, *for it reaches everywhere because of its purity* (Wis 7:24).

It does not touch everyone in the same way, however, but some are touched when the Spirit instructs them, when images of things are manifested, others by the mind's attaining to understanding, others by an inspiration in both ways, while still others are unaware. Now the Spirit's instruction occurs in two ways. The first way is by dreams, as has happened not only with many saints but also with Pharaoh[6] and King Nebuchadnezzar,[7] who saw what neither of them was capable of understanding, although both were able to see. The second way is by an ecstatic manifestation that some Latin-speakers interpret as awe (*pavorem*) (which is related but not precisely the same thing), when the mind is alienated from the body's senses so that a person's spirit, having been caught up by the divine Spirit, might be open to receiving and contemplating images, as when what Daniel did not understand was manifested to him[8] and that vessel was lowered on four lines from heaven to Peter,[9] for he too learned later what that manifestation symbolized.[10] The mind's attaining to understanding, however, occurs in one way, when the meaning and relevance of what has been manifested in images is revealed; this is a more certain prophecy, for the Apostle refers to it as a higher degree of prophecy.[11] It was thus that Joseph merited to understand what Pharaoh alone merited to see[12] and that Daniel explained to the king what he discerned but did not understand.[13] But when the mind is touched in such a way that it does not understand the images of things through observation but contemplates the things themselves, just as wisdom and justice and every immutable and divine attribute are understood, this does not pertain to the prophecy that we are now discussing. But those are granted prophecies by a twofold gift who both see the images of things in the spirit and immediately understand what they mean, or at the very least are instructed by clear words in the course of the manifestation itself,

---

4. See 1 S 10:5-6.
5. See Jn 3:8.
6. See Gn 41:1-8.
7. See Dn 2; 4:1-15.
8. See Dn 7-8.
9. See Acts 10:10-16.
10. See Acts 10:28.
11. See 1 Cor 13:2.
12. See Gn 41:1-36.
13. See Dn 2:29-45; 4:16-24.

which is how some [prophecies] are explained in the Apocalypse.[14] The spirit of prophecy touches the unaware, however, in the manner of Caiaphas who, when he was the high priest, prophesied of the Lord that it was expedient for one man to die for the whole people, although he intended something else in the words that he spoke, which he was unaware that he was not speaking in his own person.[15] There are numerous examples in the sacred books, and I am offering the most notable instances to Your Prudence. For you are not learning these things from me but in them you are testing me by your inquiry, desiring to acknowledge my contributions while being ready to correct my errors. By the phrase that has been cited, *A spirit came upon him*, an unanticipated inspiration as if from the hidden reaches of the Divinity is being signified.

In which of these ways we should understand that Saul was touched is quite clear from the fact that it is written there: *God changed Saul's heart* (1 S 10:9). For this signifies another disposition of heart, which God accomplished by changing him, so that he would be receptive to images full of meanings and foreshadowings in order to be able to engage in prophetic divination.

1,2. Now there is as great a difference between the prophecy of the prophets—such as Isaiah, Jeremiah and others who were like them—and the transitory [prophecy] that made its appearance in Saul as there is between human speech as spoken by human beings and that same speech as spoken, through miraculous necessity, by the ass that the prophet Balaam sat on.[16] For that beast received this [ability] at the time in order to make clear what God had commanded, not in order that an animal might habitually speak in the presence of human beings. Or, if this example is outlandish, it is much less remarkable for prophecy to have been bestowed on a bad man at a given moment through a transitory influence when the bestower was the one who even caused an ass to speak when he wished. For there is a greater difference between an animal and a human being than there is between a bad human being and those who have been chosen but are still human beings. For a person must not immediately be considered wise if he says something that smacks of wisdom. Thus neither should someone be numbered among the prophets if he has prophesied once, since the Lord himself says in the gospel that some persons receive the word with joy and do not have the depth for roots; they only last for a time.[17] *And so*, as the reading goes on and indicates, *it became a proverb: Is Saul also among the prophets?* (1 S 10:12) Let us not

---

14. See, e.g., Rv 1:12-20.
15. See Jn 11:49-51.
16. See Nm 22:28-30.
17. See Mt 13:20-21.

cease to be amazed, then, when something of God appears in human beings that transcends their merits and habits, since perhaps God wishes that such an appearance occur in order to signify something.

1,3. If there is some question about the fact, however, that Saul, who had first received a spirit of prophecy, was later choked by an evil spirit that attacked him,[18] there is nothing here to be astonished at either. For the former resulted from a plan to convey a meaning, while the latter represented a merited punishment. Nor should these alternations in the human soul—that is, in a changeable creature—shock us, especially at the time when corruptible and mortal flesh is being borne. Do we not see in the case of Peter himself, as the gospel indicates, that he made so great a confession as to merit to hear, *Blessed are you, Simon bar Jonah, because flesh and blood did not reveal this to you but my Father who is in heaven* (Mt 16:17), and shortly afterwards thought about the Lord's suffering in so fleshly a fashion that he immediately heard, *Get behind me, Satan, you are an obstacle to me, for you think not the things of God but of men* (Mt 16:23)? And perhaps, for people who have a deeper understanding, this contrast—by which Peter first understood, thanks to God the Father's revelation, that Christ was the Son of God and afterwards was horrified that he would die—is a model for distinguishing the visions that occur imaginatively in a person's spirit once his mind has taken flight, such as the revelation of prophecy by which Saul was first inspired and the intrusion of the evil spirit by which he was later oppressed.[19]

1,4. Now the fact that a spirit of the Lord has also been referred to as evil is to be understood in the same way as in the case of the words, *The Lord's is the earth* (Ps 24:1)—namely, as a creature under his dominion. Or, if this example of the term's usage is inappropriate, because the earth is not evil (for each of God's creatures is good[20]), another may be appropriate: Saul himself, who was already bad and villainous and ungrateful to the saintly David, whom he even persecuted when he was so savagely tormented by the stings of envy, was nonetheless still called the Lord's anointed, as David himself called

---

18. See 1 S 16:14.
19. This somewhat difficult sentence seems to be a complicated way of saying that, just as one (good) man, Peter, could veer from a good act to a bad one in a matter of moments, so another (bad) man, Saul, could host first a good spirit and then a bad one over the course of time. The changeability of the human person, to which Augustine had alluded a few lines previously, allows for such receptivity to both good and bad influences. See also II,1,6. Here, according to Augustine, Peter's behavior could serve as a "model" (*valet*) for understanding what happened to Saul.
20. See 1 Tm 4:4.

him when he was avenging him after his death.[21] But I tend to think that the malignant spirit by which Saul was agitated was spoken of as a spirit of the Lord because it was by the Lord's hidden judgment that it agitated Saul. For God uses even evil spirits as his agents to avenge the bad and test the good—in one way for the good and in another way for the others. For even though it is from him that there comes an evil spirit that is malignant because it yearns to do harm with its evil will, yet it does not receive the power to do harm except from him by whom all things have been arranged according to their merits, in certain and just ranks, because, just as no evil will comes from God, neither does power come except from God. For although it is in a person's power to will something, nonetheless it is not in his power to be able to do it to someone or to endure it from someone.[22] For even the only Son of God, at the time when he was about to suffer in humility, said to the man who spoke proudly and claimed that he had the power to kill him or to release him, *You would not have power over me unless it had been given you from above* (Jn 19:11). The devil, too, who wished to harm the righteous man Job, was indeed a devil as far as his will to do harm was concerned, but he still asked for power from the Lord God when he said, *Stretch out your hand and touch his flesh* (Jb 2:5), although if it were permitted it was he who would do it. For this was how he asked for permission, and he called his own hand—that is, the very power that he wished to receive—the Lord's hand once it had been given permission by the Lord. This is congruent with what the Lord says to his disciples in the gospel, *This night Satan has asked to sift you like grain* (Lk 22:31). The spirit of God—that is, God's agent for doing to Saul what the all-powerful judge judged should be done to him—is therefore called evil. This is the case because that spirit was not of God by reason of the will whereby it was evil, but it was of God by reason of the creation whereby it was created and by reason of the power that it had received not because of its own justice but because of that of the Lord of all things.

The words of scripture also read thus: *Samuel proceeded and went off to Armath, and the spirit of the Lord departed from Saul and a malignant spirit from the Lord seized him and choked him. And Saul's servants said to him, Behold, an evil spirit of the Lord is choking you.* (1 S 16:13-15) This, then, is

---

21. See 2 S 1:13-16.
22. Augustine comments on these words in the *Revisions*: "I said this because we do not say that something is in our power unless what we will happens. The first and most important thing is the willing itself. Without any hiatus whatsoever the will itself is present when we will. But we also receive the power from on high for living a good life when our will is prepared by the Lord."

how it is said by his servants: *An evil spirit of the Lord* (1 S 16:15). But the earlier words of the scriptural narrative say, *A malignant spirit from the Lord* (1 S 16:14). *Of the Lord,* accordingly, means *by the Lord,* because by itself it had the wherewithal to wish to do harm—that is, to lay hold of Saul—but it did not have the wherewithal to be able to do so unless it were allowed by the highest justice. For if God takes vengeance justly, as the Apostle himself says, when he hands people over to the desires of their heart,[23] there is nothing surprising if, taking vengeance no less justly, he also hands them over to the desires of others who wish to do harm, so long as his immutable justice is always observed.

1,5. It should be noticed that a spirit of God is said to be evil with a qualification. When a spirit is simply said to be "of God," even if "good" is not added, it is for that very reason understood to be good. Hence it is clear that a spirit of God is called a good spirit relative to its substance but evil relative to the function that it exercises. However, the question may still be asked as to whether, when a spirit is said to be "of God" and for that very reason is understood to be good, even if there is no further qualification, that Holy Spirit is to be understood who is in the Trinity and consubstantial with the Father and the Son, and of whom it is said, *Where the Spirit of the Lord is, there is liberty* (2 Cor 3:17); and again, *God has revealed to us through his Holy Spirit* (1 Cor 2:10); and then, *And so no one knows the things of God except the Spirit of God* (1 Cor 2:11). And in many passages the Spirit is referred to in this way as "of God" and is understood as the Holy Spirit, even if there is no further qualification, because the context gives sufficient indication as to who is being referred to, so that on occasion "of God" may not be added and yet that Spirit of God who is the source of holiness is understood. For who else is being spoken of when it says, *The Spirit himself bears witness to our spirit that we are the children of God* (Rom 8:16); and, *The Spirit himself helps our weakness* (Rom 8:26); and, *One and the same Spirit does all these things, distributing to each person just as he wishes* (1 Cor 12:11); and, *There are different gifts but the same Spirit* (1 Cor 12:4)? For in all these passages neither "of God" nor "Holy" is added, and yet he himself is understood.

But I do not know whether, after having given an example, it can be shown that, wherever the spirit of God is spoken of without further qualification, it is not the Holy Spirit that is meant in such cases but one that is, although good, nonetheless created and made. For what is cited is doubtful and calls for clearer proof, as is the case with the text, *The Spirit of God was borne above*

---

23. See Rom 1:24.

the water (Gn 1:2). I do not know what would prevent someone from seeing the Holy Spirit there.[24] For since the word *water* implies that unformed matter which was made from nothing, from which everything came into being, what prevents us from understanding the Holy Spirit of the creator here? For he was borne above this matter not by moving through space, from one place to another, which is in no way rightly said of any incorporeal thing, but by the excellence and eminence of a will that mastered all things, so that all things might be created. Moreover, that expression, as is the custom with scripture, has a certain prophetic tone and foreshadows the mystery of the future baptism in water and the Holy Spirit of a people that was still to be born. There is no compelling reason to believe, then, that what is written, *And the spirit of God was borne above the water*, refers to that spirit, as some would have it, by which the world in all its bodily mass is as it were animated for the sake of living things and of maintaining corporeal creatures in their visible form. For whatever is like that is a creature. As far as its also having been written that *the Spirit of the Lord filled the earth* (Wis 1:7), those are not lacking who would like the same spirit to be understood—namely, an invisible creature that by a kind of all-embracing sympathy vivifies and maintains everything visible. But neither do I see here what prevents the Holy Spirit from being understood, since God himself says in the prophet, *I fill heaven and earth* (Jer 23:24). For God does not fill heaven and earth apart from his Holy Spirit. Why, then, should it be surprising if the words, *He filled the earth*, were said of his Holy Spirit? For he fills in one way by making holy, as is said of Stephen *(He was filled with the Holy Spirit* [Acts 7:55]) and of others like him; in another way he fills certain saints with sanctifying grace; and in still another way he fills them, as he does all things, with his witness-bearing and ordering presence. Hence I do not know whether it can be shown from some unambiguous text in scripture that anything other than the Holy Spirit is being signified when "the spirit of God" or "the spirit of the Lord" is spoken of without further qualification. But even if perhaps this does not come to mind, I certainly think that it is not rash to say that, as often as the spirit of God is mentioned without further qualification, whether he is understood as that Holy Spirit who is consubstantial with the Father and the Son or as some invisible creature, nonetheless he cannot be understood as evil unless he is also qualified as evil. For, inasmuch as God makes good use of evil in order to carry out his judgment, he is also called the spirit of God for the punishment of the wicked and for the training and testing of the good.

---

24. See *The Literal Meaning of Genesis* I,5,11-7,13 = *Eight Questions of Dulcitius* 8.

1,6. Nor should it surprise us that it is written that afterwards the same Saul prophesied when the Spirit of God came upon him, so that after the good spirit there was an evil spirit and, again, after the evil one a good one. For this occurs not because of the changeableness of the Holy Spirit, who with the Father and the Son is unchangeable, but because of the changeableness of the human soul, as God distributes all things both to the wicked by reason of their merited condemnation or correction and to the good by reason of the generosity of his grace. Yet it could also seem that the same spirit of God was always in Saul, although it was evil for him because he was incapable of receiving its holiness. But this does not appear correct. For that understanding is safer and truer whereby, leaving aside the changeableness of the human disposition, God's good spirit has a good effect whether in prophecy or in any other work peculiar to God, whereas an evil spirit—which is itself also called a spirit of God because it is at the service of divine justice, which distributes and uses all things rightly—has an evil effect. This is particularly clear from the words, *The spirit of God departed from him and a malignant spirit from the Lord seized him* (1 S 16:14). For in no way can the same [spirit] seem to have departed [from someone] and to have seized hold [of him]. But in some manuscripts, and especially in those which seem to have been translated literally from Hebrew,[25] *the spirit of God* appears without qualification, and it is understood to be evil from the fact that it seized hold of Saul, and David reinvigorated him whenever he touched the cithara. Yet it is clear that "evil" is not added because it had already been mentioned shortly before and could be supplied and understood from its proximity in the text. For this is what is read in manuscripts of this kind: *Therefore, whenever the spirit of God seized hold of Saul, David would take up the cithara and play it, and Saul was revived and he recovered, for the evil spirit departed from him* (1 S 16:23). "The spirit of God" was not mentioned here, therefore, but only *the evil spirit,* and it was not mentioned perhaps because it appears as something that had departed or perhaps because it had been mentioned previously as follows: *And Saul's servants said to him, Behold, an evil spirit of God is troubling you. Let our lord command, and your servants who are before you shall look for a man who knows how to play the cithara and, whenever an evil spirit of God seizes hold of you, he will play and you will recover.* (1 S 16:15-16) In either case, when it was said again, *Whenever the spirit of God seized hold of Saul,* there was no

---

25. Here and in II,1,7 manuscripts translated from Hebrew are mentioned. Augustine himself did not read Hebrew, and read Greek with some difficulty, and hence was obliged to rely on translations.

need to add "evil" because it was obvious from its having been mentioned previously.

1,7. But it is an important question and one which ought not to be treated with passing interest, that when Saul, full of envy and insane with spite, was pursuing the innocent David, the spirit of God came upon him, and he walked along and prophesied. For here nothing but a good spirit, through whom the holy prophets used to discern images and visions of future things, can be understood—and that not merely because it is said, *And he prophesied* (1 S 19:23). For in manuscripts translated from Hebrew this is also found to be said as follows with reference to an evil spirit, *But after another day an evil spirit of God entered Saul, and he prophesied in the middle of his house* (1 S 18:10), and in other passages of the divine scriptures it is often the case that prophecy is called not only good but also bad, and prophets are said to be Baal's,[26] and those who prophesied in Baal's name are reproached.[27] There is no need, therefore, to understand a good spirit as having come upon Saul because it says, *And he walked along and prophesied* (1 S 19:23), but rather because it states without further qualification, *And the spirit of God also came upon him* (1 S 19:23). For *an evil spirit of God* (1 S 16:15) was not spoken of in that previous passage so that it could thus also be understood in subsequent passages; moreover, earlier passages attest even more that that spirit of God was good and truly prophetic. For David was with Samuel,[28] and Saul sent messengers to seize David.[29] But as Samuel was among the prophets and in the company of the prophets who were prophesying at that time, the messengers who had been sent received the same spirit and were prophesying, and this affected a second and even a third group.[30] Later, when Saul himself arrived, *the spirit* of *God also came upon him, and he walked along and prophesied* (1 S 19:23). For when it says, *The spirit of God also came upon them, and they too prophesied* (1 S 19:20), it was in fact the same spirit that was in the prophets, among whom Samuel was found. From these words this spirit must be understood to be good, and hence the question must be carefully discussed as to how they, when they had been sent to seize a man and kill him, merited to be touched by such a spirit, and how Saul himself, who had sent them and who had come himself in his attempt to shed innocent blood, merited to receive that spirit and to prophesy.

---

26. See 1 K 18:19.
27. See Jer 2:8.
28. See 1 S 19:18.
29. See 1 S 19:20.
30. See 1 S 19:20-21.

1,8. Doubtless there occurred here what the apostle Paul very clearly explains when he describes the loftiest way:[31] *If I speak in the tongues of men and of angels,* he says, *but do not have love, I have become sounding bronze or a clashing cymbal. And if I have prophecy and know all mysteries and everything knowable, and if I have all of faith, such that I may move mountains, but do not have love, I am nothing. And if I distribute all my property, and if I hand over my body to be burned, but do not have love, it is valueless to me.* (1 Cor 13:1-3) In this passage it is obvious that he is mentioning the gifts that are distributed by the Holy Spirit, as he says earlier, *But to each person is given a bestowal of the Spirit for a good purpose. To one person is given speech full of wisdom by the Spirit, to another speech full of knowledge by the same Spirit, to another faith in the same Spirit, to another the gift of healing in the one Spirit, to another the working of miracles, to another prophecy, to another discernment of spirits, to another different kinds of languages. But one and the same Spirit accomplishes all these things, distributing what is his to each person as he wishes.* (1 Cor 12:7-11) It is quite clear, therefore, that prophecy is one of the gifts of the Holy Spirit. Yet if someone has it and does not have love, he is nothing. As is manifest from this, it can happen that even some persons who are unworthy of eternal life and of the kingdom of heaven may be in possession of some gifts of the Holy Spirit, but since they do not have love, without which these gifts are not negligible, they are nonetheless valueless to them. No, prophecy without love, as has already been shown, does not lead to the kingdom of heaven, but love without prophecy does indeed lead to it. For when, speaking of Christ's members, [Paul] says, *Are all apostles? Are all prophets?* (1 Cor 12:29) it is clear without a doubt that even he who does not have prophecy can be counted among Christ's members. [But] what place would he have [among them] if he did not have love, without which a person is nothing? When it was a question of the members by which the body of Christ was constituted, it was never said, "Do all have love?" as it was said, *Are all apostles? Are all prophets? Do all work miracles? Do all have the gifts of healing?* (1 Cor 12:29-30) and so forth.

1,9. But suppose someone says that it can certainly happen that a person may not have prophecy and yet have love, and that therefore he belongs to and is numbered among Christ's members, but that it cannot happen that he may have prophecy and not have love, for a person who has prophecy without love is nothing. This is perhaps like saying that a person who has a soul without a mind is nothing—not because a person who has a soul without a mind can be

---

31. See 1 Cor 12:31.

found but because, if he could be found, he would be nothing. It is also like saying that, if a body has a shape but no color, it cannot be seen—not because there is a body that lacks color but because, if it existed, it could not be seen. This is perhaps how it was said that, if a person has prophecy and does not have love, he is nothing—not because prophecy cannot exist in someone without love but because, if it existed, it could not be of any value to him.

In order to respond to this question, therefore, we have to show that a wicked person had this gift of prophecy. If we found no such person, Saul himself would be sufficient evidence of it. But the Balaam whom we discussed seems to be wicked, for scripture is not silent about his having been condemned by the divine judgment, and yet he had prophecy. And, because he lacked love, he possessed a will to curse the people of Israel, which he had readied for the price furnished by their enemy, who had bribed him to pronounce the curse; but by that gift of prophecy which was bestowed on him he unwillingly pronounced a blessing.[32] And those words [of blessing] corroborate in no small way the utterance that is recorded in the gospel, which many will say on that day: *Lord, Lord, in your name we ate and drank, and in your name we prophesied, and in your name we did many miracles* (Mt 7:22). But he will say to them, *I do not know you. Depart from me, workers of iniquity.* (Mt 7:23) For we do not think that they will lie about those things in that judgment, where there will be no opportunity to deceive, and we do not read of such persons saying, "We loved you." They could say, then, even though they were ungodly and wicked, *In your name we prophesied.* But they could not say, "We observed the law that you laid down." For if they say that, the response to them will not be *I do not know you. For in this,* he says, *it is recognized that you are my disciples: if you love one another.* (Jn 13:35)

1,10. And so the example of this man Saul contradicts some proud heretics[33] who deny that anything good from the gifts of the Holy Spirit can be given to those who have no share in the lot of the saints, whereas we tell them that they can possess the sacrament of baptism which, when they come back to the

---

32. See Nm 22-24.
33. "Some proud heretics" (*superbis nonnullis hereticis*) are the Donatists who, as Augustine explains, do not believe that sinful persons can possess God's gifts, particularly the sacraments. Catholics, on the other hand, recognize the Donatists' sacraments and, when a Donatist returns to Catholic Christianity, will not allow his first baptism under Donatist auspices to be violated by a second one administered by Catholic authorities, as if the first were not valid. See *Baptism*, passim. It is tempting to see in the "some" (*nonnullis*) an implicit contrast with the many who constitute the Catholic Church, spread throughout the Roman world and not restricted to North Africa, as the Donatists were. It was a contrast frequently made by Augustine. See, e.g., *Answer to the Writings of Petilian* II,39,93-94; II,45,106.

Church, is not in any way to be violated in them or to be given [to them] as if they do not possess it. Yet they must not on that account take their salvation for granted because we do not condemn what we concede that they have received, but it is right that they should recognize that there is a fellowship of unity that must be entered into, which is bound together by love; without that they may be able to possess anything whatsoever, but, as holy and venerable as it may be, they themselves are nothing, and the more they have misused the gifts that they received in this life, which is transitory, the more unworthy they have become of the reward of eternal life. For nothing is used properly without love, and love bears all things,[34] and therefore it does not divide the unity of which it is itself the strongest bond. For that slave was not one who did not receive a talent (or perhaps the talent may be understood as something else than a truly divine gift), yet to the one who has it will be given, but from the one who does not have even what he has will be taken away.[35] What he does not have cannot be taken away, but there is something else that he does not have, and on account of its lack what he has may rightly be taken away; he does not have love in his conduct, so that whatever else he has, which is useless without love, will be taken away.

1,11. It is not surprising, then, that King Saul, at the time when he was first anointed, received the spirit of prophesying,[36] and that later, when he had been condemned because of his disobedience,[37] the spirit of the Lord departed from him and he was seized by a malignant spirit from the Lord which, on account of the function that it exercises, is itself also called *the spirit of the Lord*, because the Lord makes good use of all spirits, even bad ones, whether to condemn certain persons or to correct them or to test them; and although malice is not from God, nonetheless there is no power except from God. There was also said to have come from the Lord a sleep that overwhelmed the soldiers of the same Saul, when David removed the spear and the goblet from near his head while he slept,[38] not because there was sleep in the Lord then that would cause him to fall asleep but because the sleep that had then seized those men had been poured into them at God's behest, lest the presence of David's servant be felt in that place. Neither is it surprising, again, that the same Saul received the spirit of prophecy, although he was pursuing a righteous man and had come to the place where the company of prophets was with the intention of seizing and killing him. For this makes it quite clear that no one can be uncon-

---

34. See 1 Cor 13:7.
35. See Mt 25:29.
36. See 1 S 10:10.
37. See 1 S. 15:22-23.
38. See 1 S 26:7-12.

cerned now because of such a gift, as if he were fully acceptable to God, if he does not have love, when in fact that gift of Saul's could also have been given for some secret and mysterious reason, but it still could have been given to a wicked and envious and ungrateful person who returned evil for good and who, even after receiving the spirit, was not set right and changed for the better.

Second Question

2,1. Now let us see how it was said, *I regret having made Saul king* (1 S 15:11). For you are not ignorant in your understanding of these words, but with a fatherly affection and kindly concern you are examining my rudimentary explanations and asking how God, in whom complete foreknowledge exists, could regret anything. Now when this is said with respect to God, I myself would consider it unworthy—if there is anything that may be said that would be worthy of him. But inasmuch as his eternal power and divinity marvelously and with utmost certainty exceed all the words that are used in human discourse, whatever is humanly said of him, which may seem contemptible even in human eyes, admonishes human infirmity that even those things which one reckons are spoken fittingly of God in holy scripture are more appropriate to human comprehension than to the divine loftiness, and hence even they themselves must be transcended by more enlightened minds, just as somehow the former have been transcended.

2,2. For what person would not realize that in God, who foreknows all things, there can be no regret? And yet, of course, since there are these two words, regret and foreknowledge, we believe that one—namely, foreknowledge—is appropriate for him, while we deny that there is regret in him. But someone else may explore these matters with greater attention and ask how even foreknowledge itself may be attributed to God, finding that the sense even of this word is utterly surpassed by his ineffable dignity. That being the case, it is not surprising that both words could be said of him for the sake of human beings, even though both words are said of him inappropriately in his own regard. For what is foreknowledge except the knowledge of future things? But what is there that is future to God, who is beyond all time? For if God's foreknowledge contains these things, to him they are not future but present, and hence this can no longer be called foreknowledge but simply knowledge. If, however, future things exist neither with him nor in the order of temporal creatures, but by knowing he anticipates them, then he knows them twice—first in accordance with his foreknowledge of future things and secondly in accordance with his knowledge of present things. Whatever impinges upon God's knowledge, then, does so within the context of time, which is most absurd and incorrect. For it cannot be the case that, when they occur, he knows the things that he foreknows when they are about to occur unless he takes cognizance of them twice, both by foreknowing them previous to their existence and by knowing them after they have come into existence. Thus it would happen—which is alien to the truth—that something would impinge upon God's knowledge within the context of time, since temporal things, which are foreknown, are also known as present, which were not known before they came into being but were only foreknown. But if, since even those things that were about to take place were foreknown when they took place, nothing new impinges upon God's knowledge, but his foreknowledge will remain just as it was even before there took place what was foreknown, how may that now be called foreknowledge when it does not concern future things? For the things that he saw as future are now present, and a little later they will be past. But in no way can foreknowledge be spoken of in reference to things past, just as it cannot be spoken of in reference to things present. It comes down, then, to a situation in which what was the foreknowledge of future things becomes the knowledge of the same things, now present. And when what was at first foreknowledge in God turns afterwards into knowledge, it allows for mutability and is temporal, although God, who exists most truly and most highly, is neither mutable in any respect nor temporal in terms of any new motion.[39]

It is right, then, that we should speak not of God's foreknowledge but only of his knowledge. Let us try to understand why this is so. For we are unaccustomed to speak of knowledge in ourselves unless it refers to something that we retain in our memory as grasped and understood, when we remember that we have grasped or understood it, so that we recall it when we wish to do so. If this exists in God in such a way that it can properly be said that he understands and has understood, grasps and has grasped, then time is admitted and, moreover, that mutability gradually enters in which must be alien to the substance of God. And yet God knows and God foreknows as well in an ineffable way. For although God's knowledge is so removed from human knowledge that a comparison is laughable, each is still called knowledge. And, indeed, human [knowledge] is of such a kind that the Apostle says of it, *Knowledge will be destroyed* (1 Cor 13:8), which can in no way be said correctly of God's knowledge. Thus also a human being's anger is disordered and not without mental torment, whereas God's anger (about which it is said in the gospel, *But*

---

39. Time is the measure of motion. See *Confessions* XI,24,31.

God's anger remains on him [Jn 3:36], and by the Apostle, *For the anger of God is being revealed from heaven upon all wickedness* [Rom 1:18]) punishes the creature who is subject to it with wondrous fairness while he abides in unceasing tranquility. Likewise, a human being's mercy (*misericordia*) implies some distress of heart (*cordis miseriam*), from which it also takes its name in Latin, and this is why the Apostle exhorts us not only to rejoice with those who rejoice but also to weep with those who weep.[40] But who with any common sense at all would say that God is in any way touched by distress, even though scripture everywhere testifies that he is merciful? Similarly, we understand that human jealousy is not without the curse of ill-will but that God is not jealous in that way: the same word does not have the same connotation.

2,3. It would be tedious to give further examples, and there are numberless instances which show that many divine realities are referred to by the same terms as human realities are, although they are immeasurably distinct from each other. Nor is it without reason that the same words are applied to both sets of realities inasmuch as, when the latter are known, which are part of daily usage and which make themselves known by frequent experience, they open a path to the understanding of the former lofty matters. For when I abstract from human knowledge the quality of mutability and certain elements of transition that characterize the process of going from one thought to another, when we reflect so as to discern with the mind what it was unaware of shortly before and thus jump from one thing to another with an accumulation of recollections (which is why the Apostle says that our knowledge is partial[41]): when I remove all of this and leave only the vigor of a truth that is sure and unshaken and that illuminates everything by its unified and eternal contemplation, or rather I do not leave it, for human knowledge does not have it, and I concentrate with all my strength, then I obtain some glimpse of God's knowledge. Yet this term—based upon the fact that, through knowing, something is disclosed to a person—can be common to both [human and divine knowledge]. Nevertheless, among human beings themselves knowledge is customarily distinguished from wisdom, as even the Apostle notes: *To one person, indeed, a word of wisdom is given by the Spirit, while to another a word of knowledge according to the same Spirit* (1 Cor 12:8). In God, however,

---

40. See Rom 12:15.
41. See 1 Cor 13:9.

these are by no means two but one, whereas in human beings they are in fact customarily and fittingly distinguished in such a way that wisdom pertains to the understanding of eternal realities but knowledge to those things that we experience through the body's senses.[42] But although someone may suggest another difference, these would not have been distinguished by the Apostle if they had not been different. If it is truly the case that the word "knowledge" is to be used in reference to things that we experience through the senses, there is no knowledge whatsoever in God, for of himself God is not composed of body and soul as human beings are. But it is better to say that God's knowledge is something else and not of the same kind as that which is referred to as belonging to human beings. In similar fashion, the very thing that is called God[43] is entirely other than, for example, what is referred to in the words, *He stood in the assembly of the gods* (Ps 82:1). Yet the very shared use of the term is not intended to cause some sort of obfuscation.

Thus also I remove the turbulence from human anger so that the force of punishment may remain, and in that way I somehow rise up to an awareness of what is called God's anger. Likewise, concerning mercy, if you take away the fellow feeling of pain that you share with the person to whom you are showing mercy, and there remains the tranquil goodness implicit in helping someone and in freeing him from distress, some idea of the divine mercy results. Neither should we repudiate and scorn the jealousy of God, since we find it in scripture; but let us take away from human jealousy the pallid plague of sadness and the morbid agitation of the soul and let there remain by itself the judgment by which the corruption of chastity is not allowed to go unpunished and we shall rise up to some kind of rudimentary understanding of God's jealousy.

2,4. Hence when we read that God says, *I regret*, we should give consideration to what regret usually implies in human beings. Without doubt it includes the intention to change, but in a human being this occurs with sadness of soul, for he censures within himself what he rashly did. Let us therefore abstract those things that come from human weakness and igno-

---

42. This is Augustine's classic characterization of the difference between knowledge (*scientia*) and wisdom (*sapientia*). See *Teaching Christianity* II,7,9-11; *The Trinity* XII,4,22-XIV,19,26.

43. "The very thing that is called God": *id ipsum quod deus dicitur. Id ipsum* is a term with much meaning for Augustine when used in reference to God. See *Exposition of Psalm* 121 [122],5: "What is *id ipsum?* What always exists in the same way, not what is now one thing and another time something else." The term is sometimes translated as "the selfsame" or simply "the same." See also *Confessions* IX,10,24; *The Trinity* III,2,8.

rance, and let the intention alone remain that a particular thing not be as it was. This is how our mind can get an inkling of the general outlines within which to understand that God is regretful. For when he is said to regret, he intends that a particular thing not be as he had made it to be. But, on the other hand, since it was thus, it was supposed to be thus; and when it is no longer permitted to be thus, it is no longer supposed to be thus, thanks to a certain eternal and tranquil just judgment by which God arranges all changeable things in accordance with his unchangeable will.

2,5. But because we usually refer with praise to foreknowledge and knowledge in human beings, and because humankind generally fears rather than blames anger in great personages, we think that such things may appropriately be attributed to God. Someone who is jealous or who regrets something, because he is accustomed to being blamed or to correct what is blameworthy in himself and therefore is used to being criticized by human beings, is surprised when we read that there is something of this sort in God. But scripture, which has a view of the whole, willingly uses these terms lest things that are attractive be understood to be divine just as they are customarily understood to be human. For from these unattractive things, since we dare not understand them with reference to God as they are found in human beings, we also learn to question what we hold to be suitable and appropriate. For if a particular thing must not be said of God because it is unattractive in a human being, then we ought not to call God unchanging, because it was said critically of human beings: *For with them there is no change* [of heart] (Ps 55:19).

Similarly, there are certain things that are praiseworthy in a human being but that cannot exist in God, such as modesty, because it is a great ornament of youth, or such as fear of God, for it is not only praised in the ancient books but the Apostle also says, *Attaining the perfection of holiness in the fear of God* (2 Cor 7:1), which of course does not at all exist in God. As, then, some of the praiseworthy qualities of human beings are *not* correctly spoken of in reference to God, so some of their blameworthy qualities *are* correctly understood as belonging to God—not as they are in human beings but only through a common language whose meaning and usage are utterly distinct. For a little later the same Samuel to whom the Lord had said, *I regret having made Saul king*, himself says of God to Saul, *For he is not like a human being, that he should regret* (1 S 15:29). This clearly shows that, even when God says, *I regret,* it must not be taken in a human way, as we have now argued as much as we were able.

Third Question

3,1. You likewise ask whether the unclean spirit that was in the necromancer was able to bring it about that Samuel was seen by Saul and spoke with him.[44] But it is far more remarkable that Satan himself, the prince of all unclean spirits, who also begged to test the apostles,[45] was able to speak with God and beg that he might test Job, the most righteous of men.[46] Now this question is not a difficult one because the truth, which is present everywhere, speaks *through* whatever creature it wills *to* whatever creature it wills, and consequently it is no great matter to whom God speaks. What is to the point is what is said, because even the emperor does not speak with any number of innocent people for whose welfare he looks out with the greatest care, whereas he *does* speak with any number of criminals whom he orders to be executed. If, then, there is no question in this regard, there should be no question as to how even an unclean spirit was able to speak with the soul of a holy man. For God, the creator and sanctifier, is indeed far superior to all his holy ones. But if it is an unsettling fact that he allowed a wicked spirit to arouse the soul of a righteous man and to call it forth from, as it were, the remotest refuges of the dead, is it not more surprising that Satan took the Lord himself and set him upon the pinnacle of the Temple?[47] For, however he may have accomplished *this*, the way in which it happened that he aroused Samuel is also hidden—unless perhaps someone says that it was easier for the devil to gain permission to take the living Lord from where he wanted and to set him where he wanted than to arouse the spirit of the dead Samuel from his resting place. If what is in the gospel does not disturb us because the Lord willed and allowed it to happen, with no diminishment of his power and divinity, just as he submitted himself to be seized and overcome and mocked and crucified and slain by the Jews themselves, although they were perverse and unclean and did the devil's work, it is not absurd to believe that permission was granted in accordance with some dispensation of the divine will so that, not involuntarily or under the dominion and mastery of magical powers but intentionally and in obedience to the secret disposition of God, which lay hidden from that necromancer and from Saul, the Spirit, who was going to strike him with the divine judgment, would allow the holy prophet to make an appearance before the king. For why would the soul of a good man, if it came forth at the behest of evil persons in the land of the living, appear to lose its dignity when even good persons in the land of the

---

44. See 1 S 28:7-19.
45. See Lk 22:31.
46. See Jb 1:6-12.
47. See Mt 4:5.

living, who have often been summoned and who come to evil ones, cooperate with them in accordance with the requirements of justice, all the while maintaining the unsullied beauty of their virtue and dealing with the vices of those others as the utility or the need of temporal affairs dictates?[48]

3,2. Apropos of this event, however, there could be another and easier solution and a simpler explanation, whereby we believe not that the spirit of Samuel was really aroused from its rest but that a kind of phantasm and imaginary illusion was produced by the devil's machinations, which scripture therefore refers to by the name of Samuel because the images of things are usually referred to by the names of what they represent. For example, all the things that are painted or fashioned out of metal or wood or some other material that is suitable for works of this sort and that are also seen in dreams, and all the things that are close approximations of those things, are usually referred to by the names of what they represent. For who would hesitate to call the portrait of a man a man? Whenever, in fact, we look at portraits of particular individuals we unhesitatingly use their proper names, and when gazing at a framed picture or a mural we say, That is Cicero, that is Sallust, that is Achilles, that is Hector, that is the River Simois,[49] that is Rome, although they are merely painted images. Hence those figures of the cherubim that, although they are heavenly powers, were fashioned from metal, as God commanded, and set upon the ark of the covenant in order to signify something great,[50] are also referred to as nothing else than cherubim. In the same way, whoever has a dream does not say, I saw an image of Augustine or Simplician, but rather, I saw Augustine or Simplician (although at the moment that he saw such a thing we ourselves were unaware), so much is it taken for granted that it was not the men themselves that were seen but their images. And Pharaoh said that in his dreams he saw ears of corn and cows,[51] not the images of ears of corn and cows. If, then, it is common practice that images are referred to by the names of what they represent, it is not surprising that scripture refers to what was seen as Samuel, even if perhaps the image of Samuel appeared through the

---

48. This is a relatively rare acknowledgement in patristic literature of the possibility that the good and the wicked may work together in order to pursue a goal consistent with justice (*quod officium postulat aequitatis*) in such a way that the good do not lose their virtue through contact with the wicked. It is the beginning of a theology of politics, or at least of an aspect of it.
49. Sallust (86-34 B.C.) was a Roman historian and political figure, while Achilles, Hector and the River Simois all appear throughout Homer's *Iliad*.
50. See Ex 25:18.
51. See Gn 41:17-24.

machinations of him who disguises himself as an angel of light and his ministers as ministers of righteousness.[52]

3,3. But if it is striking that true things were foretold even by Saul's evil
spirit, it can also appear remarkable that the demons recognized Christ,[53]
whom the Jews did not recognize. For when God wishes someone to know
true things even through base and infernal spirits, although they are only
temporal and pertain to this mortal life, it is convenient and not inappropriate
for him who is almighty and righteous to grant, by the hidden working of his
ministers, some power of prediction even to such spirits so that they may
announce to human beings what they hear from angels, and thus, for their
punishment, those to whom these things are foretold will suffer through foreknowledge the evil that threatens them before it comes. But they only hear as
much as the lord and ruler of all either commands or permits. Hence also the
soothsaying spirit in the Acts of the Apostles bears witness to the apostle Paul
and attempts to be an evangelist.[54] Yet these beings mix in lies, and the truth
that they have succeeded in knowing they foretell as much for the sake of
deceiving as for that of teaching. And perhaps this is why, when that image of
Samuel predicted that Saul was going to die, he also said that he was going to
be with him, which was manifestly false. For in fact we read in the gospel that
after death the good are separated from the bad by a great gulf, since the Lord
attests that, between that proud rich man, when he was suffering torments in
the nether world, and him who used to lie with his sores at his gate and was
now at rest, a huge gulf intervened.[55] Or if Samuel told Saul, *You will be with
me* (1 S 28:19), referring not to an equality of happiness but to the equal condition of death, because each was a human being and each was mortal, then it
was a matter of a dead man predicting death to a living man.

Your Prudence sees, I am sure, that that text has an explanation consonant
with each understanding, which is not contrary to faith,[56] unless perhaps
through deeper and more complex research, which exceeds the limits of my
strength and time, it may be discovered whether the human soul, once it has
departed this life and been called back by incantations, can or cannot appear to
living persons clothed in the features of a body, so that it may be able not only
to be seen but also to be recognized. And, if possible, it may be discovered
whether even the soul of a righteous person may not indeed be compelled by

52. See 2 Cor 11:14-15.
53. See Mt 8:29.
54. See Acts 16:16-17.
55. See Lk 16:26.
56. See Miscellany of *Eighty-three Questions* LIX,1 and note 155.

magic formulas but may deign to show itself in obedience to the secret injunctions of the highest law. Thus, if it is ascertained that this cannot occur, neither understanding in the discussion and explanation of this passage of scripture will be allowed, but, with the former excluded, it will be clear that the simulated image of Samuel was produced in a diabolical fashion. But since, whether it can or cannot occur, Satan's stratagems and his crafty manipulation of simulated images are nonetheless aimed at deceiving the human senses in every way, we certainly ought not, in all caution, to object to more careful research (although we should still think that a thing of this sort was accomplished through the evil devices of that necromancer), as long as something more is not given us to reflect upon and work from.[57]

Fourth Question

4. As to your question about the scriptural passage, *King David went in and sat down before the Lord* (2 S 7:18), what else can it mean if not that he sat in the presence of the Lord where the ark of the covenant was, by which a certain presence of the Lord that is more sacred and more favorable can be understood, or that he sat down with the intention of praying, which is something that is not correctly done except in the presence of the Lord—that is, in the depths of the heart? *Before the Lord* can also be understood as the place where there is no human being who could hear a person praying. Whether, then, it was the ark of the covenant or a concealed location, far from onlookers, or the intimacy of the heart, where the disposition for prayer is located, *He sat before the Lord* is well put, unless perhaps there is a question as to why he prayed while seated, although holy Elijah did the same thing when he prayed and begged for rain.[58]

We are made aware by a number of examples that there is no objection to how the body is positioned for prayer, as long as the mind is present to God and fixes its attention [upon him].[59] For we pray standing, as scripture says, *But the tax-collector stood a long way off* (Lk 18:13); and kneeling, as we read

---

57. When Augustine reproduced this question in *Eight Questions of Dulcitus* 6, he added in section 5 that he had found another text (Sir 46:20) relating to the account of the necromancer.
58. See 1 K 18:41-45.
59. "As long as the mind is present to God and fixes its attention [upon him]": *dum animus deo praesens peragat intentionem suam*. The translation in the Bibliothèque Augustinienne reads: "pourvu que l'âme, attentive a Dieu, exprime ses désirs"("as long as the soul, attentive to God, expresses its desires"). Both translations of these few important words on prayer seem possible.

in the Acts of the Apostles;[60] and sitting, as we have seen with David and Elijah. And unless we also prayed while lying down, it would not be written in the Psalms: *Every night I will wash my bed, I will water my pillow with tears* (Ps 6:6). For when someone seeks to pray, he arranges his limbs just as it occurs to him at the time that his body is best disposed to arouse his mind. But inasmuch as the desire to pray comes not from seeking but from being bestowed,[61] when a person suddenly thinks of something that with wordless groans incites the desire to pray, however it may have found that person, prayer should by no means be put off so that we may look for a place to sit down or to stand or to throw ourselves down. For the mind's attentiveness creates a solitude for itself, and it is often even unaware, at the time when it occurs, of where it is facing or of the body's position.[62]

Fifth Question

5. Now in the words that blessed Elijah says, *O Lord, witness of this widow, since I am living with her you have acted badly by killing her son* (1 K 17:20), there should be nothing astonishing if the correct manner in which the words are spoken is maintained. For these are not the words of someone who believes that God acted very badly with that widow, who had welcomed the prophet very hospitably, especially at that time, when he to whom she had offered her small amount of food in its entirety was in such severely straitened circumstances. And so it is put as though he had said, "O Lord, witness of this widow with whom I am living, have you acted badly by killing her son?" In this way it may be understood that the Lord was indeed the witness of that woman's heart, in which he saw such great hospitality, which is why he himself had sent Elijah to her, and that he brought death upon her son not in order to act badly but in order to perform a miracle for the glory of his name, by which he might commend that great prophet to those who were living at the time and to those who would come later, just as the Lord said that Lazarus was not dead for death's sake but so that God might be glorified in his Son.[63] Events bore this out, for, thanks to the very depth of Elijah's faith, it did not transpire that the woman who gave him hospitality was afflicted with sorrow; instead God in his

---

60. See Acts 20:36.
61. "Comes not from seeking but from being bestowed": *non quaeritur sed infertur.* This is consistent with the understanding of grace that Augustine explained in I,2 of the present work.
62. There is a hint here of the ecstatic self-forgetfulness that prayer sometimes induces and that appears fullblown in John Cassian, *Conferences* IX,31: "That is not a perfect prayer in which the monk understands himself or what he is praying."
63. See Jn 11:4.

magnanimity showed the widow to what sort of servant of God she had been hospitable. As scripture says in the next lines, *And three times he breathed on the boy and called upon the Lord and said, Lord my God, now let the soul of this boy return to him. And so it happened.* (1 K 17:21-22) This petition, therefore, with which Elijah asked so briefly and so trustingly that the boy would arise, gives a clear indication as to the tone in which the previous words were spoken. And the woman herself showed that her son had suffered death for the reason that Elijah presumed when he had spoken those words not affirmatively but negatively. For when she received her son back alive she said, *See, I know that you are a man of God and that the word of the Lord is most truthful in your mouth* (1 K 17:24). But there are numerous passages in the scriptures that, unless they are spoken in that way, yield a contrary meaning, such as, *Who will accuse God's chosen ones? God, who justifies.* (Rom 8:33) If you respond affirmatively, you see how much mischief may be caused. Therefore the words must be spoken as though it were being asked, "Is it God, who justifies?" so that it is understood: "Of course not!" And in this way I think that Elijah's meaning, which an incorrect tone can obscure, is clear.[64]

Sixth Question

6. But concerning the spirit of lying by which Ahab was deceived,[65] our understanding, which I think was previously discussed with sufficient clarity,[66] is that God, the almighty and just distributor of punishments and rewards in accordance with personal merits, employs not only good and holy agents for works that suit them but even wicked ones for works appropriate to them, since these latter, by reason of their perverse desires, enjoy doing harm; but they are only permitted as much as he, who arranges everything according to measure and number and weight,[67] judges best. But the prophet Micaiah spoke as it had been revealed to him.[68] For matters that are mysterious and profoundly obscure are revealed to the prophets in a way that human instinct can grasp, since in the process of revelation it is instructed also through the images of things as though through words.

---

64. Although modern exegetes would balk at Augustine's reinterpretation of Elijah's words in 1 K 17:20 and his refusal to accept the possibility that the prophet might complain to God about the divine decisions, they would agree with his understanding of Rom 8:33. Part of the problem, at least regarding the latter verse, has to do with the lack of a question mark in the Latin language.
65. See 1 K 22:19-23.
66. See especially II,1,4.11; 3,1.3.
67. See Wis 11:20.
68. See 1 K 22:19-23.

For God does these things while being present everywhere, and everywhere always present in his entirety, and the holy angels and all the sublime and most pure spirits created by him consult his simple and unchanging and eternal truth and see in that which is eternally just what they should accomplish within the bounds of time for the welfare of lesser creatures. The fallen spirits, on the other hand, who have not abided in the truth and who, on account of their uncleanness and the infirmity characteristic of their desires and punishments, are unable to gaze upon his presence from within or to consult his truth, look for signs from without by way of created reality and are moved by them either to do a thing or not to do it,[69] and they are compelled by the eternal law by which the universe is governed, having been prevailed over and constrained either to wait upon God's permission or to yield to his command. But why all of this is the way it is, it would be too arduous to grasp and take too long to explain.

I fear, now, that what has been said by me may not have met your expectations and may have been tedious to Your Dignity, given the fact that, although you wanted a single book from me on everything that you queried me about, I sent you two books—very long ones!—and perhaps did not at all answer your questions carefully and promptly. Hence, on account of my errors, I beseech your frequent and assiduous prayers. But I also entreat your briefest and most considered opinion on this work, and, although it may be very frank, I shall not reject it as too severe.

---

69. On the demons' skill in acting in accordance with external signs see Augustine, *The Divination of Demons* 3,7;4,9.

Eight Questions of Dulcitius

Introduction

Unique among Augustine's writings, the *Eight Questions of Dulcitius* consists almost entirely of excerpts from previous works of his. Composed about the year 425, it responds to eight questions forwarded to the author by Dulcitius, who was a tribune sent by Emperor Honorius to enforce the decrees against the Donatists.[1] In *Revisions* II,65 Augustine says that, given the unusual composition of the work, he would not have included it in the list of his writings except for the fact that parts of questions 1-4 and 6-8 were new, while all of question 5 was also new. In his opening remarks Augustine explains that he answered Dulcitius' questions in this way because to have done otherwise would have been too laborious for him (he was in his early 70s at the time) and, in any event, would not have been of any more use to his correspondent.

In contrast to the *Miscellany of Questions in Response to Simplician,* in the present work Augustine seems to preserve his addressee's questions integrally. They suggest that Dulcitius was a man who, for all his official duties, was familiar with scripture and a theological dilettante. Some of his questions are of perennial importance. The first is one of precisely such importance. Dulcitius asks whether the torments of hell will ever end for those who have committed sin after having been baptized. He himself is of the opinion that these torments are in fact not eternal, and he cites two scriptural texts, Mt 5:26 and 1 Cor 3:15, as evidence in favor of this view, although a third text, Mt 1:25, creates ambiguity in his mind. Augustine responds by quoting *Faith and Works* 14,23-16,29 and *Faith, Hope and Charity (Enchiridion)* 18,67-69. His study of Paul's mysterious words in 1 Cor 3:11-15, which preoccupy him elsewhere,[2] produces the following results: faith alone is insufficient for salvation but must be supplemented by the works of love; hell's fire is eternal, and those who suffer in hell suffer eternally in that fire; some kind of purgative fire, either real or metaphorical, awaits those who were attached to this world's goods once they have parted with those goods. In his conclusion, written specifically for Dulcitius, Augustine cautions that the love which one may feel for grave sinners who have been baptized must not be allowed to dilute Paul's stern teaching in 1 Cor 6:9-10 and Eph 5:5-6 that the kingdom of God is closed to them.

---

1. See *Answer to Gaudentius, a Donatist Bishop* I,1,1. Augustine also addressed his Letter 204 to Dulcitius, on the treatment of the Donatists.
2. For a survey of his exegesis see Bibliothèque Augustinienne 1,8,503-505.

Dulcitius' second question has to do with the value of offerings made on behalf of the souls of the departed. As his answer Augustine cites *The Care to be Taken for the Dead* 1,1-2 and *Faith, Hope and Charity* 29,109-110, the burden of which is that only those whose earthly lives were neither extraordinarily good nor very bad will benefit from such offerings. Conversely, these offerings will profit neither the truly good nor the truly wicked. Hence the kind of earthly life that one lives is determinative of the value of the offerings made for one after death. Augustine ignores the comment with which Dulcitius accompanies his query—namely, that in the view of some it would be better if the soul of the deceased could make offerings for itself rather than having to rely on others.

The third question has two parts: When the Lord comes will he immediately judge? Must those who will be snatched up in the clouds to meet Christ, as described in 1 Thes 4:17, first experience death or not? Augustine answers the first part affirmatively with a curt reference to the creed. For the second he turns to his Letter 193,9-13, in which he admits that he cannot reconcile the scriptural and creedal texts which suggest that not all will die (or have died, in the cases of Enoch and Elijah) with the scriptural texts which insist that death must precede resurrection. In his Letter 59,3, written in the mid-390s, Jerome had interpreted 1 Thes 4:17 to mean that some persons would indeed escape death and that their intact bodies would then be glorified. Augustine, who may very well have known of Jerome's letter, does not refer to it to support the same position, to which he himself leans.

In the fourth place Dulcitius asks how David could have predicted in Ps 112:2 that the offspring of the upright would be called powerful or blessed when in fact both the righteous and the unrighteous have offspring both cursed and blessed. Augustine's response is taken from a sermon, his exposition of Ps 111[112],2-3, and is in essence a warning against making hasty judgments —i.e., in the present life—as to who is cursed and who is blessed.

Since his reply to Dulcitius' fifth question was composed expressly for him and not excerpted from an extant work of his, Augustine relegates it to the last place and proceeds at once to the sixth question, which is about the necromancer of 1 S 28:7-19. He had already answered a similar question in the *Miscellany of Questions in Response to Simplician* II,3 (translated in this volume), and he repeats that answer here. At the end he adds that, subsequent to writing the *Miscellany,* he discovered a further scriptural reference to the story of the necromancer in the Book of Ecclesiasticus.

Dulcitius' seventh question asks how Sarah could be said to have avoided dishonor if she barely escaped having sexual relations with Abimelech and did in fact have them with Pharaoh, as suggested in Gn 20:2-4 and 12:14-20 respectively. Building his case upon the text of Est 2:12-13, Augustine begins by saying that she probably did not have intercourse with Pharaoh. In regard to Abimelech, he briefly recalls an incident in nearby Mauritania Sitifensis in which a man was prevented by a dream from having intercourse with a widow whom he had kidnapped. Then, in defense of Abraham, Sarah's husband, who seemed to have put her in a compromising situation, Augustine quotes a passage from his *Answer to Faustus, a Manichean* XXII,33, excerpted from a longer section of that work (XXII,33-40) which discusses these two incidents in detail and relies mostly on allegory to interpret as justifiable what was, at least on the surface, the patriarch's morally dubious behavior. Roughly the first half of Augustine's response to this question is new material, and it is fascinating as a combination of exegesis and anecdote in the service of maintaining the respectability of the patriarchal couple.

As his eighth question, Dulcitius wonders whether the Spirit of God that was borne above the water, as recounted in Gn 1:2, was the third person of the Trinity or some lesser spirit. Augustine's answer from *The Literal Meaning of Genesis* I,5,11-7,13 takes it for granted that this was the Holy Spirit and offers possible explanations for why he was appropriately said to be borne above the water—water being a symbol here either of inchoate creation or of the unconverted and hence fluid soul. The Holy Spirit, however, was borne above this unfinished being in terms not of location but of love and power. And with this mention of the Holy Spirit in Gn 1:2 Augustine finds, as he does also in *Confessions* XIII,5,6, an allusion in Gn 1:1 to the other persons of the Trinity as well, while in Gn 1:3-4 he finds a second allusion to the Trinity.

At last Augustine turns to Dulcitius' fifth question: Why would the Lord, who foreknows all things, say that he had chosen David, a man after his own heart (in the words of Acts 13:22), when he knew that David would be such a great sinner? (Both Dulcitius' question and Augustine's response make better sense in the realization that the citation from Acts 13:22 is actually a conflation of as many as three Old Testament texts—1 S 13:14, 1 K 8:16 and Ps 89:20.) Augustine replies that these words apply historically to David, who did indeed sin greatly but who also repented of his sins, and can apply prophetically to Christ, who is often referred to under the name of David in the Hebrew scriptures and who was truly the man after his Father's heart. In his identification of David with Christ, Augustine follows a long tradition in the early Church.[3]

---

3. This tradition is conveniently summarized in Angelo Di Berardino, ed., *Encyclopedia of the Early Church*, trans. by Adrian Walford (New York 1992) I,220-221.

Revisions II,65

The book that I entitled *Eight Questions of Dulcitius* was not supposed to be listed among my books in this work because it was composed from items that I had previously written elsewhere, except that there is some discussion in it that we included, and to one of those questions I gave a response that is not in any of my works but that succeeded in coming to mind then. The book begins thus: "As far as possible, my dearest son Dulcitius, it seems to me."

Eight Questions of Dulcitius

As far as possible, my dearest son Dulcitius, it seems to me that I have not delayed in responding to your questions. In fact it was during the Easter season this year, when I was at home with those closest to me, that on the third of the kalends of April[1] I received the letter of Your Love that had been sent to me from Carthage. Following those holy days, however, I set out at once for Carthage, and in that city the overwhelming number of tasks—of which there can be no end there—gave me no time to dictate anything. But after I came back from there and had spent two weeks with my own people, who after my long absence insisted that I attend to other affairs (for I was allowed to return after three months), I did not put off answering the questions that you sent, which I had already dealt with in several of my works, and from those same works I obtained either an answer or at least an opinion. The only thing that I was unable to retrieve [from my earlier works] had to do with your question as to why the Lord, with his infallible foreknowledge of future events, said, *I have chosen David,* [a man] *after my own heart* (Acts 13:22), although he committed such great misdeeds; where I dealt with this, what I said about it, and whether it is in a book or a letter of mine I do not know. Hence, since this obliged me to research the matter anew, I kept it until the end in this treatise of mine, desiring first to set down what I had that was already at hand in my other volumes. In this way I would neither fail Your Holiness' zeal, which is particularly precious to me, nor, on the other hand, be constrained to write what would be very toilsome to me and would not be of any further help to you.

First Question

1. That brings us to your first question, which is: "Do those who are sinners after baptism ever leave Gehenna? For," you say, "there are a considerable number of persons who have a different view in this regard and who say that the torments of sinners, like the reward of the righteous, will have no end. Their desire is to maintain that punishment will remain as unending as does reward. Directed against them are those words from the gospel that say, *You shall not leave there until you pay back the last penny* (Mt 5:26). The implication, therefore, is that once this has been paid back a person can leave. We hold to this and to the statement of the Apostle: *He shall be saved, yet as though by fire* (1 Cor 3:15). But because," you say, "we read elsewhere, *And he did not*

---

1. I.e., March 30th.

241

know her until she gave birth (Mt 1:25), which we are unable to interpret in this way, we wish to be made more certain in this regard." That is the extent of your question.

2. To this I respond from my book entitled *Faith and Works,*[2] where I spoke thus on this matter: "Now James," I said, "is so vehemently opposed to those who think that faith without works counts toward salvation that he even compares them to demons when he says, *You believe that God is one, and you do well; the demons also believe and tremble* (Jas 2:19). What could be said more succinctly, more truthfully, more vehemently, since in the gospel as well we read that the demons said this, when they confessed that Christ was the Son of God—which was praised in Peter's confession [of faith][3]—and were rebuked by him?[4] *What good will it be, my brothers,* says James, *if someone says that he has faith but does not have works? Will faith be able to save him?* (Jas 2:20) He also says that *faith without works is dead* (Jas 2:20). How long, then, will they be mistaken who from their dead faith promise themselves eternal life?

3. "Hence it is well to pay close attention to how the following words of the apostle Paul should be taken, which are clearly difficult to understand: *For no one can lay a foundation other than that which has been laid, which is Christ Jesus. But if anyone builds upon this foundation gold, silver, precious stones, wood, hay or straw, the work of each person will be made manifest. For the day will declare, because it will be revealed in fire, and fire will test the work of each person, as to what sort it is. If the work that a person has built upon remains, he shall receive a reward, but if a person's work burns up, he shall be condemned. But he himself shall be saved, yet as though by fire.* (1 Cor 3:11-15) They think that this should be understood such that those who add good works to the faith that is in Christ may be seen to build gold, silver and precious stones upon this foundation, while those whose works are bad, although they have the same faith, [are seen to build] wood, hay and straw. On this basis they believe that, thanks to their foundation, they can be cleansed by certain punishments of fire in order to obtain salvation.

4. "If this is the case, we acknowledge that it is with an admirable charity that they are trying to admit everyone without exception to baptism—not only male and female adulterers who claim marriages that are false in opposition to the Lord's words but also brazen prostitutes who remain in this most sinful profession, whom certainly no church, not even the most careless, has been in

---

2. *Faith and Works* 14,23-16,29.
3. See Mt 16:16.
4. See Mt 8:28-32.

the habit of admitting unless they have first been freed from prostitution. But with this reasoning I do not understand whatsoever why they are not *all* admitted. For who would not prefer that they at least be well cleansed by a fire of a specific duration, thanks to having a foundation laid down, even if they constructed it of wood, hay and straw, than that they perish forever?

"But then those words will be false that are without obscurity or ambiguity: *If I should have all faith, such that I may move mountains, but do not have love, I am nothing* (1 Cor 13:12); and: *What good will it be, my brothers, if someone says that he has faith but does not have works? Will faith be able to save him?* (Jas 2:14) These words will be false too: *Make no mistake: neither fornicators nor idolaters nor adulterers nor the effeminate nor those who sleep with men nor thieves nor the avaricious nor drunkards nor slanderers nor the greedy shall possess the kingdom of God* (1 Cor 6:9-10). These also will be false: *The works of the flesh are clear. They are fornications, impurities, worship of idols, sorcery, enmities, disputes, jealousies, animosities, dissensions, here-sies, envies, drunkenness, gluttony and things like that. I declare to you, as I have declared, that those who do such things shall not possess the kingdom of God.* (Gal 5:19-21) These [words] will be false. For if they merely believe and are baptized, although they persevere in such evildoing, they will be saved by fire; and therefore those who have been baptized in Christ, even if they do such things, will possess the kingdom of God. But in vain is it said, *And that is what some of you were, but you have been washed clean* (1 Cor 6:11), if, even after they have been washed clean, they stay that way. What Peter said will also be seen as vain: *Baptism saves you as well by a similar form, not the putting off of the flesh's filthiness but the questioning of a good conscience* (1 Pt 3:21), because [according to this opinion] baptism saves even those who have the worst consciences, filled with every disgraceful and criminal thing, and have not been turned by repentance from their misdeeds, for they will be saved on account of the foundation that they laid at their baptism, although by fire.

"I also do not see why the Lord said, *If you wish to attain to life, observe the commandments* (Mt 19:17), or why he spoke of the things that have to do with virtuous behavior,[5] if, even when these things are not observed, a person can attain to life by faith alone, which is dead without works. How, finally, will this be true, which he will say to those who are placed on his left: *Go into the eternal fire that has been prepared for the devil and his angels* (Mt 25:41)? He does not rebuke them because they have not believed in him but because they

---

5. See Mt 19:18-19.

have not done good works.[6] For no one at all should promise himself eternal life on the basis of a faith that, without works, is dead. For that reason he said that he would separate all the peoples who were intermingled with each other and used the same pastures, so that there would appear those who will say to him, *Lord, when did we see you suffering this or that and not minister to you?* (Mt 25:44) They believed in him, but they did not trouble to do good works, as if by dead faith itself one could attain to eternal life. Will perhaps those who did not do works of mercy go into eternal fire[7] but not those who took what was not theirs, or those who destroyed the temple of God in themselves[8] and were unmerciful to themselves? As though works of mercy would have any value without love! As the Apostle says, *if I should distribute all my property to the poor but do not have love, it is of no use to me* (1 Cor 13:3). Or as though someone who does not love himself could love his neighbor as himself![9] For he who loves wickedness hates his own soul.[10] Nor can it be said here (which several persons have let themselves be fooled by) that it was an eternal fire that was spoken of and not eternal punishment itself. They think that the persons in question will indeed pass through a fire that will be eternal, and to them, on account of their dead faith, they promise salvation by fire. In other words, the fire itself will be eternal, but their being burned—that is, the effect of the fire—will not be eternal for them. But the Lord, foreseeing this too as the Lord, concluded his words in this way and said, *Thus they shall go into eternal burning, but the righteous into eternal life* (Mt 25:46). There will be, then, an eternal burning like fire, and the Truth said that they will go into it who, as he declared, were lacking not faith but good works.

5. "If, then, all these and other things that can be found stated unambiguously and frequently throughout scripture are false, that understanding of the wood and the hay and the straw—[namely,] that those who have neglected good works while maintaining mere faith in Christ will be saved by fire—is true. But if they are both true and evident, then certainly another meaning will have to be sought in the Apostle's words, and they will have to be classified among those things that Peter says are difficult to understand in his writings and that people must not pervert to their own ruin.[11] Thus, against the clearest witness of the scriptures, they assure the gaining of salvation for those who are

---

6. See Mt 25:41-43.
7. See Mt 25:45-46.
8. See 1 Cor 3:17.
9. See Mt 19:19.
10. See Ps 11:5.
11. See 2 Pt 3:16.

most wicked, who cling most obstinately to their own wickedness and who have not changed through correction or repentance.

6. "Here it will perhaps be asked of me what *I* think about Paul's words themselves and how *I* believe they should be understood. I confess that at this point I would rather listen to those who are more intelligent and learned and who could explain them in such a way that all those things that I mentioned previously, and whatever else I did not mention, would remain true and unshaken.[12] Scripture testifies most openly in regard to these things that faith is of no use unless it is as the Apostle describes it—that is, working by love[13]—and that there can be no salvation without works, neither apart from fire nor by fire because, if there is salvation by fire, then it is really [faith] itself that saves. But it is said openly and apodictically: *What good is it if someone says that he has faith but does not have works? Will faith be able to save him?*

"Nonetheless, I will say as briefly as I can what I myself think, too, about those words of the apostle Paul that are difficult to understand, as long as what I said is taken into consideration—namely, that I would rather listen to my betters.

"Christ is the foundation in the structure of the wise architect.[14] This does not lack an explanation, for it is clearly said: *For no one can lay a foundation other than what has been laid, which is Christ Jesus* (1 Cor 3:11). But if Christ, then certainly faith in Christ. By faith Christ dwells in our hearts, as the same Apostle says.[15] But if faith in Christ, then surely that which the Apostle described, *which works by love* (Gal 5:6). For it is not the faith of the demons, although they themselves believe and tremble and confess that Jesus is the Son of God,[16] which can be taken for the foundation. Why is this so if not because it is not the faith that works by love but that is expressed by fear? Faith in Christ, then, the faith of Christian grace, which is the faith that works by love, allows no one to perish once it has been laid as a foundation.

"But if I should try to discuss in greater detail what it means to build upon this foundation gold, silver and precious stones, or wood, hay and straw, I fear that this explanation will be harder to understand. Yet, with the Lord's

---

12. Augustine's modesty in confessing that he would prefer to listen to others in this matter is almost certainly genuine. He expresses this kind of sentiment frequently. See, e.g., Letters 157,41; 166,9; 202A,15. See also question 3,3.6 and note 55.
13. See Gal 5:6.
14. See 1 Cor 3:10.
15. See Eph 3:17.
16. See Mt 8:28-29.

help, I shall make an effort to set out as briefly and clearly as I can what I think.

"Recall the man who asked the good master what good thing he should do in order to possess eternal life, and he heard that, if he wanted to attain to life, he should keep the commandments, and when he asked what the commandments were, he was told,[17] *Do not kill, do not commit adultery, do not steal, do not bear false witness, honor your father and your mother, and love your neighbor as yourself* (Mt 19:18-19). If he did these things with faith in Christ he would undoubtedly have the faith that works by love. For he could not love his neighbor as himself unless he had received the love of God, without which he could not love himself. But if he also did what the Lord added to this when he said, *If you wish to be perfect, go, sell all that you have and give to the poor, and you will have treasure in heaven; and come, follow me* (Mt 19:21), he would be building upon that foundation gold, silver and precious stones. For he would be thinking only of the things that are of God and how to please God,[18] and to think along these lines is, in my view, gold, silver and precious stones. But if he were in the grip of a kind of fleshly affection for his riches, even though he gave alms from them and did not strive to increase them by fraud and theft or, through fear of lessening or losing them, slip into criminal or disgraceful behavior (since in that way he would be withdrawing himself from the solidity of that foundation)—on account of a fleshly affection that he had for them, then, as I have said, which would not allow him to lack such good things without distress, he would be building upon that foundation wood, hay and straw, especially if he also had a wife, so that for her sake he would be thinking of the things of the world and how to please his wife.[19] These [riches], then, are not abandoned without distress when they are loved with fleshly affection. Therefore those who possess them in such a way that they have for their foundation the faith that works by love, and who do not, by any calculation or desire, prefer them to it, suffer pain at their loss and attain to salvation by a distress that is like fire. A person is that much more secure from this distress and pain the less he loves those things or if he possesses them as though he did not possess them.[20] But the one who, in order to keep them or to acquire them, commits murder, adultery, fornication, idolatry or anything like that will not be saved

17. See Mt 19:16-18.
18. See 1 Cor 7:32.
19. See 1 Cor 7:33.
20. See 1 Cor 7:29.

by fire on account of his foundation; rather, because his foundation has been destroyed, he will be tormented in everlasting fire.

7. "Hence, in their desire to prove that faith alone suffices, they also cite the Apostle's words: *If one who is unfaithful departs, let him depart, for there is no brother or sister who is under obligation in such a case* (1 Cor 7:15); in other words, for the sake of faith in Christ even one's own wife, to whom one is bound in a lawful union, may be abandoned without any culpability if she does not wish to remain with a Christian husband because he is Christian.[21] On the other hand, they do not consider that she may be justifiably dismissed if she says to her husband, 'I will not be your wife unless you rob in order to make me rich, or unless, even as a Christian, you engage in the pimping that you used to do in our home,' or if she knew anything else criminal or disgraceful in her husband that used to please her and would either satisfy her lust or make her life comfortable or even allow her to go out better dressed. For then, if he sincerely repented of his dead works[22] when he came to baptism and has as his foundation the faith that works by love, he to whom his wife speaks will undoubtedly be held more by his love of divine grace than by his wife's body, and he will bravely cut off the member that is an obstacle to him.[23] But whatever sadness of heart he may endure in this separation on account of his fleshly affection for his wife, this is the loss that he will suffer, this is the fire by which—as the hay burns—he will be saved. But if he had a wife as though he did not have her,[24] for the sake not of lust but of mercy, so that he might save her,[25] and paying rather than exacting the conjugal debt,[26] he will experience no fleshly sorrow whatsoever when he is separated from such a marriage, for while he was in it he was thinking only of the things that are of God and how to please God.[27] And to the extent that by those thoughts he built gold, silver and precious stones, to that extent he will suffer no loss, and his structure, which was not made of hay, will not be burned up by any fire.

8. "Whether, therefore, people suffer these things in this life alone or similar things pursue them after this life as well, the understanding of these words, in my opinion, is not inconsistent with the law of truth. But even if

---

21. The issue of pagan-Christian marriage is also briefly discussed in the *Miscellany of Eighty-three Questions* LXXXIII. See note 469 there.
22. See Heb 6:1.
23. See Mt 5:30.
24. See 1 Cor 7:29.
25. See 1 Cor 7:16.
26. See 1 Cor 7:3.
27. See 1 Cor 7:32.

there is another [understanding] that should be chosen instead, which does not occur to me, as long as we hold to this one we are not obliged to say to the unrighteous, the rebellious, criminals, the defiled, parricides and matricides, murderers, fornicators, men who sleep with men, kidnappers, liars, oath-breakers and anything else that is contrary to sound doctrine, which is in accordance with the gospel of the glory of the blessed God:[28] 'If you merely believe in Christ and receive the sacrament of his baptism you shall be saved, even if you have not changed the worst sort of life.'

9. "Hence that Canaanite woman does not establish a precedent for us because the Lord gave her what she asked for, since he had previously said, *It is not good to take away the children's bread and give it to the dogs* (Mt 15:26), because he who sees into the heart saw that she had changed when he praised her. And therefore he did not say, 'O dog, great is your faith,' but, *O woman, great is your faith* (Mt 15:28). He changed his way of talking because he saw that her disposition was changed, and he observed that his rebuke of her had borne fruit. I would be surprised, however, if he praised in her a faith that was without works—that is, a faith not such as could work by love, a dead faith and, as James did not hesitate to call it, a faith not of Christians but of demons. If, finally, they are unwilling to see that the Canaanite woman changed her errant behavior when Christ reproached her by his disdainful rebuke, and if they have come across some persons who merely believe and do not so much as conceal the basest kind of life but even openly profess it and have no intention of changing, let them heal their children if they can, as the daughter of the Canaanite woman was healed,[29] yet let them not make them into members of Christ when they do not discontinue being the members of a prostitute."[30]

10. And similarly, in the book entitled *Faith, Hope and Charity*,[31] which I wrote to my son and your brother Laurence,[32] these are my words on this matter: "It is believed by some that even those who do not abandon the name of Christ and are baptized in the Church by his bath, who are not cut off from it by any schism or heresy, may live in whatever sins they please, which they need not wash away by repentance or redeem by almsgiving but may obstinately persevere in until the last day of life, and they will be saved by fire, although on account of the magnitude of their crimes and misdeeds they will

28. See 1 Tm 1:9-11.
29. See Mt 15:28.
30. See 1 Cor 6:15.
31. *Faith, Hope and Charity* 18,67-69.
32. Of this Laurence, who requested Augustine to write the treatise in question, nothing else is known. He is undoubtedly referred to as Dulcitius' brother in the sense that both belonged to the Christian family.

be punished by fire at great length, even if not eternally. But those who believe this and are still Catholics seem to me to be in error because of a certain human kindness, for divine scripture, upon investigation, gives another response. But I wrote a book on this question entitled *Faith and Works* in which—in accordance with holy scripture and, with God's help, to the best of my ability—I showed that a saving faith is that which the apostle Paul described with great clarity when he said, *For in Christ Jesus neither circumcision nor a foreskin is of any benefit, but a faith that works by love* (Gal 5:6). If, however, it works not good but evil, without doubt, according to the apostle James, it is dead in itself.[33] As he says, once more, *If someone says that he has faith but does not have works, will faith be able to save him?* But if, however, a wicked person is saved by fire on account of his faith alone, and what the blessed Paul declares—*He shall be saved, yet as though by fire*—is to be understood in that way, his faith will then be able to save him without works, and what his co-apostle James said will be false, and what the same Paul himself said will also be false: *Make no mistake,* he says. *Neither fornicators nor idolaters nor adulterers nor the effeminate nor those who sleep with men nor thieves nor the avaricious nor drunkards nor slanderers nor the greedy shall possess the kingdom of God.* For if they will nonetheless be saved on account of their faith in Christ while persevering in these sins, how will they not be in the kingdom of God?

11. "But because these very clear and obvious apostolic testimonies cannot be false, that obscure saying about those who build upon the foundation, which is Christ, not gold, silver and precious stones but wood, hay and straw—for it says that these persons will be saved by fire because, on account of their foundation, they will not perish—is to be understood in such a way that it is not contrary to those clear testimonies.[34] Now wood and hay and straw can reasonably be taken to be desires for things that are worldly, albeit lawfully conceded, and which are of the sort that they cannot be abandoned without distress of mind. But when this distress burns a person, if Christ has a place at the heart of his foundation—that is, so that nothing is preferred to him and the person who burns with such distress would rather lose the things that he loves in this way than lose Christ—he is saved by fire. If, on the other hand, in his time of trial he would rather hold on to temporal and worldly things of this sort than hold on to Christ, he did not have him as his foundation because he had

---

33. See Jas 2:17.
34. Augustine states here a famous principle for interpreting scripture: obscure passages are to be interpreted in light of clearer ones. This exegetical rule was known since at least the end of the second century, as witnessed in Tertullian, *On the Resurrection of the Flesh* 21, and is cited again by Augustine in *Teaching Christianity* III,26,37.

those things in first place, since in a building there is nothing that precedes its foundation. For the fire that the Apostle spoke of in that passage should be understood as one that both persons pass through—that is, both he who builds upon his foundation gold, silver and precious stones and he who builds wood, hay and straw. For when he said this he added, *Fire will test the work of each person, as to what sort it is. If the work that a person has built upon remains, he shall receive a reward. But if a person's work is burned up, he shall suffer condemnation; but he shall be saved, yet as though by fire.* Fire, then, will test the work not of one but of both of them.

12. "The trial of tribulation is a kind of fire, about which it is plainly written in another place: *The furnace tests the potter's vessels, and the trial of tribulation tests righteous persons* (Sir 27:5). For a time in this life this fire accomplishes what the Apostle spoke of. If it happens to two of the faithful—to one who thinks of the things that are of God and how to please God and who builds upon Christ the foundation gold, silver and precious stones; and to another who thinks of the things of the world and how to please his wife and who builds upon the same foundation wood, hay and straw—the work of the former is not burned up, because he is not tormented by the loss of the things that he loved, but that of the latter *is* burned up, because things that have been possessed with love do not perish without sorrow. But since, in the one example that has been proposed, the person in question would rather lose those things than Christ and would not abandon Christ out of fear of losing such things, even though he is sad when he *does* lose them, he is surely saved, *yet as though by fire*, because distress over the lost things that he had loved burns him, but it does not overthrow or consume his defenses, thanks to the solidity and inviolability of his foundation.

13. "That something similar might happen even after this life is not out of the question, and whether this is the case—that some of the faithful are saved by a kind of purgative fire,[35] either over a long time or quickly, depending on their greater or lesser love for passing goods—can be searched out and either be discovered or remain hidden. But the people to whom this applies are not like those of whom it was said that *they shall not possess the kingdom of God* (1 Cor 6:10), unless at an opportune moment these same crimes are forgiven them upon their repentance. But I said 'at an opportune moment' so that they may not be barren in almsgiving, which is so greatly emphasized in divine

---

35. By a kind of purgative fire: *per ignem quendam purgatorium.* The tone of the entire sentence suggests that Augustine believed that the existence of a post-mortem purgatorial fire was a debatable point. In *The City of God* XXI,13, however, he leaves no doubt that at least for some there will be punishment after death but before the final judgment, and that it will not be eternal—although he does not speak of it as fiery.

scripture that the Lord declares that he will reckon its fruit alone to the account of those on his right hand and barrenness in it to those on his left hand.[36] This will happen when he says to the ones, *Come, blessed of my Father, receive the kingdom* (Mt 25:34) but to the others, *Go into eternal fire."*

I think that these responses to your question from my two books are sufficient.

14. But there was no need for me to respond concerning those words of the Lord, *You shall not leave there until you pay back the last penny*, because you yourself answered the question based on a similar gospel passage, where it is written: *He did not know her until she gave birth.* Indeed, so as not to conceal from you my thoughts on the matter, I would like, if possible, or rather I really want, if possible, to be vanquished by the truth in this question. For what is said—that those who die in the Catholic communion will be freed from the vengeful punishment at one time or other, even if it be after a great deal of time, despite their having lived to the end of this life in a way that is most disgraceful and sinful—touches closely upon the love that we have for those who communicate in the sacraments of Christ's body and blood along with us and whom, although we despise their depraved conduct, we are unable to correct by church discipline or keep away from the Lord's table. But I want to be mastered by that truth which does not resist scripture's clearest statements. For that which resists it must on no account be referred to or thought of as truth. But for the moment, until we hear of or read something of that sort, let us pay attention to him who says, *Make no mistake. Neither fornicators nor idolaters,* and so forth, *shall possess the kingdom of God.* Because if what is said to the contrary is such as to be able to give another meaning to these straightforward apostolic words, the same Apostle has in fact instructed and sought to equip us against it when he says, *But be aware of this, you who are intelligent: no fornicator or person who is impure or avaricious, which is to be in bondage to idols, has an inheritance in the kingdom of Christ and God; let no one seduce you with empty words* (Eph 5:5-6). But when we heard that certain fornicators and impure and avaricious persons were being saved by fire, so that they would have *an inheritance in the kingdom of Christ and God* (Eph 5:5), we could not be deaf to him who cried out and said, *No fornicator or person who is impure or avaricious has an inheritance in the kingdom of Christ and God* (Eph 5:5). And, lest we look for any comfort in such words, he adds at once, *Let no one seduce you with empty words* (Eph 5:6).

---

36. See Mt 25:31-46.

Second Question

1. Your second question is: "Does an offering that is made on behalf of those who are at rest confer anything on their souls? For it is clear that we are either lifted up or weighed down by our own deeds, since we read that in the nether world no one can confess to the Lord anymore.[37] In response to this there are many who say that, if there is a possibility for something beneficial in this [place] after death, how much greater would be the forgiveness that the soul would gain for itself by confessing its own sins there than to have an offering made for their forgiveness by other persons."

2. I have said something about this in the book that I recently wrote for the holy Paulinus, bishop of Nola, when he asked me whether the practice of burying the dead at the memorials of martyrs would be of any benefit to the spirits of the dead.[38] From there I insert this passage for you:[39] "For a long time, venerable Paulinus, my brother bishop, I have owed Your Holiness an answer, ever since you wrote to me by way of the persons who came from the household of our most devoted daughter Flora and asked me whether it would be of benefit to anyone after his death if his body were buried near the memorial of some saint. For the widow whom I mentioned had asked this of you with respect to her son, who had died in those parts, and you had written back to console her and to tell her that what she had wished with motherly and dutiful feelings for the body of the faithful young man Cynegius—namely, that it be placed in the basilica of the most blessed confessor Felix[40]—had been accomplished. On that occasion it happened that you also wrote me a letter, delivered by the same bearers, raising a question on this issue and, so that I might respond as seemed best to me, begging me and not concealing what you yourself think. You say that it seems to you that the inspirations of religious and faithful persons who attend to these matters on behalf of their loved ones are not foolish. You also add that the fact that the universal Church has been accustomed to make supplication on behalf of the dead cannot be meaningless, so that from this it can be deduced that it is beneficial to a person after his death if, through the faith of his loved ones, such a place is provided for burying his body, thereby also manifesting the sought-for assistance of the saints.

---

37. See Ps 6:5.
38. Paulinus (c. 355-431) was born near Bordeaux and died as bishop of Nola, near Naples. He and Augustine were regular correspondents, but the letter of his which elicited the treatise *The Care to be Taken of the Dead* has been lost.
39. *The Care to be Taken of the Dead* 1,1-2.
40. This basilica had been built by Paulinus to honor Felix, a third-century priest and confessor of Nola whose cult was promoted by Paulinus.

3. "But, although this may be the case, you do not sufficiently indicate that you see how what the Apostle says is not contrary to this opinion: *For we shall all stand before the tribunal of Christ so that each person may receive recompense in accordance with what he did in his body, whether good or bad* (2 Cor 5:10). These apostolic words are certainly a warning to do *before* one's death what can be of benefit *after* one's death, and not to leave it to the moment when each person is due to take responsibility for what he did before his death. But there one finds the answer to the question, because it is by a certain kind of life, while a person is living in this body, that the wherewithal is acquired to help the dead, and hence, in accordance with what they did in the body, they are helped by the things that have been devoutly done on their behalf after [they have left] the body. For there are those to whom these things are no help at all, whether they be done for persons whose merits are so wicked that they are not worthy to be helped by such things or for persons whose merits are so good that they do not stand in need of such assistance. Thanks to the kind of life that a person has led in his body, then, whatever is piously done for him will either be beneficial or not once he has left his body. For these things bear upon merit to this extent: if none has been obtained in this life, in vain is it sought after this life. Hence the Church, and its concern for its own, is not foolish in expending what it can, in a righteous spirit, on the dead, and yet *each person will receive recompense in accordance with what he did in his body, whether good or bad*, when the Lord gives to each person according to his works.[41] For, in order that what is expended might benefit a person after [he has left] his body, it was acquired in the life that he led in his body."

4. I also said something along these lines to Laurence,[42] as follows:[43] "But the time," I said, "that comes between a person's death and the final resurrection detains souls in secret refuges, according as each is worthy of either repose or toil on account of the lot that it was assigned while living in the flesh. And it must not be denied that the souls of the dead are comforted by the piety of their loved ones who are still living, when the Mediator's sacrifice is offered on their behalf or alms are given in church.[44] But these things are of benefit to those who, when they themselves lived them, merited that afterwards they could be of benefit. For in fact there is a certain way of living that is neither so good as not to require these things after death nor so bad

---

41. See Rom 2:6.
42. On this Laurence see note 32.
43. *Faith, Hope and Charity* 29,109-110.
44. The eucharist and almsgiving are mentioned together in the same breath, as is the case a few lines later. Augustine, however, understands almsgiving in a very broad way. See *Faith, Hope and Charity* 19,72.

that they will not benefit it after death. But there is a person who is so very good as not to require these things and, on the other hand, one who is so very bad that, once this life has passed, he cannot be helped by these things. It is for this reason that all merit is acquired here by which, after this life, a person may be comforted or burdened. But no one may prepare himself, when he meets the Lord, to merit what he has neglected here. The things that the Church practices for the sake of commending the dead, therefore, are not opposed to that apostolic text in which it says, *For we shall all stand before the tribunal of Christ so that each person might receive recompense in accordance with what he did in his body, whether good or bad*, because each person has also acquired this merit for himself so that these things might be of benefit to him. For they do not benefit everyone. And why do they not benefit everyone if not by reason of the difference in the lives that persons have led in their bodies? When, therefore, the sacrifice either of the altar or of some form of almsgiving is offered for all the dead who were baptized,[45] there is thanksgiving for those who were truly good, there is propitiation for those who were not truly wicked and, in the case of those who *were* truly wicked, even if there is no help for them now that they are dead, there is some sort of consolation for the living. For those whom it benefits, however, the benefit is either that there is complete forgiveness or at least that the punishment itself becomes more bearable."

Third Question

1. Your third question is: "Should it be believed that at the Lord's coming there will be an immediate judgment, or will a space of time intervene? Since," you say, "we read that at the days of his coming those who survive will be snatched up in the clouds to meet Christ in the air and thus will always be with the Lord,[46] I want to know whether judgment will follow soon upon his coming and if those who are snatched up into the clouds will pass over into death, unless we should perhaps understand this very change as a substitute for death."

2. I think that the faith of the creed, in which we confess that Christ will come from the Father's right hand to judge the living and the dead, ought to

---

45. The reference to "all the dead who were baptized" is an indication to the present-day reader of what Augustine's fellow Christians would most likely have taken for granted—namely, that pious practices were of benefit only to those who had been baptized (and not even to all of them) and that the unbaptized were utterly out of the running.

46. See 1 Thes 4:17.

suffice for your question as to whether it should be believed that judgment will occur directly at the Lord's coming. Since this is the very reason for his coming, what else will he do as soon as he comes if not that for which he came?[47]

Concerning those who will be snatched up in the clouds, however, you may read in what follows the argument that I laid out in a letter that I wrote to my son whose name is Mercator and who is doubtless very well known to you.[48] He had approached me regarding some questions of the Pelagians, who deny that death is a punishment for sin. As I said,[49] "When the Apostle was speaking about the resurrection of the dead he said, *And we who have been left alive shall be snatched up in the clouds together with them to meet Christ in the air, and thus we shall always be with the Lord* (1 Thes 4:17). Now those of whom he spoke raise a question, to be sure, but on their own account and not because of them [*istos*, i.e., the Pelagians].[50] For if they [i.e., those who have been left behind] are not also going to die, I do not at all see what may help them [*istos*, i.e., the Pelagians] when the same things can be said of them [i.e., those who have been left behind] as were said of the two"—namely, Enoch[51] and Elijah.[52] "But in fact, as far as the words of the blessed Apostle are concerned, he seems to maintain that there are some persons who will not die at the end of the world, when the Lord comes and the resurrection of the dead takes place; instead, having been found still alive, they will at once pass over into that immortality which is also given to the other saints, and together with them, as he says, they will be snatched up in the clouds.[53] As often as I have pondered these words, no other explanation has seemed plausible to me.

---

47. Note that, in order to answer Dulcitius' question regarding an immediate judgment after the Lord's coming, Augustine resorts to the creed rather than to scripture, which is less clear on the matter (see, e.g., Acts 10:42; 2 Tm 4:1; 1 Pt 4:5).

48. Mercator had written against the Pelagians and was living in Rome. It is not certain why he should have been known to Dulcitius; perhaps Augustine is simply exercising a form of courtesy.

49. Letter 193,9-13.

50. Without recourse to the preceding section of Letter 193, from which Augustine is quoting, this and the following sentence would be incomprehensible. Sections 5-8 of that letter say that it is a common belief that Enoch and Elijah will die before the final judgment but that, in any event, God may remit the punishment of death to whom he will. Hence the Pelagians cannot build an argument based on the case of these two exceptional persons.

51. See Gn 5:24.

52. See 2 K 2:11.

53. See 1 Thes 4:17.

3. "But in this matter I would like to listen to those who are more learned,[54] in order to see if the Apostle may also be found to say to those who think that there are some who will pass on to eternal life even though they have not first died and been restored to life: *Fool, what you sow is not restored to life unless it dies* (1 Cor 15:36). For how could what we also read in numerous codexes—*We shall all rise* (1 Cor 15:51)—be possible unless we all die? For there is no resurrection if death does not come first. And what several codexes have—*We shall all fall asleep* (1 Cor 15:51)—promotes this meaning more clearly and more obviously. And whatever else of the sort is found in holy scripture seems to demand that no human being be thought to attain to immortality if death does not come first. Consider, accordingly, what the Apostle said: *And we who have been left alive at the Lord's coming shall not precede those who previously fell asleep. For the Lord himself will descend from heaven with a command, at an archangel's voice and with God's trumpet, and those who have died in Christ will rise first, and then we who have been left alive shall be snatched up in the clouds together with them, to meet Christ in the air, and thus we shall always be with the Lord.* (1 Thes 4:15-17) Concerning these words, as I have said, I would like to listen to those who are more learned and, if they could be explained to me in such a way as to mean that all human beings who are living or who will live after us will die, I would correct what I otherwise once believed in this regard. For we must not be unteachable teachers, and certainly it is better that a crooked man be straightened than that an unbending one be broken, since our frailty and that of others is exercised and instructed by what we write, although there is nothing like scriptural authority in it.

4. "But it may be that in these words of the Apostle no other meaning can be discovered, and that this has made clear that he wished to be understood what the words themselves seem to cry out—namely, that at the end of the world, at the Lord's coming, there will be some who will not be stripped of their body but will cover it in immortality, so that what is immortal will be swallowed up

---

54. This idea is repeated at the end of the present section and then taken up again in section 6, where it is expanded into a reflection on learning and teaching in a Christian context that serves as the coda to the entire question. In fact it is repeated in the final sentence of the treatise. Augustine likes to present himself as at most a secondary teacher and Christ and the Holy Spirit as the principal teachers. See *Exposition of Psalm* 126 [127],3; *Homily on the First Epistle of John* 3,13. In *Instructing Beginners in Faith* 2,3 he worries about his teaching skills. Yet, in *Teaching Christianity*, pref. 4-9, he acknowledges both the necessity of having human teachers and the wisdom of God's plan, according to which human beings teach one another rather than receive their instruction from God himself. See also question 1,6.

by life.[55] Then it will certainly be in conformity with this position that we confess in the rule of faith[56] that the Lord will come to judge the living and the dead—not with the understanding that the living are those who are righteous while the dead are the unrighteous (although righteous and unrighteous are to be judged),[57] but with the understanding that his coming will find alive those who have not yet left their bodies and dead those who have already left them. If this is the case, those words will have to be interpreted so that we understand *What you sow is not restored to life unless it dies* and *We shall all rise* or *We shall all fall asleep* as not contradictory to this position, in accordance with which it is believed that there are some who will live forever with their bodies without having tasted death.[58]

5. "But whichever of these meanings is found to be more truthful and insightful, what does it have to do with the matter at hand whether all are struck by a deserved death or some are spared from this condition, when it is still obvious that the death not only of the soul but also of the body would not follow if sin did not precede and that the righteous come back from death to a life of eternal beatitude by a more marvelous power of grace than if they did not experience death? Let what has been said regarding the persons about whom you wrote to me suffice, although I would not think that they still say that, even if Adam had not sinned, he would still have experienced death in his body.

6. "But as to what pertains to the question of the resurrection and of those who, it is believed, will not die but will pass from this mortality to immortality without the intervention of death, careful research must be undertaken, and if you have heard or read of or even been able to think through yourself, or if in the future you succeed in hearing or reading of or thinking through, a definitive solution, arrived at by way of a rational and conclusive process, I beg you not to hesitate to send it to me. For, as I must confess to Your Charity, I would rather learn than teach. We are also urged to this by the apostle James when he says, *But let every person be quick to hear but slow to speak* (Jas 1:19). In order to learn, then, the sweetness of

---

55. See 2 Cor 5:4.
56. See *Miscellany of Eighty-three Questions* LIX, 1 and note 155. The "rule of faith" seems to be identifiable with the creed.
57. Touching upon an issue secondary to whether there are some who will not die but simply be snatched up into the clouds alive, Augustine here argues against the allegorization of "the living" (as meaning the righteous) and "the dead" (as meaning the unrighteous) in the words of the creed: "He will come to judge the living and the dead."
58. See Mt 16:28.

truth must attract us.[59] In order to teach, however, the necessity of charity must compel us. There it is rather to be desired that that necessity, whereby one person teaches something to another person, may pass away and all of us may be taught by God,[60] which is the case when we learn the things that pertain to true piety, even when a human being seems to be teaching them, because neither he who plants nor he who waters is anything, but God who gives the increase.[61] And so, if the apostles who planted and watered were nothing unless God gave the increase, how much less am I or you or any men of this age, even though we seem to ourselves to be teachers."

Fourth Question

1. Your fourth question is: "Why did David say, *His seed will be powerful on earth; the generation of the upright will be blessed* (Ps 112:2), when we know that there are children of the righteous who have been and are accursed and children of the unrighteous who have been and are blessed?"

2. To this question I respond from the explanation of a psalm on which I preached to the people. As I said,[62] *"For blessed is the man who fears the Lord, who delights greatly in his commands* (Ps 112:1). God, who alone judges both truthfully and mercifully, sees how much progress that man makes in his commands, because, as saintly Job says, *Human life upon earth is a trial* (Jb 7:1). And again it is written, *The body that is perishing weighs down the soul, and the earthly dwelling oppresses the mind that ponders many things* (Wis 9:15). But the Lord is the one who judges us. We ought not to judge hastily, until the Lord comes and illuminates our dark and hidden places and reveals the thoughts of our heart, and then everyone will have his praise from God.[63] It is he, therefore, who sees how much progress each person makes in his commands. Yet he delights greatly who loves deeply the peace of that building in common,[64] and he ought not to lose hope, because *he delights greatly in his commands* (Ps 112:1) and there is *peace on earth to men of good will* (Lk 2:14).

59. "The sweetness of truth must attract us": *invitare nos debet suavitas veritatis*. The phrase is a beautiful one and points to Augustine's conviction that truth has an affective as well as an intellectual quality. See *Confessions* III,6,10; IV,15,27 (*dulcis veritas*).
60. See Jn 6:45.
61. See 1 Cor 3:7.
62. *Exposition of Psalm* 111 [112],2-3.
63. See 1 Cor 4:4-5.
64. "The peace of that building in common": *pacem illius coaedficationis*. *Exposition of Psalm* 111 [112],1 is being referred to here, in which Augustine cites Eph 2:19-22 and discusses the building of a spiritual temple as the task of the Christian people.

3. "Hence *his seed will be powerful on earth.* The Apostle bears witness that the seed of a future harvest is the works of mercy when he says, *But let us not be remiss in doing good, for at the proper time we shall reap a harvest* (Gal 6:9); and again, *But* [I say] *this,* he says, *He who sows sparingly will also reap sparingly* (2 Cor 9:6). But what, brothers, is more remarkable than the fact that not only may Zacchaeus purchase the kingdom of heaven with the half of his property[65] but also the widow with her two small coins,[66] and that each may possess just as much there? What is more remarkable than the fact that the same kingdom is worth both a rich man's treasure[67] and a pauper's cup of cold water?[68] But there are those who do these things who, as they pursue earthly goods, are either hoping for a reward from the Lord here or seeking to please human beings. But *the generation of the upright will be blessed.* This refers to the works of those whose God is the good God of Israel because they are upright of heart[69] (but an upright heart means one that does not resist the Father when he corrects and that believes him when he makes promises) and not of those whose feet are shaken and whose steps slip and slide, as it says in another psalm, while they envy sinners on seeing sinners' peace[70] and think that their own works are perishing if a perishable reward is not given to them. But the man who fears the Lord and, because of the manner of life of an upright heart, is well prepared for God's holy temple neither seeks the glory of human beings nor desires earthly riches, and yet *glory and riches are in his house* (Ps 112:3). For his heart is his house, where he dwells more opulently with God's praise and the hope of eternal life than he would in marble houses under paneled ceilings with the adulation of human beings—and the fear of eternal death. For *his righteousness remains forever* (Ps 112:3): that is his glory, that is his riches. But that other man's purple and fine linen and splendid banquets[71] are passing away, even while they are present, and when they come to their end he will cry out with burning tongue in his desire for a fingerful of dripping water."[72]

As for your fifth question, I have promised to discuss it after dealing with all the others.

65. See Lk 19:8.
66. See Mk 12:42.
67. See Mt 13:44.
68. See Mt 10:42.
69. See Ps 73:1.
70. See Ps 73:2-3.
71. See Lk 16:19.
72. See Lk 16:24.

Sixth Question

1. Your sixth question is: "Did the necromancer, according to the story, call forth the prophet Samuel himself from the nether world?"

2. Simplician, bishop of Milan, of blessed memory, once asked me this. What I wrote for him, then, you may read as follows:[73] "You likewise ask," I said, "whether the unclean spirit that was in the necromancer was able to bring it about that Samuel was seen by Saul and spoke with him.[74] But it is far more remarkable that Satan himself, the prince of all unclean spirits, who also begged to test the apostles,[75] was able to speak with God and to beg that he might test Job, the most righteous of men.[76] Now this question is not a difficult one because the truth, which is present everywhere, speaks *through* whatever creature it wills *to* whatever creature it wills, and consequently it is no great matter to whom God speaks. What is to the point is what is said, because even the emperor does not speak with any number of innocent people for whose welfare he looks out with the greatest care, whereas he *does* speak with any number of criminals whom he orders to be executed. If, then, there is no question in this regard, there should be no question as to how even an unclean spirit was able to speak with the soul of a holy man. For God, the creator and sanctifier, is indeed far superior to his holy ones. But if it is an unsettling fact that he allowed a wicked spirit to arouse the soul of a righteous man and to call it forth from, as it were, the remotest refuges of the dead, is it not more surprising that Satan took the Lord himself and set him upon the pinnacle of the Temple?[77] For, however he may have accomplished this, the way in which it happened that he aroused Samuel is also hidden—unless perhaps someone says that it was easier for the devil to gain permission to take the living Lord from where he wanted and to set him where he wanted than to arouse the spirit of the dead Samuel from his resting place. If what is in the gospel does not disturb us because the Lord willed and allowed it to happen, with no diminishment of his power and divinity, just as he submitted himself to be seized and overcome and mocked and crucified and slain by the Jews themselves, although they were perverse and unclean and did the devil's work, it is not absurd to believe that permission was granted in accordance with some dispensation of the divine will so that, not involuntarily or under the dominion and mastery of magical powers but intentionally and in obedience to the secret dispensation of God, which lay hidden from that necromancer and from Saul,

---

73. See *Miscellany of Questions in Response to Simplician* II,3.
74. See 1 S 28:7-19.
75. See Lk 22:31.
76. See Jb 1:6-12.
77. See Mt 4:5.

the Spirit, who was going to strike him with the divine judgment, would allow the holy prophet to make an appearance before the king. For why would the soul of a good man, if it came forth at the behest of evil persons in the land of the living, appear to lose its dignity when even good persons in the land of the living, who have often been summoned and who come to evil ones, cooperate with them in accordance with the requirements of justice, all the while maintaining the unsullied beauty of their virtue and dealing with the vices of those others as the utility or the need of temporal affairs dictates?

3. "In regard to this event, however, there could be another and easier solution, whereby we believe not that the spirit of Samuel was really aroused from its rest but that a kind of phantasm and imaginary illusion was produced by the devil's machinations, which scripture therefore refers to by the name of Samuel because the images of things are usually referred to by the names of what they represent. For example, all the things that are painted or fashioned out of metal or wood or some other material that is suitable for works of this sort and that are also seen in dreams, and all the things that are close approximations of those things, are usually referred to by the names of what they represent. For who would hesitate to call the portrait of a man a man? Whenever, in fact, we look at portraits of particular individuals we unhesitatingly use their proper names, and when gazing at a framed picture or a mural we say, That is Cicero, that is Sallust, that is Achilles, that is Hector, that is the River Simois, that is Rome, although they are merely painted images. Hence those figures of the cherubim that, although they are heavenly powers, were fashioned from metal, as God commanded, and set upon the ark of the covenant in order to signify something great,[78] are also referred to as nothing else than cherubim. In the same way, whoever has a dream does not say, I saw an image of Augustine or of Simplician, but rather, I saw Augustine or Simplician, although at the moment that he saw such a thing we ourselves were unaware, so much is it taken for granted that it was not the men themselves that were seen but their images. And Pharaoh said that in his dreams he saw ears of corn and cows,[79] not the images of ears of corn and cows. If, then, it is common practice that images are referred to by the names of what they represent, it is not surprising that scripture refers to what was seen as Samuel, even if perhaps the image of Samuel appeared through the machinations of him who disguises himself as an angel of light and his ministers as ministers of righteousness.[80]

---

78. See Ex 25:18.
79. See Gn 41:17-24.
80. See 2 Cor 11:14-15.

4. "But if it is striking that true things were foretold even by Saul's evil spirit, it can also appear remarkable that the demons recognized Christ,[81] whom the Jews did not recognize. For when God wishes someone to know true things even through base and infernal spirits, although they are only temporal and pertain to this mortal life, it is convenient and not inappropriate for him who is almighty and righteous to grant, by the hidden working of his ministers, some power of prediction even to such spirits so that they may announce to human beings what they hear from angels, and thus, for their punishment, those to whom these things are foretold will suffer through foreknowledge the evil that threatens them before it comes. But they only hear as much as the Lord and Ruler of all either commands or permits. Hence also the soothsaying spirit in the Acts of the Apostles bears witness to the apostle Paul and attempts to be an evangelist.[82] Yet these beings mix in lies, and the truth that they have succeeded in knowing they foretell as much for the sake of deceiving as for that of teaching. And perhaps this is why, when that image of Samuel predicted that Saul was going to die, he also said that he was going to be with him, which was manifestly false. For in fact we read in the gospel that after death the good are separated from the bad by a great gulf, since the Lord attests that, between that proud rich man, when he was suffering torments in the nether world, and him who used to lie with his sores at his gate and was now at rest, a huge gulf intervened.[83] Or if Samuel told Saul, *You will be with me* (1 S 28:19), referring not to an equality of happiness but to the equal condition of death, because each was a human being and each was mortal, then it was a matter of a dead man predicting death to a living man.

"Your Prudence sees, I am sure, that that text has an explanation consonant with each understanding, which is not contrary to faith, unless perhaps through deeper and more complex research, which exceeds the limits of my strength and time, it may be discovered whether the human soul, once it has departed this life and been called back by incantations, can or cannot appear to living persons clothed in the features of a body, so that it may be able not only to be seen but also to be recognized. And, if possible, it may be discovered whether even the soul of a righteous person may not indeed be compelled by magic formulas but may deign to show itself in obedience to the secret injunctions of the highest law. Thus, if it is not ascertained that this

---

81. See Mt 8:29.
82. See Acts 16:16-17.
83. See Lk 16:26.

cannot occur, neither understanding in the discussion and explanation of this passage will be allowed, but, with the former excluded, it will be clear that the simulated image of Samuel was produced in a diabolical fashion. But since, whether it can or cannot occur, Satan's stratagems and his crafty manipulation of simulated images are nonetheless aimed at deceiving the human senses in every way, we certainly ought not, in all caution, to object to more careful research (although we should still think that a thing of this sort was accomplished through the evil devices of that necromancer), as long as something more is not given us to reflect upon and work from."

5. That is what I wrote in reply at the time with regard to the necromancer and Samuel. But how reasonable it was of me to say that we should think that in this occurrence the simulated image of Samuel was made present through the evil devices of the necromancer but that we ought not, in all caution, to object to more careful research my own subsequent research made clear, when I found in the Book of Ecclesiasticus, [in the passage] where our forebears are praised in chronological order, that Samuel himself was praised as one who was said to have prophesied even in death.[84]

Seventh Question

1. Your seventh question is: "How should one answer those who say that Sarah did not avoid dishonor, since they say that Abimelech was restrained by a dream from taking her to himself[85] and that Pharaoh was allowed to have sexual relations with her?"[86]

2. I do not see how they can say that Pharaoh was allowed to have carnal relations with her when scripture does not compel us to believe it. For he took her as his wife, to be sure, and immediately thereafter Abraham was enriched with many gifts from the Egyptians because of her,[87] but it is not written that Pharaoh slept with her and had intercourse with her because God, by afflicting him with numerous great misfortunes, did not allow him to do this.[88] For women whom kings viewed as marriageable did not also enter into carnal relations right away. But, as we read in the book entitled Esther, for a few months, or rather for a whole year, their bodies were treated

---

84. See Sir 46:20.
85. See Gn 20:2-4.
86. See Gn 12:14-20.
87. See Gn 12:15-16.
88. See Gn 12:17. It seems more likely from the scriptural text that God inflicted misfortunes on Pharaoh precisely because he *did* have sexual relations with Sarah.

with unguents, washes and perfumes before being joined to the king's body.[89] The things that have been set down in writing [in the Book of Esther], then, were done during this space of time until Pharaoh, contrite and terrified, restored the wife to her husband.[90] Because Abimelech, however, was forbidden by a dream from having intercourse with her,[91] those who contend that Sarah did not avoid dishonor think that the king, in order to have a dream, was unable to sleep until he had had carnal relations with her.[92] As if, quite apart from the time when women's bodies were prepared for the king's pleasure, as I mentioned previously, God could not have plunged him into sleep and warned him by a dream before they came together.

3. Let me tell you what happened in Mauritania Sitifensis.[93] For it is not true that the God of our holy fathers is not himself our God as well. A certain young catechumen named Celticius, in order to have a wife, seized a widow who had embraced a life of continence. Before they could have sexual intercourse, he was overwhelmed by sleep and terrified by a dream, and he sent her back untouched to the bishop of Sitifi, who was most anxiously looking for her. Those of whom I speak are still alive. He was baptized and, having been converted to God by a miracle of which he was the object, advanced to the episcopate, thanks to an admirable virtuousness, while she remained in holy widowhood.

4. I have appended what I said in response to Faustus the Manichean when he slandered our father Abraham for having sold his wife to two kings to sleep with them:[94] "But when he calls a righteous and faithful husband the infamous vendor of his own marriage for the sake of avarice and his stomach—because at different times he deceived two kings, Abimelech and Pharaoh, by saying that his wife Sarah was his sister, since she was very beautiful—and asserts

---

89. See Est 2:12-13. This is an excellent example of the patristic practice of allowing one scriptural text to interpret another despite vast discrepancies of time and culture—as if the world that scripture described were static and there were no difference between royal marriage customs in Pharaoh's Egypt and Esther's Persia (leaving aside the question as to whether the description of the latter is historically accurate).
90. See Gn 12:19.
91. See Gn 20:3-4.
92. Those against whom Augustine is arguing seem to show awareness of the fact that sexual intercourse is such an exhausting experience for many men that they fall asleep after it. The following sentence argues that a man may just as well fall asleep *before* planning to have sexual relations, and the paragraph after that (section 3) is, at least in part, an illustration of that argument.
93. Mauritania Sitifensis was in north Africa to the west of Hippo. Its chief city was Sitifi. The story of Celticius that Augustine recounts is otherwise unknown.
94. *Answer to Faustus, a Manichean* XXII,33.

that he sold her into concubinage, he does not with a truth-telling mouth distinguish between goodness and wickedness but with a malicious mouth turns the whole thing into a crime. This deed of Abraham's, to be sure, looks like pimping—but [only] to those unable to tell the difference, thanks to the light of the eternal law, between upright deeds and sins. To them even steadfastness can look like obstinacy and the virtue of courage brings the vice of rashness to mind, to say nothing of whatever other objections are made by those who do not see aright against those who do not seem to act aright. For Abraham did not concur in his wife's disgrace and sell her adultery at a price. Instead, just as she did not yield her servant to her husband's sexual urges but brought her forward of her own volition for the sake of procreation,[95] without at all disturbing the natural order where his authority lay by commanding his obedience rather than acceding to his desire,[96] neither did he have any doubt whatsoever about her soul, where the virtue of modesty dwells. He called not wife but sister[97] the chaste spouse who clung to him with a chaste heart lest, if he were slain by impious foreigners, she be taken captive,[98] for he was certain that his God would allow her to suffer nothing evil or disgraceful. Nor did his faith and hope fail him, for Pharaoh, terrified by strange happenings and afflicted on her account by numerous woes, returned her unharmed and with honor when he learned by divine intervention that she was his wife.[99] And Abimelech did the same when he was warned and instructed in a dream." [100]

Eighth Question

1. Lastly you ask for an explanation of the Spirit of God who was borne above the water.[101] "For," you say, "certain people assert that this is the Holy Spirit, while others call it a this-worldly spirit, saying that the author of the account could not have listed the creator among his creatures nor assigned a particular location to him who, with the Father and the Son, is everywhere in his entirety."

---

95. See Gn 16:1-3.
96. I.e., according to the natural order (*ordine naturali*) it was the husband's right to exercise his authority by commanding his wife, not the other way around. Augustine does not tell us how Sarah succeeded in not usurping that authority when she was commanding his obedience (*iubens . . . oboedienti*), but he at least wants us to know that it remained inviolate, since an infraction of it would have been unimaginable in the patriarchal couple.
97. See Gn 12:19; 20:2.
98. See Gn 12:12; 20:11.
99. See Gn 12:17-19.
100. See Gn 20:3-16.
101. Gn 1:2.

2. In this short work I have copied what I think about this matter from the first book of the twelve that I wrote about Genesis, treating it to the best of my ability not allegorically but in accordance with a faith based upon actual events.[102] "In God," I said, "there is a lofty, holy and just benevolence directed towards his works and a love for them that proceeds not from need but from kindness. Therefore, before *God said, Let there be light* (Gn 1:3) was written, scripture first said, *And the Spirit of God was borne above the water* (Gn 1:2). Perhaps this is the case because it wanted to refer to all of corporeal matter by the term 'water'; in that way it could give an indication of what everything that we can now distinguish according to species was made of and shaped from, calling it water because we see that all things on earth, in their various species, are shaped and formed from moisture. Or perhaps it is the case because it wanted to refer to the spiritual life as something fluid before conversion shaped it. [In any event] it was certainly the Spirit of God that was borne above, because whatever he had begun had still to be shaped and completed and was subject to the good will of the creator; thus, when God said, *Let there be light*, what was made would remain, according to its type, in his good will—that is, it would remain pleasing to him. And so it is right that it pleased God. As scripture says, *And light was made, and God saw that it was good* (Gn 1:3-4). Thus, at the very beginning of the unfinished creation, which is suggested by the phrase *heaven and earth* (Gn 1:1) because of what was still to be completed from them, the Trinity of the creator is alluded to. For when scripture says, *In the beginning God made heaven and earth* (Gn 1:1), we understand the Father in the mention of God and the Son in the mention of the beginning. He is the beginning not for the Father but, originally and chiefly, for the spiritual creation created through himself and then also for the whole of creation. And when scripture says, *And the Spirit of God was borne above the water*, we see the Trinity mentioned in full. Likewise, in the conversion and perfection of creation, in the arrangement of the species of things, the same Trinity is alluded to—namely, the Word of God and the Word's begetter, when it is said, *God said*, and the holy goodness by which whatever pleases God pleases him as being perfect according to the measure of its own nature, when it is said, *God saw that it was good*.

3. "But why is creation, albeit imperfect, mentioned first and afterwards the Spirit of God? For scripture says first, *But the earth was invisible and unformed, and there was darkness over the abyss* (Gn 1:20), and then it says,

---

102. *The Literal Meaning of Genesis* I,5,11-7,13.

And the Spirit of God was borne above the water. A poor and needy love shows itself in such a way that it subordinates itself to the things that it loves. When the Spirit of God was mentioned, by whom his holy benevolence and love are meant, was he said to be *borne above* lest God be thought to love more through needy desire than through abundant goodness the works that he had yet to accomplish? Mindful of this, the Apostle, when he is about to discuss love, says that he will show a more lofty way,[103] and elsewhere he speaks of *the lofty love of the knowledge of Christ* (Eph 3:19). Since, therefore, it was fitting that an allusion be made to the Holy Spirit by saying that he was *borne above,* it was all the more appropriate that an allusion be made first to something unfinished above which he could be said to be borne—in terms not of location but of a power that overwhelms and surpasses all others."

Fifth Question

1. Now on to what I had put off discussing for a short while. For you ask: "Why did the Lord, with his unerring foreknowledge of future events, say, *I have chosen David,* [a man] *after my own heart* (Acts 13:22),[104] although the man himself committed such great misdeeds?"

2. If indeed we understand that this was said of that very David who was the king of Israel after Saul had been condemned and was dead, all the more because God possessed foreknowledge of future events did he see in him such great piety and such true repentance[105] that he was numbered among those of whom he himself says, *Blessed are those whose iniquities are forgiven and whose sins are covered over. Blessed is the man to whom the Lord has imputed no sin.* (Ps 32:1-2) When, therefore, God foreknew that he was going to sin and that he would blot out his sins by his pious humility and sincere repentance,[106] why would he not say, *I have found David,* [a man] *after my own heart?* He was not going to impute sin to one who had done so much good and was living with such piety and, by reason of that piety, had offered the sacrifice of a contrite spirit[107] for his sins. On account of all of that it was said with the utmost truth, *I have found David,* [a man] *after my own*

---

103. See 1 Cor 12:31.
104. *I have chosen* (elegi) *David,* [a man] *after my own heart* hereafter becomes *I have found* (inveni) *David. . . .*
105. See 2 S 12:13; 24:10.
106. See 2 S 11:12; 24:10.
107. See Ps 51:17.

heart. For although there was a time when he was not after God's heart because he sinned, nonetheless he was after God's heart because he made satisfaction for his sins with appropriate repentance. This one thing in him, then, which God did not impute to him, was not after God's heart. And so, once it was removed—that is, not imputed—what remained except the basis on which it could be said with the utmost truth, *I have found David,* [a man] *after my own heart*?

3. But if we wish to take it that this was spoken prophetically of Christ, there would be no impediment unless perhaps we were to question how Christ could properly be called by this name. But we respond that it is because of David's seed, from which Christ took his flesh,[108] and we can give an example for attributing this name to Christ. For we find that Christ Jesus is very openly referred to as David in the prophet Ezekiel, when we read in the person of God the Father: *I will raise up over my sheep one shepherd who will pasture them, my servant David. And he himself shall pasture them, and he himself shall be their shepherd. But I the Lord will be their God, and my servant David shall be the leader in their midst. I the Lord have spoken.* (Ez 34:23-24) And in another place: *And there shall be one king,* he says, *ruling over all. And no longer shall there be two peoples, nor shall they be separated any more into two kingdoms, nor shall they any longer be polluted by their idols and their abominations and by all their iniquities. And I will save them from all the dwellings in which they have sinned, and I will make them clean. And they shall be my people, and I will be their God, and my servant David shall be king over them, and there shall be one shepherd for all of them.* (Ez 37:22-24) The prophet Hosea, too, when he announced what sort of time the Jews now have, and that they will later believe in Christ, prophesied of the same Christ under the name of David when he said, *For the children of Israel shall stay many days without a king, without a leader, without sacrifice, without an altar, without a priesthood, without manifestations* (Hos 3:4). Now no one doubts that these are the Jews. But consider what the apostle Paul said when he spoke to the gentiles: *For just as once you did not believe in God but have now attained to mercy through their* [i.e., the Jews'] *unbelief, so also those who now have not believed will themselves attain to mercy through your mercy* [i.e., through the mercy shown to you] (Rom 1:30-31). To this the prophet added when he predicted long before: *And afterwards the children of Israel shall come back, and they shall seek out the Lord their God and David their king, and they shall be amazed by the Lord and by his good things in the last days* (Hos 3:5). You see here as well that Christ was prophesied under the name of David because, when those

---

108. See Jn 7:42.

things were prophesied, the David who was the king of Israel had already fallen asleep a long time before. But the Lord Jesus, who was going to come in the flesh, was of his seed, and for that reason he was called David in a prophetic manner of speaking.

But it seems that the apostle Paul put this testimony in the Acts of the Apostles such that it could be understood only of that King David who succeeded Saul. For among other things he says, *And then they demanded a king, and God gave them Saul, son of Kish, a man of the tribe of Benjamin who was forty years old. And when he was removed, he raised up for them King David, to whom he also bore witness when he said, I have found David, the son of Jesse, a man after my own heart, who will carry out all my desires.* (Acts 13:21-22) But he adds this, saying, *According to his promise, God brought forth from his seed a savior for Israel, Jesus* (Acts 13:23). In this way he indicated that the testimony was to be understood on a higher level of the Lord Jesus, who truly carried out all the desires of God the Father,[109] rather than of King David. Although, as was said before, his sins were forgiven and not imputed to him on account of his pious repentance and he could rightly be said to have been found after God's heart, nonetheless how did he carry out all of God's desires? Although he was highly praised when scripture narrated his times and his deeds, yet he was censured for not having destroyed the high places, where the people of God used to sacrifice against the precept of God,[110] who had ordered that sacrifices be made to him only in the tent of the covenant,[111] even though sacrifices were being made to God in those same high places as well. Shortly thereafter, King Hezekiah, who was born of the seed of David himself, overthrew these high places to his own great glory.[112]

I have responded to your questions as well as I could. If you have found or will be able to find something better concerning these matters, we shall be most grateful if you let us know. For, as I mentioned previously about myself, I would rather learn than teach.[113]

---

109. See Jn 4:34.
110. See 1 K 3:2.
111. See Dt 12:4-14.
112. See 2 K 18:4.
113. See question 3,6 and note 54.

Index of Scripture

(prepared by Michael T. Dolan)

The numbers after the scriptural reference refer to the section of the work

Miscellany of Eighty-three Questions

Revisions I, 26

Old Testament

Genesis

6:7	1

Psalms

39:6	1
73:28	1

Song of Songs

6:8	1

Wisdom

1:13	1

Sirach

11.14	1

Jeremiah

1:5	1

New Testament

Matthew

5:32	1
24:36	1

Luke

23:43	1

John

4:1-2	1

Romans

7:1	1
7:14	1
7:24	1
8:10	1
8:11	1
8:18	1
8:21	1
8:24	1
9:13	1
9:20	1
12:2	1

1 Corinthians

3:16	1
11:7	1
15:28	1
15:54-56	1

2 Corinthians

3:18	1

Galatians

6:2	1

Ephesians

5:29	1

| 13:8-9 | I, 1, 17 |
| 13:10 | I, 1, 17 |

1 Corinthians

2:10	II, 1, 5
2:11	II, 1, 5
2:14	I, 2, 17
3:1	I, 2, 17
3:1-2	I, 2, 17
3:2	I, 1, 7; I, 2, 17
3:3	I, 2, 17
3:17	I, 2, 2
4:7	I, 2, 9
9:24	I, 2, 10
12:4	II, 1, 5
12:7-11	II, 1, 8
12:8	II, 2, 3
12:11	II, 1, 5
12:29	II, 1, 8
12:29-30	II, 1, 8
13:1-3	II, 1, 8
13:8	II, 2, 2
13:12	II
15:22	I, 2, 16
15:56	I, 1, 15

2 Corinthians

2:15-16	I, 1, 17
3:6	I, 1, 17
3:7	I, 1, 15
3:17	II, 1, 5
7:1	II, 2, 5

Galatians

| 5:17 | I, 2, 21 |

Ephesians

| 1:4 | I, 2, 6 |
| 2:8-9 | I, 2, 3; I, 2, 6 |

Philippians

| 2:12-13 | I, 2, 12 |

1 Timothy

| 1:8 | I, 1, 6 |
| 2:14 | I, 1, 4 |

2 Timothy

| 4:7-8 | I, 2, 3 |

Eight Questions of Dulcitius

Old Testament

Genesis

1:1	8, 2
1:2	8, 2
1:3	8, 2
1:3-4	8, 2
1:20	8, 3

1 Samuel

| 28:19 | 6, 4 |

Job

| 7:1 | 4, 2 |

Psalms

32:1-2	5, 2
112:1	4, 2
112:2	4, 1
112:3	4, 3

Wisdom

| 9:15 | 4, 2 |

Sirach

| 27:5 | 1, 12 |

Ezekiel

| 34:23-24 | 5, 3 |
| 37:22-24 | 5, 3 |

Hosea

| 3:4 | 5, 3 |
| 3:5 | 5, 3 |

New Testament

Matthew

1:25	1, 1
5:26	1, 1
15:26	1, 8
15:28	1, 8
19:17	1, 4
19:18-19	1, 6
19:21	1, 6
25:34	1, 13
25:41	1, 4
25:44	1, 4
25:46	1, 4

Luke

| 2:14 | 4, 2 |

General Index

(prepared by Kathleen Strattan)

Miscellany of Eighty-Three Questions

of God, LII
grandeur, XXXI,3
and justice, LIII,3
princes and powers, LXIX,4, 9
of the wicked over the good, LXXIX,5
praise
See also flattery; honor
adulation, LXXI,5
and glory, XXXI,3
for good deeds, LIX,3
greed for, XXXVI,3–4
from human beings, LIX,3
prayer, LXIX,4
preaching, LVIII,1; LXIX,9
precedent, XXXI,1
pregnancy, LIX,4
conception, LVI
pregnant soul, LIX,3
presence, divine, XII; LIX,3; LXXIX,3
the present
See also time
everything as present to God, XVII
pride, XXX; XXXVI,3, 4; LXXI,5
priesthood, LXI,2, 4
princes and powers, LXIX,4, 9
prophecy, LVIII,3
prophets, XLIV; LVIII,2; LXI,2
See also individual names
and anointing, LXI,2
false, LXXIX,3
providence, divine, XXIV; XXVII;
XXXVI,1; LIII
See also usefulness
and accident/chance, XXIV
and example, XXXVI,1
and individuals, XLIV
by means of a bad person, XXVII
and the order of things, XL; LII; LIII,2;
LXII
perfection by, XLIX
rebirth by, XLIX
and the universe, XXIV
usefulness as, XXX
and the whole human race, XLIV; XLIX;
LIII,1; LXVIII,2
prudence, XXXI,1; LXI,4
punishment, XXIV; LIII,1, 2–3
See also discipline; free choice; justice;
merit; suffering
death penalty, LIII,2
as deterrence from sin, XXXVI,1
ease in committing sin as, LXXIX,1
hardening of the heart, LXVIII
infliction of (by humans), LIII,2
by means of a bad person, XXVII
penance, XXVI
righteous rule and, XXIV

and suffering of the wicked, XXI
Whom the Lord loves he corrects,
LXXXII
purity
See also under specific topics, e.g., soul
and impurity, LXXVI,2

quadragesima and quinquagesima, LXXXI
queens, LV
questions: three sorts of, XVIII

rational soul, XLVI,2; LIV; LXXX,1
See also intellect; mind
reality, LIV
See also existence; substances; truth
allegory and, LXV
reason, VII; XIII; XXX; LI,3; LXXX
See also knowledge; mind
and the body, XXX
and creation, XLVI,2
and intellect, XII
perfected, XXX
perversion of, XXXVI,1
and virtue, XXX–XXXI
the word, LXIII
reasons: ideas and, XLVI,2
rebirth, XLIX
See also salvation
struggle with sin after, LXV; LXVI,5
recklessness, XXXI,2; XXXIV
redemption, LXXIV
See also salvation
Red Sea crossing, LXI,2
regeneration, XXXVI,2; LVII,2; LXXXI,3
See also baptism
regret, LII
reign of Christ/reign of the Father, LXIX
religion, XXXI,1; XXXVI,1; XLVI,2
See also Christianity
and superstition, XXXI,2
remission of sins, LXXIV
repentance, LXVIII; LXVIII,5
reputation, XXXI,3
resurrection of Christ, LXII; LXXXI,3
risen Christ, LXVI,2; LXIX,2; LXXXI,2
resurrection of Lazarus, LXV
resurrection of the body, IX; XLVII; LIX,3;
LXVI,7; LXIX,2, 10
revelation, divine, IX; LXI,3; LXVIII,1
revelation of the sons of God, LXVII,2
reward, XXIV; XXXVI,1; LIII,1
See also free choice; justice; merit
riches. *See* wealth
righteousness, LXXXI,3
See also goodness
and charity, LXVI,1

Miscellany of Questions in Response to Simplician

Eight Questions of Dulcitius